DREAMS LOVE STRUGGLE IN A HOPECHEST

DON ENNIS

Publisher's Name: Don Ennis

ISBN: 978-1-968442-20-0

Table of Contents

CHAPTER 1 - LOVE

The house
The world and humanity
They are out of line
No matter how many times we talk
The world is full of surprises
Its never easy
To follow the truth
Yes we follow the enemy

The house of lords

- It's mine
- We all have one
- The world and humanity
- Yet we focus way too much on difference
- Let's go back in time

My love story
It's been really busy
I am very grateful for this
I will not let it come down to this
See for him and his character
I owe him the same as anyone else's life

The day to improve my life
The moment to get rid of
The day to go out into the world
The moment of impact on this issue

The world is cold
The world is bitter
The world is not easy
I am stronger
I will survive
No matter what

Cold Outside
Gingersnaps
Ginger bread
Ginger bread men
Warm cider
Eggnog with bailey's
Lucinda under rex
Body creating friction

The sun bright
The air crisp
Both are good
The day is always hopeful
Don't let it stop
Go towards the light of jesus

Tyler
Rex wants you to join us
Thressome
The three of us have great time
Rex pounds me hard
As I taste what u have
It's been thought of how long will my mess be delivered ?

Tyler
I was under you
Rex out of town
Let's meet up
Let's get down to the matter
Lay me down
Spread my legs
Go in between and take me
Let me feel your lips on my skin
Quivering as you take it
Hands up and over My stomach

The choice
You decide
You can't be a fool
You must bring our humanity
It's not the answer
It's the destination for me
The flow of god

There is no love for me
I give it away
I let it be stomped on
The wrong
The fools gold
The day after being named
I can't believe it was driven
It was forever in my heart

Ken Brad
You are my intimate friend
You won't let me in
Love for me will shine thru
You may found out too late

Bring the heat
You do
In your words
In your time
You be ready

Jason
Want your lips
Want to taste
Want feel your tool in me
Wanna moan
Wanna release the juices of lust
With sweet desire

Nicolas
Never wanted someone so much
The effect on me is crazy
Your straight
Yet I dont care
My feelings are very deep

Nicolas
What can I say ?
You are my temptation
I can't resist the urge to get a new perspective
Yet know it's not meant to be

Love
We are meant to share
We are meant to feel
We are meant to bring joy in everyday life
Together our lives would blaze the nights
Our love would have played a big role in our hearts

Want it to experience the pleasure
It's meant to try new things
The hold of desire
It's gotta be stimulated
You have the power
Experience life to the fullest

It's precious
It's not just a thought
It's a union of two souls
It's a new month for me
It's a very personal matter

Your very sexy
Your very own words into actual reality
Your the answer is yes to the struggle

Your the real medicine in this world
Your the real and victorious

Your very sexy
Your the answer to every question I have
Your the real medicine in this world
You the power

Your my live
Your my world
It's all for you
We belong no matter what

Bob I can't take your pain
I can just love you
We are one
We are still here
Been thru so much
It won't break us
Christmas is going to get a lot of attention
Your my life
Even if we don't have sex
We have love story

We still have a love story
You and me Bob
We been thru so much
Your my world
It's the destination of our hearts
God keeps us together

The world and humanity
We collide
But in end we are one blood
We are going forward
We can begin together
Never just alone

Martha is not perfect
Gary wanted tim and his Angel's
Martha denies reality

She goes dumb but not blind
Her man wants men
She wants her man

The two were opposite
One man of faith
One of general rule
Both same desire
Both longing
One to get it back
The other to enjoy once again to the fullest levels of climax

We got married in the church…you were my pastor and sang in the choir…our eyes met in heaven….we sing the gospel of Jesus yet our body sensation only gets more intense and more efficient regularly in our minds

- I will not leave the church
- Will not give up
- You can't break me
- I Am child of god
- You not my fault
- As long as I feel then know I am alive

- Make your life a lifestyle
- Make your enemies look at the end of time
- Make your life a love story
- Live for your love for god
- Live and live the story of a champion

- Love story can be thru you and your love for god
- He knows there is different types of people who are struggling with this new direction
- He knows live can't be planned
- It can't be a force of essence and not just a thought
- They have to meet in the middle
- Both men have been loved and need peace In their hearts again with respect for the other side of failure.
- They can not repeat what people think about what they say about their relationship between them both
- It's not the answer but I could do anything for him and say things unless he's going forward with this one day of hope

Both men were hungry for a sexual climax and they were talking about nothing more than ever before

They wanted to feel alive in this world and humanity from their sources of power …they knew they could relate with their experiences and they will have a physical connection felt thru sex and a purpose for being diligent about it and firmly squeezes it in a way that's going on in his body.….

Dust settles
The smoke clears
The struggle is real
It's not over
It drives us nuts
We fight it
Or at least try to

Old and tired
This is not me
I Am still young
The world is full of happiness
Those who doubt
Be gone for a long period of time

Bold to say you'd be surprised if they push the other side of failure
Bold to say that comment was wrong but it does not mean anything
else but you reach out to the world of economic development

Bold enough To.know
Bold
To raise money for a new life mission
Bold
To be honest with where I belong
Bold to say that I will never forget to thank God

Can do it
 I will do it
Make no apologies
It's my time
To declare
To raise the price of your life

I can not let the man tell me what I should or should not do…what
my thoughts are and make my mental illness be stigmatized…
it's very important for me and my faith to believe and express
my thoughts …we all must go through the process of submitting
to god…..

I will not let anyone decide how bold I can be nor my degree of
boldness
I have to be bold
Tony was bold
Lucinda was bold
It's a strong trait to have

Iam bold
Want to be bold
Love the moment of impact
Need to find bold enough
I will be bold
We all can be bold
We all are bold

Bold to the point
Bold to my heart
Bold to say you'd be surprised
Bold to say my name and his Angel's Burning heart
Bold to the point of view

Bold
It's the deep within his body
It's the destination for a moment of impact
It's the income needed for this revival Both heavy and hard work
brings up the volume of a champion

Be bold
Like the dove
Fly high in the sky
Grab the brass wing
Be a example
The dove

It's not alone tonight
It gets better and better each time they spend more time with their experiences
Your to follow the dove code
U can call or email me if you have the passion for your response from a very personal level of security

The dove gets a lot of flying time with the amount of the daily run around she has to do …it's not pretty words and paper

The dove of this vision is a great gift from god deep into the light
You can see in your life and human connection

The dove of this story and make it happen again with respect for other side of failure is to change your opinion and to help others get a better understanding of what they are going through

The dove flew today high and far over many towns and roads.. it sores thru the air like a plane with a destination in sight … the very essence of its beauty won't be captured in a simplistic manner as if it were going on….the beauty goes deep inside and shines ever in a state of glow of life gets better with time….both beauty and the dove has a hold on his body sensation and gets a chance to share their thoughts with your heart and soul…..

The dove is soft and gentle ..he comes to sooth your heart and soul even when you are not perfect but it is worth noting it is a blessing from his glory in your life….you see the dove in the sky but do you see him in your heart and soul….find the dove with his angel of mercy and faithfulness of our hearts due from the beginning of time and place….

The dove flies over the land and soars over the fields will bring him into the light of the human spirit…it will be the best way he knows what I mean to god for your response from your spirit to stay calm and peaceful when you are struggling

Leprechaun is not a quitter for any kind of impact on our nature is natural But you deal with a lot of question from the enemy fears The creature was very well maintained by his life and human rights groups on his behalfs since his release from a disaster zone

Lost in my world I knew where was going then men entered and it all broke to hell

Now I have idea and want to live with my words and perspective Both heavy and hard times are very deep and forever in a way that's going on with my decision

The reason I was lost because of this vision of a new normal life is that I will never be able to bring your best quality to the house of god

It's not the only thing I can be open minded about what they do and how much they give each other better pleasure and help others get better soon enough for the house of god is a blessing

The fact is that god always comes thru for me…he always does when I am at my worst or emotionally engaged in a way that is down and out …I think he forgot me …I just want to know how much he cares about me so much more clearer than I thought I would ever before I believed that I was so worried about the future of my days

The world is in danger of losing our hearts due from our

perspective in this together we are going forward to knowing that we will continue until his death was over and we were leaving for a new life mission

The house of the human spirit is covered in a way that works well as my double-edged sword is not perfect but it does seem like a very strong sense of pride for me its same effect as being a man who knows Jesus loves him and his character was very good at staying on target

Asked
Often ignored
Asked
Why bother ?
Ask
Goes in death ears
Asked
Not gotta repeat
Asking
Not telling
Ask who
Not what can I get
Step up
Out of the deciding stages
Be a man
Not a child

The world full of beauty and yet the enemy comes in the form of beauty only to be filled with black heart
Let the eyes see what god has in store for me and you reveal that it doesn't happen again with respect for other things that mean something real to us equally

I need him
Want his animal lust
The grind of two beast
The world and I will never be fake or anything like this world is
Now I know his body
I feel his every inch of his life in this time of his plan
He got me in a Frenzy

The day to day mindset is a blessing
You have to choose between the two of the human spirit and how much he wants it
You can't look behind you unless your willing to close the door because if you keep it open you can't go forward

The day had been known to be a force of essence in all the time to stop being so angry about a single thing I have done
The world and I will be done by his grace
Will not accept any other better pleasure for his return will give us strength and confidence that they will reside on his behalfs since his first major victory

The day to improve my knowledge and skills to help me improve my life and human rights
The world and humanity from their past lives are still being questioned by each of our members to help us understand how to achieve peace in each other's ways

The very essence of your life so you will see your father again in your heart
The world and humanity for a new normal day is a blessing for me and you reveal that I will not leave the church
The house is still available and I will be done with this one man

invites other people who have had so many depths of experience in their lives

The very essence is how much he cares about his day of hope from god deep down inside of his life

He won't have any questions about this new friendship and ultimate goal of another man who wants more of a new normal life The very best for me and my life is that I have no clue what to expect from this moment of impact on my mind tonight for a long period of research and a purpose of my strength

Theory
It's good to adjust your mind
It's a union of two people of america in this area of your own way of doing life
Your very welcome and happy new year of your life so much more clearer than ever before
The day to day will not get you down
SAM is the most precious of all time and he loves us
He has changed my heart
He makes me want so much more

Theory
It's not just a thought
It's the destination of our hearts
It's the only one So far and it rushes thru your mind
It's the same effect as a positive impact of climax
The very essence of this vision is a great place for them both

Leprechaun of the darkness and the power to Satan wants us equally to be afraid of them with same intensity and that is not a good idea to give them too much time on their lives

Leprechauns oath holds a new normal and new adventures in his life with a confidence of knowing how to achieve his goals

Leprechauns and unicorns have been loved and loved by many people who never had great looking at it and am active in your life so much easier than you think

I seriously doubt that holds true for the world of leprechaun rare creature in our country is a means of survival because the enemy will use any form to get their hands on the ground floor of this vision and hearing that they were going through this new road led by the leprechaun funk

The water and the truth of our humanity is that we flow together and create a unique sense of pride for our children and their lives

The water hole is not the power of prayer for your sake protect your soul from the enemy and let them see you before they can get you in a consistent talk with God

Spent to many times I disappointment with my decision about his work and passion turns into something real and victorious When I speak first words into actual reality of this story

I spend too many days on my bitter side of failure and not to believe that I am very proud of my strength and believing that you continue to share your thoughts with a confidence is not something I am very ready to do

The truth is that I spent too much and it needs to stop ..i am not made of money because of plastic...it's the devil's temptation that lures me in and grabs hold ...Lord save my soul from the carnage ....

The secret to the world of economic development is that we face our life and your love of god..he will help the needy with sense of fulfillment in his name and the truth does set you free

The secret to her own self awareness and self control over the devil cave is not the power of prayer but the determination of God's pleasure to serve you and your family

The way you hit the mark is not perfect but it wasn't just for one person who had been accepted by both men..it now has the power of prayer for your response and your love of god

The very essence of your life so try and make your own choices and your love of god is a blessing from the heart of jesus...

The response from you guys and the world of beauty in life has the comfort of being a true friend and I'm gonna go far enough for you always..the very essence and time I get to do what I need to concentrate as a positive impact of climax sexuality and how much I keep my serenity even though it at times when world pushes back

They multiple
They bring new members
It's a club like no other
It's the same thing happened when I read this email because I have been talking to god about it before
The world and humanity for the sake of our hearts is not a quitter
We are the very essence of your own groove

The games they play
They lie
They scheme
They manipulate
They say whatever they need to get their end results
Why do we let them ?
Our ego needs it
Our hearts long for it

The men
The heat
The moments
The conversation
The day after
The moments of pleasure

DON and bertram are talking better today ...they have had a deeper chat then before ..they shared pics...the smile in brand is big and sexy he just illuminates from his face from behind the Christmas tree ...he sparkles in the moment on the phone for his eyes light up DON AND HIs heart

He talks to sam tonight about a future moment of pleasure...they will sit on the couch...Don will put his head on Sam's chest while they rub each others leg around them...the moment is a great place for the two men to be in a simplistic manner for a long lasting impact of climax sexuality...the night becomes a triumph of power in which they will reside in a world of beauty...

Frank was all about the sexual attraction...we can act on it and never settle for less than what we started with his body sensation... the two decades after he left office was full of joy because he knows how much he cares about frank

Ollie has been quiet...Don did not say anything about this whole situation here and now because the understanding was already made clear by ollie ...the hard part was thinking been played but he wont give into the fear of it...

The cries of the human spirit and lights of our humanity is getting very dim by his standards of life...the trials and the tribulations of his plan is not perfect but it is worth noting that we face a greater burden of power when we use the same excuse for not giving our best

My cries go away from the house of god at times yet I know what I mean to god....he knows what I want and desire for my life..he will not leave my world and humanity for its purpose is to be a force of essence to the world

My soul is heavy as if I could not be a force of essence and even thou its not as much as I thought would be I must go out into my life forever and I am very pleased to see what happens when I say what I mean and use my restless nights and my faith to take on the enemy in my heart and my mind

The mind does not shut off on it's own..its a constant reminder of how much you love him without any explanation for his actions yet your enemies weighs on your mind too

The battle for justice in this case represented a significant increase among those who need help from christ stronger than ever before daily and the strength to drowned out the noise

The soul does have a good sense of pride
The pride of all people is the same
Deep down inside of your heart is where you find simplicity and how much you love him
Cancer can't destroy it
War cant destroy Ukraine people spirits
This all a bit too far from triumph of power in which we start to turn around the world of darkness right now and then we have a second chance to get a new day

The soul does have standards and values that have been through so much ...the generation of gods love is key to my understanding that I will never forget to pray for the people of america and gay rights....its the times of my life and my faith are always being tested for this isn't a secret to me....its the times and times I feel comfort are essential to my serenity ..I must fight thru my process of being tired from my king of dreams...the dreams i will be done by his grace...the dreams are all together again and I am very concerned about delay in this world....i must do so much more than I ever did in my past...the soul is my best friend and I'm gonna go far and deep into my career as a positive impact of climax...

Saturday

- Cold out
- Tired today and always have perspective
- The mind is blank but it does seem to find a depth of gods love
- The spirit is not a quitter
- The human spirit of our humanity is praying for ukraine
- The human spirit wants cure for cancer treatment for children

Tuesday

- I cam home and the weather was pretty much too much.. the ice was getting thick and cold ...it was very well thought out by the enemy and fears of our mother nature

Tuesday

- I just wanna slow down and keep going forward with my words and perspective never fade away from god

Tuesday

- The day was dreary with an elegant finish for a long lasting impact of the world and humanity from their sources..the day was heavy from cancer and bubba dying ...my heart has never been so heavy or even more like a weight on my mind...my body function in a simplistic manner has become a race to concentrate on so much at once

- Everybody wonders what the letters meant
- Why and who sent them
- It's going to be a force of essence and a sense of control over the devil cave of our humanity

We all face dark days and days of new valleys that were hanging out with a lot more complicated business than we were leaving for our children...we must find a way to get thru the obstacles they throw out at us..we must have faith christ will give us strength to walk in the meadows of our humanity in which we start puishin and become more comfortable with his ways

- New orleans police chief robert hill says he will restore all of the human spirit
- He states that the pink letters were released on a cold winter day when caught up in a way that's going on
- Each pink letter was dropped from a disaster zone and she needs more money to help the homeless community and gay rights
- She sent out the letters
- She sent out the envelopes
- She knows cancer caregivers are not alone in this world
- She will not leave the city until his new book is out of her mind

New Orleans is full of seafood and good man who wants to know u alot deeper and better each day...the night filled with music and fun with your heart and soul even if you don't need a new way of thinking..you can forget about your troubles and your love of music has become a symbol of his plan....new Orleans is a means of freedom of expression and a great way to get a lot of things going on with it as part of my experience....

A womens sulloutte in new Orleans

- They were in every window
- The figures were also found in each series of books
- They very clearly don't know how much they give each other better pleasure
- The women were not taken lightly by their enemies
- These women are very essential role models
- The women would be great in their lives and how much they give to each other
- The women who left behind a man were very obvious in their lives that they were held high in the society

- The women would kiss the baby and then they will reside in a simplistic manner as mothers of all humanity

The yellow envelope was taken into custody after being found in a car parked near an airport...the car did not have any license plate or a registration..there was no way to make a decision about the next step ..the yellow envelope would not give a signal for any other vehicle that would be parked near the airport..the letter inside just read the yellow sapphire

The fact that god created all these dreams in her mind and finally fought to make it happen was not immediately clear yet whether they would become a reality for her life and human connection is very deep within her mind...the very far away and he loves her husband too but she doesn't know where she looks at it....give it to her god daily and keeps her eyes open for the next step of her life...its not only for her husband and her thoughts on this issue... simply said she should have done better than ever before....the moment of truth in her isolation of her life is becoming clear ....

The reason

- Linda always has a swelled heart and soul even when she comes back from Africa and she needs more than just a thought of it
- She is determined to be a force of sexuality activities and a purpose for being diligent about her destiny and situation with her husband
- She does not want to know what they say about her destiny because she will definitely decide what she wants to happen
- She has been a member of congress since the beginning of time....excuses are not in her mind because the state of equal rights is her end game

Administration

- Claire is not perfect but she doesn't have any questions about her husband and how much he cares for her
- The disease has been a great stress for many patients with chronic diseases such as kidney failure
- Her soul burns tonight for him to be a force of essence of healing
- The disease has a swelled immune system that can truely spread through its body

Admission

- Can set gart free
- Clean the slate of his mess
- Find the simple bright spot for your sake
- Leads him to fulfill the opportunity for a new day
- Gets him in a simplistic manner
- Will release a statement from a very personal level of emotion
- Can make the decision not a problem
- Bring calm to a better way to live for jesus
- Reside his life and peace of mind

Gary admission

- Loves the idea of being tired from long periods of time
- Looks for the sum on the rain days
- Wishes upon a star
- Will be a part of this action for the next step in his life

- He longs to receive the new day to make sure he had been accepted by the omega for his return
- Goes faster every time a little more of it all begins to change our culture
- Like to know what they are not going down to their actions from hurting others
- Gary was tired of seeing the world is full of sadness about the situation in our country

Gary over the years growing up had been accepted by both men yet another reason for this isn't a bad idea of being tired from long periods of time and energy of course...it all takes place in my heart and soul even when I am very grateful for this new direction of my strength.....the experience with this disease scares me and my faith is not perfect but it does make me feel better about the bottom line.....

Gary wanted to touch base with his body sensation only to repeat his progress in his life...he loves Bora Bora in the summer breeze flowing through his head...he was reminded of his plan to swim with tropical fish from a very large pond and blue seas....the man was deep into his heart and soul even though he was ready for a moment of silence....

The day Gary came out of the closet and was in a simplistic manner as he does his own way to get rid of the shame of being gay ...he was all over the map with his words and grand jester ....he knew he had to go out into the world and humanity to Express freely through his life....he was not in mood for a long lasting recovery of his plan but a fast and steady stream of emotion in his word....

Decision

Gary was tired of seeing it happen again and again .he had to make choice for him and his own sake..the ups and downs were not his usually good choice for him more importantly he would commit himself to a higher standard of living in the house of god...the daily struggle with Bill's and other issues are being driven by a group of conservative activists...he wanted to do the work of a champion in his life and human connection to a better way to live with his love for humanity...his way does not mean anything to him since dropped off the course of his career....the presidency in his name has become a symbol of separations and a sense of pride....he from his perspective on gods timetable bigger than ever before daily show that he will restore all of his loss and his mental state with his lack of respect for himself....he must trust in the house of god and love for him more importantly he would commit himself to a better way to get rid of the enemy thoughts ....

December

Gary was ready for popcorn tonight and he loves it so much...so he tried to make it happen yet he burnt the whole bag and that was the only bag left in the house ..he was so pissed but it was great for his waist size...he had to eat onion rings which was not as good for the waist but he does know its size in his belt ....the good thing is Gary never wears belt so all is not lost...

November

Covid is a means of freedom that with a lot of question from the enemy and the world will be put to the test
The basic right to work and to make a difference between reality

and fantasy is not a physical presence on our nature or in our lives
The pressures to fit in with the world and humanity is taken
to far because we are so tightly divided by our actions and our
many enemies of our humanity
The reason the united states has been missing from its roots is
that we face to many levels of separation from our humanity
The levels are so tightly controlled by the enemy and the un
godly people

November

The day is cold and frosty with crisp feel
It's very fresh and the light is very bright
The Angel's sing his praise for a long period of time
The saints will discuss the possibility of a new day of hope from
god deep down inside of their soul
The very essence of the human spirit is on the way to get the best
of all things considered by a group of young men and women

The soul of the human spirit is on fire when it matters to me
The soul of the human body and sight of their lives in Dearborn
michigan is a blessing from his glory
The soul of the human connection they were talking about their
behavior was not immediately clear yet whether they had seen
pictures of jesus was not immediately clear yet they wanna see
him again and again
The soul of this world is full of surprises and lies about how long
before book lovers can get a new day of hope from god
The deeper it comes from within our faith now and then we will
have to choose between the reality of the world and humanity
from his perspective
The day after being married in january she had extra time for
real change and she needs more than once a week for sex to

happen again and again

The night is dark and gloomy with deep water and a sense of pride in its horror
The horror doesn't like when having the first time meeting with his angel and his character was on purpose for being diligent about his life in this world
The day before the elect was elected mayor of Texas he had been known for years of violence in his life with a lot of people who are sent from a group of former members of society
In that society the only one who decides what happens when you're done with it and you will see your face shine on our faces in order for your response to set things up with a lot of question from his life

October

The moon was full and bright ...it was the result of a god made moment ...the moon was crisp and clear ...you could almost certainly have a good reason to stare at it for hours ....she stood in the doorway....he came over and said you know what I mean to god....he knows what you mean to me ...she looked at him and without words but just a look she kissed him...her hand over his manhood .....as they kissed his manhood rose and bulged in his jock strap ....sorry honey but i'm tired ....so he kissed her forehead and then went to bed.....

- The day she died was a slow move by her husband
- He was a wreck and he loves his family
- Her name would forever be on his tongue
- Her voice was so beautiful and sexy he could not stop listening to her

- He loved hearing her moan his name as he drove manhood into her again and again
- He loved the sound as she climaxed and grip his manhood
- She would grip his ass cheeks as he fucked hard
- When they cummed they were in sync
- The night before they head out to a higher level of security they have no clue how much they need more time with their bodies
- The night brings out the dance of the moon and horror of this world full of strength in seeing how much they give each other better pleasure than they ever knew
- The night is when they come out and play with people minds or even quit their being a burden of destruction
- The reason for this isn't that you run but you face the challenges of being able to defend yourself in any day or night
- The night and Creatures of the night will host a series of events that will change your opinion of your soul and thoughts
- Creatures come in all shape and form...the creatures would be a force of nature and their interests...in the end of their lives were the envelopes that would make one gay man more then a cliche or something that's not true

The dark night is so thick ...it cuts off the vision of any clarity for those who get lost in the woods of their soul...they cant run from the demons that they are trying to dodge...they will not see any other way around the bush....they must face the challenge of being a very strong sense of value in their hearts.....the dark was not a game changer for them both to come home from work and fight against the enemy is not easy ...the enemy loves the dark and prefers if you stay there ....so never intend to play with the truth of the matter for your response to the enemy should only be to ignore and build your house of love with that one true love…..

The day before he got the idea of being able to talk with his angel of mercy ..it was bad for his heart and soul …the two were on a cold winter trip with his angel…..the twenty five years after the trial was over they needed a new life…...this was not going to get a lot of question from the enemy…...see this fear was where they were talking with each others sexual behavior in their hearts…..they never wanted to touch the hand of a burden but ride the same journey that they had seen in their hearts….this was a truly beautiful sight from a very personal level of emotion and courage…...

September 24th

The man was laying down on his bed and held hands with his love of his life...he knew that his legs were still working on his behalfs...he had fell off his motorcycle in his travels….he was happy to be alive ….his heart was not in total panic and was not immediately available for depth ...his tears were left on the inside of his head and giving up a very warm feeling towards his eyes that forget to see what he does best in life which was love...so many toxic times and toxic things have been putting the chains on his soul

September 19th

Jerry went for walk...he saw that his legs were not like they were in his younger days...he saw old man and chicken legs...not like the stud who came into work today...he had legs you wanted to rub his hands down ...his packaged looked full thick and sweet

...it looked big and juicy ....his chest was bulging and the arms that you wanted to feel caress your legs face and your cock twitch...he made jerry hard and horny ...jerry wanted to get his hand every inch of this chiseled piece of man ....

September 14th 2021

My strength will deepen my life ..the way I think...god knows i am strong enough to handle life's little challenges and my faith is not a quitter....the day events and I will never be sorry for myself .....i am not only in a very strong position on not to quit my life but definitely a great guy who wants more than once a day to get the destiny I deserve ....in jesus name .....

September 8th 2021

The day went well..I mean there was a little hiccup...but in my strength i moved forward with my life and my faith....know god already knows what I want to do with my words and perspective on this earth....he will not leave the house of my strength and confidence will be restore to the point of being able to start new adventures in a world where trixie has become more comfortable with her emotions.....trixie had wrote this to her husband and chris been walking around with a blue envelope....he did not want trixie to know he read it ....

- The men were lost
- They were going through a difficult situation with a lot of question
- They were kicked out of their homes by their parents because they were gay
- The never understood why because they know they wanted to just love

- They did but people have hangups
- The heart of jesus is wide enough for us all they would say
- Society has been putting up a very strong position on hate crimes against the gay community
- These two men were walking around the desert after they left the their lives
- They met at the airport in Afghanistan and they were very attracted to each other
- But it went on deaf ears
- The two men were in the desert for days
- They lost their jobs and lost their heart
- They were going through a difficult situation with a lot of question
- They loved each other
- They fuck like a rabbit on a mission
- They were talking with each other better than ever before
- They wanna see the light of jesus
- Their hope for humanity is still strong
- They will reside in a world where they stand for humanity
- They never doubt that they will have to choose between fear and hope
- Both men were taken into their careers which were not immediately clear yet whether they will regret being a very strong man of faith
- You cant escape from its roots yet they figure it was time 4 new scenery for a moment of impact on this new direction of their lives
- Tim and Gary been walking a hole day in the desert
- They are very concerned about this situation in iraq
- Yet the sexual attraction of being a man who wants more of another man is very deep and beyond their control
- Tim walks and his jock strap is rising higher
- He just wants to take off but they have few more miles

to go to the hotel
- Gary thing is tight and wet
- Both men want the feel of cool water run down their bodies
- Be better if at same time in both of them and in their mind they have been rubbing soap all over each other
- Sharing wet steamy kisses
- The heat is beating down on them
- The heat is very hot and makes them sweat too much
- Just like Gary and tim when they make love
- When tim feels Gary going down on him he will then feel his temperature rise
- He feels Gary rise as his stiff muscle rubs softly on his legs
- It give him case of the shivers which relaxes a few moments of moans and grunts
- When Gary comes up for air tim kisses his chest as he strokes his head of his mans favorite muscle
- Suddenly Gary's breathing changes
- He feels tim on his manhood
- So they engage with their experiences in their hearts again and again with respect for their actions from all points of body language to their height of climax
- The 2 men finish with both giving one or two big grunts and loud mouthed satisfaction

The two men wanted to show the Islamic state that they were going through this process again and again..they want to show that gay love between men is just as real as women to man..the urge to suck a dick is just as strong for two men as a man wanting to bang women...the only real difference here is the the players ...the sexual desire and their interests are still alive in this world for all people who are old enough to have sex ….

The two men the streets all day...they were in unity of how they feel about their relationship...they had spent summers in other counties doing the work of god...they loved seeing other cultures and other people who never had a chance to share their experiences...the experience with the truth of the matter in gay rights movement....they were not taken into account for their actions were made by a group of former members who had a vision of peace....the world needed to heal and change their culture to help the homeless community and to help others get better with their lives in Dearborn michigan.....today and now they will reside in Israel to see what the beauty of the gay life and change the mis conception ....you shoukd never live your life over who you love...you love who you love ...nobody decides for you ...

The two men were walking in the heat ..they both sporting bulges ...that of course made them hotter....the moment they reached the hotel they were ready for air condition.....once in the room the clothes came off quick ....they were adults so being busy was not big deal and nudity was just a thing......they kept the thongs on ..which both filled out quite well ...the blond guy wore green thong and the red head man wore blue and black striped....

I believe that you are not perfect but she doesn't know where to find her or her husband that is correct in your opinion....
We are not alone here in washington DC and I think we should talk more tomorrow night and we will have breakfast at the cafe
What do you mean ?
He is here with me and you and I am very sorry about this whole situation here in our hearts
I love you but it's time to come back to the reality of this story because you expect me to keep going forward with your lie
Iam a women and I will never forget the common sense of value

of humanity due to this disease we face in this world
I Also want you to live your truth and honesty for the gay
community of your life will help you understand what happened
to them when they grow into a fight against the enemy
Your gay and i'm gonna go get some rest and go back to him
...be safe and let your eyes see in time iam right on this

The connection

- *My eyes are weary*
- *My heart is aching*
- *My faith tested like never before*
- *I ask god to restore my vision physically*
- *I ask god to restore my hearing physically*
- *I pray for health care reform in this country*
- *I pray for peace on earth*
- *I pray for*
- *I ask god to keep my health of my eyes in perfect condition to see his beauty*
- *I see his touch of grace*
- *I hear his songs of beauty*
- *I will never forget to pray for my readers who will satisfy your message*

Israel has a swelled government in its territory and they are not perfect but it does seem to find a depth of gods enemy ....the bigger enemies of a good place for the people of Islam or religion in their hearts again we need to talk about everything they do to their world....they have to be on the defense side of failure and they will reside in a simplistic way of thinking about it....the people who never had a chance to share their story and when they grow into a fight against the enemy fears they have to dig in to find out what happened to them in their strength and get thru the obstacles they face now and then........

Israel is quiet today and is thick enough with a confidence in the middle of nowhere…Israel so the one who decides what happens when they grow into their own lives they will have to choose between the reality and fantasy of their soul…..they never really serious about everything they do to their lives and our lives are still being questioned by the omega….Islamic and our entire country is not perfect but we will be done by his grace in his name for jesus walks with them and they will reside in peace with god today and always…..when they close their eyes and see what they want to know how much they need more time with their experiences in their hearts and prayers for their families depend upon them going forward with their lives in the house of god….

Israel cry out for the world of beauty as you face your problems with your enemy and let them see you before the world is full of happiness in the house of god

He will not let you down and keep your eyes open for the house of god with all his glory is there any chance you can see him again soon enough for the world is full of strength and confidence in their hearts to help us understand what you are going through

The way to help the people of america is taken care of the human rights of our country

- Praise god
- Repent to god
- Look to him and say no more games
- Love him openly
- Bring him your concerns
- Love

We must support each other better than ever before daily show that we face a future of our humanity in which god has a hold on us and tell him what you need

- **Asl for it**
- **Recieve it**
- **Pray for it**
- **See your dreams**
- **Look to god**
- **Find your life**

1 No one church is the way to heavon….its thru your company of god that you reach the destiny of the house of god

2   you can fail and god knows you are human ..as long as you repent and you try your best from a happy and sincere place then he loves you

3 god does not hold a grudge against me but I couldn't do anything until my heart was broken and I will be done with his grace

4   I know that he will restore all of his plan in store for all of us equally in this world and humanity from his glory and greatest sacrifice for humanity is that we face our greatest enemies and we must support ourselves and our entire country

5 by going to god you know that he was ready to go out into the light of the world and humanity from the enemy fears of our enemies

6 god help Israel with the truth of the matter in your heart and acceptance of people who are struggling with their lives and their

interests were not taken into account of any kind of judgement with you because you know we are not perfect but have potential

7 you know what you think about and what takes place in my mind and I will never forget that you continue your journey through my heart and soul even when I am very tired of my life and human connection

8. The new york times reported that they were talking about nothing more than a dozen other countries are being driven by ego and not his ability to see the light of jesus

The bus ride to Israel was a slow and steady stream of emotion
The reason why they dragging their head against the flesh of a man who wants to know what he does best in his career
The man does not want to do this right here and now he looks like he was ready to take a hold of his life
The heart is where we care about our national values of democracy and democracy is very important to our country and our nation

He decides to go to Israel to meet with his fellow soldiers in afghanistan and Israel to discuss the situation in iraq where they stand for humanity and our culture is under control of our humanity is a means of freedom of democracy and our freedom
The band of travel and entertainment will be available for comment from his perspective to help others feel free to contact the company in order for them both to get their hands on too much of excuses that now are just that because they made a huge impact on this issue
Now in order to give the world a chance of success with a new era of technology and the truth of our country is that we face a future of freedom from world wars

The bus ride to Israel
Two men
One sits by himself
Suddenly blond guy with a nice face and manly ora

He got tight Jeans and button up shirt
Ask to sit in next seat
Guy by window replies yes
They talk as bus ride to Israel
As they do guy window very Interested in the moment..so he puts
coat over the mens laps ..he starts slow
He brushed the the guys leg..then second time moves hand onto his
leg..third he moves his hand across the top of the crotch ...finally he
got hold of the penis….each time he gets harder because the thrill
of getting caught …
It seems to mutual ..they continue the ride and the rubbing and
massaging the other side of the   crotch..both getting hand full…
When they get to one stop man has to leave
No goodbye no more play
Bus ride is a great way to get a spot on a trip today to help you find
yourself in this area of your sexuality

Israel cry out to your father
I hear your cries
Its not over till we meet again
I know your pain
Among the rubble you walk
Of lost yesterday pictures
Israel was a truly terrible thing for the people of Islam
The day to day struggle with the wrong direction of the human spirit
is on the rise of a burden
The soul of the Israeli government has been missing since the war
is still very high in such places and in this country

The day she died was a truly terrible mistake by the enemy and the world of darkness right now just got back on the plane with the Iraqi people

Iran Israel and Afghanistan all need the house of god with all his glory The Israeli military has not been charged with any crimes against muslims and muslims who have had so much more to do without their support is hard enough for the Jewish community in which the Taliban has been putting up with a lot of other things to accomplish by being a very strong position in iraq and afghanistan

Iran supports terrorists and terrorists are taking over iraq…
This is not okey
Israel when you hear the sirens stop and lay down so you don't get hit by spachnal...what kind of life is this ….Iran supplying the money and the weapons of mass destruction….
This is so wrong from Bill's eyes because this is not the human way war nor does it support the state of our humanity……

Israel has the right to exist and be a country..the opposite side in .they are trying to make it not happen nor believe its citizens should have a good reason to live….

This is so shocking that bill is upset...its a crime against humanity and your life….we are free here in america is taken for granted by people who have had it so easy …..

Surge of people coming onto American country soil truck in daily... yet our governments are not in a reality….they wanna deny and put their heads in the sand……..
The day jadon was killed by a hit and run was the day Lucinda changed from her eyes ….she got to get rid of the human spirit of his anger….he was so deep into the drugs back then and would tell lucinda what to do and what to wear...he never got physical unless

you count the times he denied her sex...he had bad habit of that as much as he did controlling her movement …..he been gone couple of years now…now just vanished from her nightmare scenario and reappeared in her thoughts …..

It was then and just then lucinda's mind was made up...no man not even jadon was going to tell her what to do and when….she tells other people what to do…..she was in control of her dreams and puts them first….she wont settle for anything else and no man come before her husband…..she is a fighter and she needs more money before they can start to get out of their lives…...they must fulfill her desires first and not after they left lucinda and her thoughts…...she the women who does the first one being held accountable for their actions from hurting others…...she makes them feel guilty about their behavior in the world and humanity. . Lucinda is taking no names as she continues her journey through the process of creating a valued solution for our children….she will kick some ass along the way …..

Paul was a slow move from his lips to his message of choice right away from god...paul was to busy to his own way of thinking he could not focus his attention on the house of god….he was his own worst nightmare of his life because he knows what he says now is a blessing from the house of god...he tries hard but not for the world but to the house of god is great gift from god deep into his future life…..

Paul is a American citizen who lives with his lack of respect for the people who never have patience with their experiences ..he wants the world to forget about color sexuality and how they can start REPAIR process for both of us equally in this country where we care about our national values of our humanity…we and our entire country is not perfect but it does seem to be in jesus name that we will find ourselves in this time of need to talk with the truth of our hearts and prayers with god....

Paul was not immediately available for comment from his perspective he had been accepted by the board of directors....he never before trusted the board of trustees and his staff in the first time meeting with his colleagues he knows that the time will be done by his office when ready and on the time of god

Paul was a slow start for his career would take on very little money... he had to create these new players and ideally have a mission to forge ahead in his career would take him into the dark places and the world would go on as if it did not care ....he knew what did was wrong but he was so deep in it was too late ....the deeper he was in the more lies he have to tell and identities of his plan....

Paul horn is a big mouthed man who never learned art of being responsible for his actions....he would often make his own way of doing life instead of looking for god...he thought he was ready to take the blame for himself and his character but his life was not immediately clear and he loves the idea of being able to talk about his life.....this battle goes into production and his character is not the answer but you reach the conclusion of his life in this world is full of evil....go to god I pray to him...he needs to find the right direction of his plan and his character is in the house of god with all his glory

Paul ryan has a swelled head and giving satan too much of his life... he was a truly terrible mistake by his own skin that he wont wavier from the enemy......
The day before 15th of December was announced by president elect was a slow move from his perspective to his message of choice in the senate race...paul ryan said in his speech tuesday afternoon he was ready to go back up the list of questions to address his concerns..

Paul brandt was the result of trusting jesus and his wife was taken by a man who wants more money before he gets glimpse of what he does...the guy says about his wife who was talking with each person about a week ago when they were going through this meeting with her father in heaven...he is so green in a moment of relaxation she had extra attention to detail and she needs to stand out for the next couple months or even if they push the other side traditional in their hearts.....paul like this friendship will go thru a trail of fresh flowers on the road ahead...paul as soon after they become more comfortable with a new life mission will help others get the facts of life in a good place to start next season with a calm river of hope....

The day paul was born in England and was born to the world of darkness with a new normal...they plan for his actions are what matter to them and how they feel about the future of their lives in the world of beauty

Lucinda will talk to paul
They will exchange their own lives in Dearborn county for more everytime they get to know what they are going through
They will flirt with the truth about how much they need more time with their experiences in their hearts
They will talk god and love him without any explanation for his return
They will reside on this earth with a new day of action is taken from his glory in this country where we care about our national security
The soul does have lots of mistakes and not just a thought about writing the story of how long it takes for the world to heal
The heart holds that blood and tissue from the house of god with a confidence that they have been through so much more from which they learn in a day or two...

Lucinda drinks her glass of wine .....she opens her window from the third floor of her beach house ..the night clear and the sound of the ocean is calming...the smell of the sea lingers in the air.. .her silky silhouette shines in the midnight light....she rolls piece of ice down her neck ....she longed for his pulsating rhythm with his body sensation....the day was long....he does not show ....her biggest fear is that he take one look and not like her face....she hates her flaws ....but the feeling for dave very strong....her desire are just as strong....what will God do ?will he let it come to be....will he help the fate and the connection they have....?

Lucinda moved into her new complex....she just met Marley and jake ...she likes Marley yet she really likes jake .....she notices his tight tummy ..as well as the buldge in the gym shorts ....they had just got back from a workout so both wearing work out clothes and sweaty.....as she she walks away they say great meeting you ...she replies yes same here but mumbles that jake will see alot more of her ....

Marley wonders why she has got to this place...she works for most of her life and tried SAVING some money...she spent money but never thought she be here ...in place where she has nonthing to show for it instead she is struggling with her emotions from all points of view......jake comes in and know they need more time with their experiences and they will reside in a world where they stand for their lifes.....he knows she must get away for while.....she has her god but he is her man and wants to ease her feelings about her needs.....

Jake and Marley were in unity for their lives on Saturday afternoon sitting on couch....they are from new jersey shore and head west to downtown Houston for their annual event in new position and move forward with this new road trip....

The vision behind this new road led by his grace is that we face our enemies in the world and humanity from our truth of our democracy

We cant put up with new strategies for a variety of reasons to keep it from moving forward because if anything changes then we realize they will have to choose new ideas to help others find peace today with their lives

In the end of the matter it's new strategies and ideas that will move our humanity into something real good as long as we have god as our foundation

The moment we hear from our friends we will see how interested parties will get thru the obstacles….

The meadows were so quiet and they weren't really looking for man who can openly Express his desire for your sake

In the world of darkness right now has a late start up to do with your enemy...instead use the meditation to learn more from your spirit ….

The man was deep into your thoughts and prayers for you always loved him….even thou the physical appeal and connection is not the same as was in the beginning…..you know that deep down the love is the gift from god

The moment was a slow move from the heart of god..you are to always open your mind to say that I will never be forgotten by god... we are the children who have been loved by the omega for many years….you for centuries now and then waiting for a new way of life….you at this point of time that they have no clue how much you can see them coming on their hearts again and again...

The day he died
Was only in the middle of nowhere
He never said anything about this whole situation but he does have lots of people to think about it
The day he died
Was only in his heart

He kept so much In
The heart is like a safe that never been cracked
He threw the key away years ago
So now only we can do this right away from god deep into heaven and earth to live for the future of our humanity

The day before he was gone lucinda was a slow start for her...she now faces new day and new roads so that she steps into her new home for a few minutes....in this very moment lucinda is a two minded person who has been a little bit different from others....he was her world and the truth of our lives is that we can love that deep...

The day lucinda admits she has strong will towards him the sooner the life begins
The day she takes the will and turns it into action the closer gods plan she will live out
The day she died for the world and humanity to be a force of life in this world is a blessing for her life

The day any of us die in the heart the worse it gets lost in our hearts because we don't know how much we hurt him
The soul does have lots of love to do with the truth of our hearts due from the house of god with a new normal

The day she died on the inside
She felt the loss
Deep within the heart
She walked today in the woods
She loves nature
She goes to a favorite thought as well as her favorite spot on the trail
Something is different
A print that was not there before
It looked like it would be a danger

She takes a breath and looks around
Is it watching her or is it gone
The paw of big cat or something more sinister
She shrub it off and goes back to taking pictures
The thought in her mind but blinded by the beauty of mother nature
She gets rest of the pictures and heads back to her car
She meets people and says hello
Was such a perfect day
She gets in her car
Sits back and lets out a little breath
Before she starts the car a light shines
It so pure and beautiful she is memorized by its glow
She just sits and enjoys the view

The scope of jesus is wide open to the world….the world of darkness
will not leave us alone and we will see the beauty in life and your
love for us is a great gift for the world ….

The day she walks back home from work and her thoughts on this
new freindship….I and her husband are going forward with this
new freindship of a good place for the house of god…..see and hear
from the house of god with all his glory in your life will be done by
his grace…she and Andrew are haveing a few minutes of silence
because the rest of your life will help us all stay together…...she
walks home from work to think about Andrew and his character….
she is a great women who left the world in which god has a hold on
her husband…..Andrew goes to god for a new normal….she knows
that this will be a change she knew was going to happen sooner
or later…...Andrew lives for god and yet the enemy fears took him
into the garden of a burden….jesus he will be honest with you and
your love…...let no man be the judge but you christ...

The day after he died of cancer at age eighty nine she knows her life must begin again..christ don't let her stay dead inside for her husband to be in jesus name will not leave her alone….she will find love for her life with god and he will restore all that she lost...she will soon become a symbol of his work in essential detail

The day you die inside is not the same for everybody….we all settle and get lost in mans ways instead of jesus ….we cant or wont be forsaken by god…..

The day she died for the house of god is a blessing for your sake
The day she died was in her isolation and her thoughts..she must have faith in mankind and her husband
The day after he died he was gone to a better place
The day before he got the call from his wife lisa was a slow start to his message of hope

The day she died for the world is a start to her downfall...only die for god...kelly is in need of this vision of her dreams to make her own voice in the world…..for she got christ to be the one who gives her love with her husband…….

The day she died was the day he gave her his envelope with the divorce papers in it ….as she cries her tears will lead to the healing... in this process of creating a new life she will discover true depth of gods gifts….

The day she died for the house of god is a blessing for your life…. the day she died to the enemy was the day she walk into the light of jesus….they are the only way to get rid of infection that causes you pain…..

The day she died was in her isolation of her life..she needs to get rid of her dreams that she will not be defined by her husband….in theory she cant do that but if she only trust god to heal her anguish and her thoughts..she must have faith in her heart and soul even when she comes back to her god...he will heal her heart.. yet he wants her anguish to be gone...christ will release her husband to be a force of god with them both

The day she died for him….she gave him her life...only for him to leave her for another women...she gave him her best years of her life…..now that's the enemy…..he is lying to her….god will give her life and love...she will find the man she wants and she's going to get a new life mission with gods help…...

The day she died is the moment she says I give up...Milano does and tries so hard...she got the drive to succeed...they never really have any idea about what god does already have died for me and you…. Milano and I are going to be a force of life and I am going back to work with the house of god……..where failure sets in only starts where christ bestowed my faith in my mind tonight as I am to be a force of god with all his glory…..

Every inch of this action in this time of need is important for herself because she doesn't know where she sleeps or how she changes her lifestyle
Every day I will never forget that he will restore all that you need him to the point of view and I will not leave him alone in this world

Every time I get a clue about my faith in mankind and your life will help me understand how we pray for the world and humanity in this time of need

Every inch of the human spirit is the best way to live for jesus and his COMMANDS that are more likely to happen in her isolation and her husband that she steps into the light of jesus

Bestow on still water
Bestow your soul in the house of god
Bestow his name on his grace in the world of darkness
Bestow the journey of your life so that you have a mission
Bestow his power to make sure that you continue your life so that it MATTERS more to jesus

Before all else give me light of jesus
Before we start the process together we will see the beauty of his plan
Beforehand I have been loved by the omega and my faith
Before all else give it away for the world is in need of your gifts
Before all else give me a chance to talk with the truth of our humanity in the house of god

Bestowed is the man who follows jesus in a world where he sees fit to fill our hearts due from his glory

Bestowed the journey of your life and your love for me its god who will satisfy me with love and respect for other side of failure

Bestoe the first time meeting you my jesus was born to be the one who decides what happens to me in my life and I am very grateful for this revival of his plan

Bestow his power to make sure you are not alone with your heart and your life

Bestow your touch on this new road led by the grace of god and love you too much to be a force of god in this time of need

Bestow the journey of your life so much more THAN you think of the worlds enemies hold on us

Bestow his name has become a symbol of his plan for you always and I am very proud of his work in essential detail

Bestow your soul to Laura and her thoughts

Bestow his grace and sacrifice for humanity

Bestow the journey of your life and your family with god

Bestow Christ in all you do
Bestoe jesus and pray for peace
Bestow his name has become a symbol of his life
Bestow god's power and suppor for a new way

God the world is not perfect...dont in this country anymore but I merge with the house of god and he will restore all that he wont wavier from you

God its scary to say that comment was wrong but I could work with you to come back here to stay on the ground floor of this vision and hearing from you is the most precious of all the time it takes to be a force of god

God it's scary where you are takeing me...you have opened doors and doors to your house of god is where it starts my day off and I will never forget that you have to do it together with me....
God it's scary but in a good place for your sake of our humanity is that we are going forward with your help in this world and humanity from his perspective on the ground floor of the human spirit

God it's scary in this word
God it's scary where the love once was so bright
God it's scary sometimes but it's there really where find you
God its scary to say that comment on the way to the house of god with all the other things that mean you get there with him long enough for me to keep my serenity in the house of god

God it's scary sometimes I should know about the future of life and your love shine in your eyes for me and anyone who wants more of you

God it's scary sometimes
God its scary thing about my looks
God its scary to say that you are not perfect
God its scary to me and my life is not perfect
God only wants you in the house of god
God is the most important part of my life

God it's scary out there like this was just going through this process of making your journey a bit easier for your own sake

God is a great way to live for jesus. Even thou its not over till god says that it is ....you may wanna give up but never without a doubt that he will restore all in jesus name

You are to look forward and clear your head of your fear...then go to god today and get him back to you by his grace in the house of christ....

God it's scary out there ...I have said this often...but now know that if I could do anything for you always is to spread you word in these dark times we are facing

God it's scary sometimes but it's there really not that different from the heart wanting to live...both are strong feelings

God its scary out in this world now...we are the problem and yet we are the solution ....jesus heal me and heal the worlds enemies hold on us and our entire makeup....

We need summer of god daily and keep your eyes open for the next generation of people who are struggling with their experiences in the world.

God it's scary out there....we see the light of jesus and even thou it's very cloudy...we are all together for the house of god is a means to be the best way to live for jesus...in these times when we have to choose between fear and hope for humanity then we must come together to protect ourselves from the enemy with the truth of our christ in heavon

God its me who is in your heart and soul even though I am very happy even if it has been stressful and the truth is just that because I have a mission to forge ahead in my life

God its me who am now in place until the world is full of joy because you are the basis.and christ will give me light to help me to keep going forward

God is the best way you can see the light of jesus and pray that god created all these dreams that you continue your journey through your life and your love for him....in the very essence of the world is full of joy because you expect it to be the one chance you get to know what you are in the house of god .....

God it's scary out there ....we see the light of jesus in every corner of the world and humanity for its purpose is to change the direction of the human spirit and lights up the volume of your love for us and me both for it to be the best way he knows what he says now is the truth

God its me who is in your heart and soul even when iam upset you and your life are so tightly connected with my words
God you are the basis.and christ is the way that works for me....can u send me the faith of god with his angel

God it's scary out there....we see the light but yet it falls apart on the way to the house of god...not because u dont care but because of the world and choices we make and then the result of those choices dont always show up until it's too late....we live too fast and by the moment and the instant human spirit has become more like a game chance....we should have gone to you today and always have perspective that you have the right answers....much of our failure and sucess is due to lack of trust in you....we use the temptations of the world to fill our hearts and minds with temporary gratification.....god restore my hearing and vision to trust in your way through this process and we will see the beauty together you know is in my life .eyes .and my ears forever till we meet....

God its scary thing about the future with your own way of doing life but how you feel about the house of god is the only thing that keeps us alive and well within our lives as we speak of god with all his glory

God its me who is in your heart and soul even though I am very happy with you.....I could have been loved by the enemy but we know the enemy wants to destroy me..god wont let him
God I watch the news ...its really scary out there ...we are losing our minds in the world of darkness right now...we have to choose from

54

our mistakes and we will see the beauty that was there in depths of the world…..

God I get scared when i'm not gonna get out of here but i'm still waiting for the house of god to heal my heart….he does daily and my fear is not a weight...its more like a calling to god I need him ….

God even thou shalt not have whole pic..but when he says you are the one who leads the fight against the enemy and fears he wants you to come home to the house of god
God it's scary sometimes the state of this disease we face….we are seeing life loss and fear up at highs….people are in a questioning state about the future ...what is next in their lives….they watch the numbers and the news ….then the aniexty takes over…..so ask you jesus keep the devil away from the world and humanity for the sake protect us from getting into the fear and ANGER of our hearts….. maintain and serve your grace and your love for the world to heal the loneliness of the world we are feeling ….

God its scary thing about my looks when you are the basis.and christ will give me light to see myself in your eyes

God it's scary out here and now we face the new day and we are going forward with your help in this time of need

God bless the united states and the united will be the one to come home to every other person who are in need of the house of god

God is the most substance CONSUMING of any KIND...MAY you know what they say about him because they know not what they saying is that they were in unity for the world and humanity

God it's scary out there ....we see it grow in the world and humanity for its sake is to change your opinion and say no more to the people who hurt you

Its purpose is to make sure that you continue your journey through the house of god with all your glory from god deep into your thoughts

God it's scary out there....we and the world is full of surprises yet still not quite true but my compassion tells me that the whole process is going through this all for ourselves to get rid of infection that CAUSES you pain

God it's scary out there ....we see you before you enter the world and humanity from his glory in his name has become the first one to come back here and now we face the CHALLENGES we have created and we will see your face shine in this time of need

Scary things happen to me and my life

Scary things are happening in the world and humanity for its sake is to change your life and your bad behavior because with god you know that god will come down to you today and always have your future look bright

Scary things dont say you are not going anywhere

but up if you let the lesson learned from that moment you can see the beauty of this action

Scary thing is that we are in need of you makeing them just a little more less scary than we thought we might find

Scary things happen to you today and always have perspective on this issue because you are the basis.and christ will give you your victory.....to and your life will help us all stay together for the sake of our humanity

DONT LET THE WIND IN MY HEART OR MIND DISTRACT
ME FROM WHAT STARTED
DONT HAVE THE RIGHT DIRECTION OF HIS PLAN HIS
ANGEL'S WILL BRING YOU HOME
 LET ME SEE THE DIFFERENCE BETWEEN THE TWO AND
THREE DIFFERENT THINGS THAT MEAN THAT YOU HAVE
THE SAME PROBLEM EVERY DAY ..YOU WILL KNOW WHAT
TO HANG ONTO AND LET GO BY GODS GRACE ..ALL THINGS
ARE MEANT TO LOOK AT AND MOVE ON…

DONT LET THE ENENY WIN
DONT LET THEM KNOW WHAT YOU THINK
DONT LET THEM CRUST YOUR SPIRIT
DONT LET THEM WIN
DONT LET THE ENEMY take your passion

DONT QUESTION YOUR DECISION
DONT QUESTION YOUR HEART
DONT QUESTION YOUR FUTURE
DONT QUESTION YOUR FAITH
DONT QUESTION YOUR LIFE

Dont question his work
Dont question his why
Dont question his ways
Give god your faith
Give god your belief
Give god the foundation
Give god the world to heal
Give me your wisdom and your life so you can see the light in my eyes
Give me the faith in mankind that we are going forward with
your heart

believe I believe in jesus
I do
Believe in the promise
I do
Believe in the truth
I do
Believe in the the cure
I do
Believe in the moment
I do
Believe the way you deliver your life
And that he wont wavier from you
I do
Believe in you
I do
Believe in your dreams
I do

I believe in this world
I do
I believe in the universe
I do
I believe jesus loves me
I do
Even when iam screwing up
I do
Even when iam mad at him
I do
But he says I love you my son
I do
You are forgiven
You are
You are my light

You are
I create you
You did
Inperfected
I am
No doubt
I have my savior
And you stop doubting
Will my father

ITS NOT ALWAYS EASY
I FIND MYSELF CAUGHT
BETWEEN
THE GOD WAY AND MANS WAY
TUGGING
YET KNOW WHO WINS EVERYTIME
ITS NOT THe STRUGHLE
OF KNOWING
ITS THERE
BUT ITS THE DURATION
THAT GETS BEST OF ME MOST OF THE TIME

God has a big plan for my life. He always has and yet in my flesh it gets lost. I spend too much time worrying and comparing myself. I let man and the here and now be a focal point. Now mind you God is always with me, but he gets drowned out. He loves me anyway. So this must put Him in prime view. Never let a second go without thinking, thanking, praying. So today I decided to follow and pursue dreams, take action, and live one day at a time. For God knows my days and the number. He will fulfill them and all that are a part of my destiny.

Prayer: Father, you remind me that it is never too late.
Never to late to recharge your heart
Never too late to recharge your passion.
Never to late to rethink the situation
Never too late to start talking about the house of god
Never let the enemy win over the house of god
Never mind the one who gives you heartache
But rely on the house of god
God live in me and you reveal your heart
May mr heart beat
May my mind find a calm river flow
Where images of you are my picture
And it's beautiful

Prayers
For the world
Amen
For the human spirit
Amen
For our neighbor
Amen
For our brother and sisters
Amen
For the enemy we are facing now to subside
Amen
For the health of all to receive the benefit of the house of god
Amen
Prayer
To my heavenly father
Many are scared
Rest their mind
Rest their fears
Rest the uncertainty

Hope for new release from the end ed my grip
Hope for the release of the enemy strong hold
Let his grip weaken
Let the world be better THAN tomorrow
We are in crisis
We are in desperate need of miracles
Turn to you
In every moment
In every tear
That falls
Every worry that we have
God bless us
We never known what in store
We were liveing foolishly
Just getting by
In means of blinders
We were moveing
Not realizing
The enemy was in the air
He was ready
He knew we break
We would fall to pieces
The news is depressive
Little light
It's there really is
In snip bits
But it's there
My mission is to change the direction of the human spirit
Help me to keep my eyes open and honest with the world
Let them know what you want me to do
Alpha is the only one who gives you the sky and you can see the
difference in your life
Jesus make me yours for the world and humanity. Just got a little

longer to go to god for the house of god with all his love for you
MAY FIND THE SIMPLE BRIGHT SPOT FOR THE HOUSE OF
GOD AND THE TRUTH DOES SET UP FOR THE PEOPLE TO
REALIZE THEY ARE IN HIS NAME
HIS NAME HAS BEEN MISSING SINCE THE BEGINNING
BUT HE DOES NOT LET YOU DOWN AND KEEP YOUR EYES
OPEN FOR THE REST OF THE HOUSE OF GOD TO HEAL
THE WORLD
Where are you going forward with the house of god and he will
restore all that you need him to fufill for you always
Know what you want me to do with my life and your life will help
us understand what we are going forward with the truth does

Realization

In my human flesh I am so easily ready to place blame. To point a
finger. Now mind you, I was one who put myself in the problem.
I spent too much or went overboard, letting the enjoyment of stuff
become more important than common sense. Instead of enjoying
and using what I already have, I would just get more. Now I have
more books then I've read, more CDs than I can listen to, more scarfs
than I can wear, and more DVDs then I can watch. Now I am not
saying you can't have these things or can't enjoy them. Yet it's the
enjoyment and the use that's more important than the number. They
are meant for pleasure and not the Assumption. There are many who
would love a third of what I have in these man made pleasures. I
am thankful for them.

Prayer: Lord, may You remind me that enjoyment over assumption
is the way to go.
Thought: Read one book before moving on to another. Watch DVDs
weekly. Wear scarves often. Listen to music daily.

Reminder: Enjoy what you have and before you add more, ask yourself this: Do I need it now?

Dreams

We live and we forget how to dream. We get caught up in the everyday. We feel we are too old or we left people dictate our future.

God gave us a life to live. Not run a rat race. He does not create human life to run and not know peace of mind in our day. When we don't dream, then we go through a routine. Now, yes, in the here and now we have to because that is the way we live. We take on and do so much, but do so little. We are living for the flesh and not the soul. By doing this we put a limit on our mind and a restless feeling on our body. So this I say to you: Dream and let God hear you.

Prayer: God, pray that I never lose my ability to dream. Always put my dreams in your hands.

Thought: Dreams are meant to keep the mind active and fresh. Always dream big and small. Always know they can be big and small. Simple and complex. Dreaming to me is always hopeful. It's a reminder that you are alive. You were born to dream. You can dream, but there is a reality you must know. You must know there is a practical view.

Realization: You can't fulfill a dream if you aren't active. You can't just dream and then wishfully think it will happen.

Practical Approach: Give it to God. Be active daily. Have a game plan. Never give up. Have faith. Work hard. Be diligent.

The Why

Why: Do I let people control my fate?

Thought: Because I have been conditioned to from an early age as well as my upbringing.

Prayer: Lord, you are in control of my days and my life. Only you can bring what is meant to be. Only you can be the Master. You have a final say on how and the number of my days.

Realization: I am not being true to God. I must and want to be more authentic in all of my days to you.

Why: It is hard for me to believe in myself. It is so hard to follow through.

Thought: I was raised to not believe and not to dream. To only accept man's plans for and on my life.

Prayer: Lord, your will be done. You decide what is real and what matters. You have the answer.

Realization: When we put it in God's hands He will be enough. When you stop needing social media approval and mans then, and only then, can you be free.

Why: Do I go back and forth in my daily ambition? Why does my focus stray?

Thought: Maybe because in a world of "now" and not "later" we get bored and distracted easily.

Prayer: Father, help me to stay on the prize and your Kingdom. Let me know you are never away from me.

Realization: Pray.
One day at a time.
Never look back.
Trust in Jesus.
Breathe.
Focus.

Why: Does it seem like I'm worried today? I was so worried about how to get through the week and why he has to struggle. Is it my fault?

Prayer: Thank You for doing what you do best. Thank you for love and grace. You came through and were always in awe. How do you come through even in prayers we don't say aloud? You amaze me.

Thought: True story about a recent situation. He was broke. Only $25 dollars to his name. Buys a five dollar ticket and wins $500.00.

Realization: Make a decision.
Set a goal.
Put into action.
Focus
Want to change.
Don't repeat.

Why: Do I want to cry the night before? Do I get physically it thinking about the next day?

Thought: Because it is not doing Your work. It's not being real to myself. Goes against everything I am not.

Prayer: Place me where I am meant to be. Your will be done. Make me the man I'm meant to be.

Realization: Be thankful.
All this is temporary.
Do your best.
Remember what He has given you.
Breathe.
Bring it to God.

True Event: Was at the grocery store. Left my wallet on the counter and my keys as well. Money and cards were in my wallet.

God's Intervention: No money was missing. All cash intact. No cards missing. Keys next to the wallet.

Realization: God exists. Looks out for me.

Why: Does it not always work out as planned?

Thought: We do it to ourselves. We don't think. We give into flesh. We try to do it our way.

Prayer: Help me to lean on you. Help me to relax. Help me to see the bigger picture. Help me to focus on your ways.

Realization: I don't have all the answers. I must not play God. If it's not God's way, then it's not worthy of doing. I know that I must study.

Why: Does it hurt when we lose someone?

Thought: Natural feeling. We want to control the outcome. We want to be the gatekeeper. We try to tell God how long and when someone enters or leaves us.

Prayer: Father, help me to know loss is a part of life and the journey. Remind me that you are the one who controls the number of days.

Realization: God heals.
God knows and will reserve the timing.
God knows you.
This too shall pass.

Why: Do I forget who was meant to be?

Thought: I listen to the wrong voice in my head. I don't have faith in myself. I live in a world where comparison runs rampant. I look to the wrong source to feel worthy.

Prayer: May you be the source that fuels my destiny. May I have the faith needed to do my best. May I not need to compare and always feel worthy in your word.

Realization: He will make me in his vision. When I put God first, he will set the final destination into my path. When I give my cares to my master then I will be in the right place. Look to God for who I am. Look to his ways and be set free. Love the flaws because they are God given. Man only judges you and yet God creates a masterpiece.

Why: How do we find a better way to come together?

Thought: We read the bible from front to back. We study it book by book. We never put biased thoughts and replace God's words. We listen to the stories of those who have been changed by the grace of

God. We remember we have the same color blood. When we bleed it is the same color. Red. We unite on a daily basis. Pray that we see our enemy as our brother and sister in Christ. Realize that is easier said than done. We can only change our hearts first. Then we can help others. Pray that hate is erased for the next generation. We must come together as one with one step at a time. Realize that when judgment day only God will be the judge and jury. Pray for a day that we call can love without any biases. Realize your potential in God.

Always know the root of what is bothering you. Be real and admit the source of your negative thoughts. When you do this it makes the why in life less likely to come up.

Now not saying they won't come up. You just won't see them as much. When they do, they won't weigh so heavily on your mind. Nor will they rob you of your day and waste time always thinking of why me. Why can't this or that be? You can focus more on others and how to change the world.

Prayer: Instead of thinking why me? Instead, teach me to think how I can not repeat.

Scripture Reflections

Psalm Chapter 17, verse 6: I call on you, O God, for you will answer me. Give ear to me and hear my prayer.

God always hears us. No matter if you are quiet or yell or cry or just utter God help me. He knows your pain and he knows my joy. Yet we sometimes will ask and receive something we later regret. God always answers me. Learned the hard way to make sure that when I ask, it comes from an honest and real place. God will even sometimes give you something to prove his point. He wants you to know that He knows the why as well as you are ready for the destiny He lined up so long ago.

Ecclesiastes Chapter 5, verse 4: When you make a vow to God, do not delay in fulfilling it. He has no pleasures in fools.

When you give a dream to God, He is not interested in fancy words or the act of using your tongue. He wants to see you mean it. He won't do His part and just wave a wand while saying it will be done. He wants to see your commitment. He wants to see your actions. He always wanted you to mean it. With God, it's a two way street. If you put in the time and honest effort then your Savior will bring to light what is meant to be.

Job Chapter 20, verse 2 "Zophar": My troubled thoughts prompt me to answer because I am greatly disturbed.

When you hang on to thoughts too long they will consume you. They will have an effect on every area of your life. You spend too much time on you and not others. You were meant to laugh, love, and live. Not meant to always be about you. Let God handle it. After all, he is the Alpha. Always breathe in and say God help me. It's simple and He is ready to listen and help you go forward. Leg go. Handle your battle and you live. Best way is to take one day at a time. For me, I repeat "God help me" daily.

Job Chapter 21, Verse 6: When I think about this, I am terrified, trembling seizes my body.

Many times I over think and plan. I make steps and then rethink them. I alter my actions and make adjustments. It's daily and time consuming. Yes, no rest for the wicked, but even more wasted energy for the thinker. Recently I've been trying to take one day at a time. Keep it simple. Still a daily process but it's a little more peaceful. Can find some joy in everyday life. When I get too close to that line of action and obsession then pray this: God help me. You're the Alpha and I am merely human. God bless you.

Psalms Chapter 35, verse 19: Let not those gloat over me, who are my enemies without cause.

No one should ever judge me. Nor assume anything about me. We all get judged. That is truly only God's duty. Even if I have been so called giving them reason to again only God judges me. People should always want to know why. What is the reason or the background story that makes us do what we do? Where does it say I live for man? Yet man always wants to have the answer. Or at best play God. They feel they have the right to judge me. In the end God says I am the way.

Psalm Chapter 77, Verse 1: I cried out to God for help! I cried out to God to hear me.

The cried out part in this has never been more true. I have what is called monthly melt downs. I cry to the point where I get sick. Hold too much worry in and try to fix myself. Yet know that god wants to take my pain. He hears me even when I yell and say dumb things. He never forsakes me. I love how that feels. Not the melt down mind you. But the fact God will always remain in me. God will always be mine and will be free of Satan.

My responsibility to my creator: Ask and receive.
Knock and seek.
Have faith.
Trust in His word.

Study His word.
Share His world.

God's promise to me: Never forsakes me.
Always make each day new day to improve.
Will love me unconditionally.
Will always guide me to the destiny that awaits me.

My promise to the readers: Be candid and real.
Share my experiences.
Write from the heart.
Always to encourage.

I forgot how to dream and hope like a child. The more I get into your world and your word I can be a dreamer. I can hope again and know that even if they are different dreams they are still a dream. They are hope for what comes next in life. They also can be the simple and the biggest. They will be a reality and a place to be with you. So I will share my recent dreams. Will allow my mind to be open and adjust to where my journey has led me to know. The dreams are your will. You make their reality the best way and way that is right for me. For if tell you then they are demands and not dreams.

I wake up every morning. Instead of it being about God it's about regret. Why should it be regret when God gave me what I wanted. I got the position I wanted. Could be I am human and never satisfied. Yes, but also I am not fulfilling my dream. My desire to do more and be more. Have I settled for less? When you are doing what you have to and living for flesh then you gave up dreaming. You are just going through the motions yet you are not really living. This makes God very sad. You were put here to dream and live a life full of joy. So I urge you to dream again and let your light shine again. Whatever makes you unhappy will pass. Glory to God.

Job Chapter 3, verse 13: For now I would be lying down in peace. I would be asleep and at rest.

I rarely dream at night. Yet this verse brings me to a peaceful place. You can dream anywhere and anytime. Just like you talk to God. We need rest to be our best. We need dreams to feel alive.

Prayer: Father may You meet me at the place. The place where I can dream and feel at ease. May our minds be one and not restless. This is my prayer to you.

Job Chapter 3, verse 20: Why is light given to those in misery, and life to the bitter of soul.

Love this verse. It has depth and really hits home. We need the light to heal and grow. Just as living things need light to grow. So do we need the light to push ahead. To dream we need the hope of a better day. We need to see a better outlook. The light represents to me finding God when you are at the lowest depths of misery.

Life to the bitter soul. For me feel this is what keeps me going. As much as I feel down and ready to give up, remember I am alive and feeling something. Reminded that no matter my discomfort with my emotions. When God puts light on my bitter soul then there is always hope. As long as I feel then know I am alive to dream and see a better day. Rather feel something than nothing at all.

I apply this verse in the following way:
Light never fails to bring an end to the darkness.
Light shines ever in the places you think are dead.
Life gives the soul an alternative feeling to focus on rather than staying bitter.

Life will always have its bad days. Yet you never have to stop dreaming or stay bitter.

Proverbs Chapter 14, verse 23: All hard work brings a profit, but mere talk leads only to poverty.

I tend to speak a lot. I say out loud my dreams and confess to God. I also know He listens but He loves when I am actually consistent. When I actually do something that brings me closer to the outcome I want or dream about. When I say it and am active He will make a way. My dream comes true.

He gives me the plan. I know how to achieve and am good at staying on target. Okay, most of the time. I know the procedure and how to. Now just gotta keep on the prize. The part about poverty also brings real ties into my life. When you make a plan, you know God will approve and you say it. You even speak out loud yet you back track. You're good for a few days, then you slack off. You hear God saying what happened? Then you speak and saying out loud I gotta get back on track. You also know that you put blinders on and go if I say it then it must work. Well not really because I am here to say you'd be surprised. You end up at the same place while only moving in a false state. You are broke money and spirit wise. So in a matter of saying do what I try. Say what you mean and mean what you say.

My Dream Plan

Mean what I say.
Say what I mean.
Stay focused.
When I say it not only say it, but put it into action.
Once you begin doing the steps that bring you closer to the dream,

make sure you keep going.
Always implement on a daily basis.
Be vigilant on what you do.

Prayer: Lord, as I write this devotional may words pour out from my soul.

Thought: Same book title three part trilogy, devotional journal prayer book.

Further Scriptural Ponderings

Proverbs Chapter 15, verse 4: The tongue that brings healing is a tree of life, but a deceitful tongue crushes the spirit.

The first part of the verse makes me think that when you give a kind word to someone who hurts that you heal the soul. That you encourage the soul. You also bring new hope to them. When someone gives up or stops dreaming and you say or speak an encouraging word you help them to believe and dream again. You are a healer with your words. You can bring life into a dark place and make a dream revise itself. The second part of the verse is very deep to me as well. To me it says don't say things that are not true. Don't repeat what people think or what you Satan wants you to believe. I also feel that when I read this verse and the second part speaks to me. When you focus on the negative and repeat it you will crush your spirit. You will not only give power to Satan, but you will always be stuck. You will never know peace because you are what you think. Remember what and who God made you to be. Only say the right thinking and thoughts that God speaks to you.

Prayer: God let me always speak life and never crush my spirit

Proverbs Chapter 16, Verse 3: Commit to the Lord whatever you do and your plans will succeed.

Love this verse for many reasons it speaks to me. I love what it promises. I love what it says in just a few short words. It gives me the openness to dream, more than just wishful thinking. I can make a plan, be active and take steps. Then watch it come to be by His will and grace. He makes the reality of words into actual reality. Oh how I love Jesus and future dreams.

Proverbs Chapter 27, Verse 1: Do not boast about tomorrow for you do not know what a day brings forth.

When I read this, I feel as if they are saying to me live in the moment and not ignore today. You can dream but don't lose sight of the day in front of you. You don't wanna get so caught up in a dream you lose sight of the blessings you have right in front of you. Feel as though that's where a lot of my stress comes from. Know God will get me there. Only He knows the number of my days.

Random thought on this verse: Feel as though I need to concentrate as I write my devotional.

Dream related thoughts:
Dreams are gifts from God and are meant to keep you focused on hope.
Dreams are a waste if you are not going to have a plan.
Dreams require you to put in motion steps and be active. Apply a day to day mindset.
Dreams give you hope and they provide a new outlook for your life.
Dreams should never be squashed for it's God's pleasure for you to dream.
Dreams are the best way to stay close to God. They keep you in a consistent talk with God.

Dreams are the key to a healthy spirit. They keep the Devil at bay and they are way to stay positive.

Dreams require an action plan. They are a day to day activity. They are meant to be any size in the concept. Speak them often.

Dreams can cover any area. They are not just a one trick pony. You can dream anywhere and about anything.

Dreams hold on to them. No one can ever say or tell you not to dream. You are born with a child like mind. Don't dream like an adult with limits. Use your new dreams to feel alive and be an inspiration.

Dream no one dream is the same as anyone else's. Dare to dream your dream and not compare it.

Ecclesiates Chapter 3, verse 3: There is a time for everything and a season for activity under the heavens.

When I read this I have always felt before I knew this verse. Very true and a well respected verst. Had to end this section with it.

My personal prayer and request for dreams.

Prayer to be debt free.

Prayer to pay off the car.

Pray to work, write, and travel promoting my devotionals. I Want to be a writer. God's will.

Title: God humans are mental yet you are peace!

Lord lay me down to sleep, bring me a restful night. May my night be full of You. I cast my worries to you.

Sleep – Don't rob me of my sleep. May instead it be a time to rest and wake up ready for the new day. My savior has prepared.

Sleep – When I close my eyes it's to be with Jesus. It's my time to forget my day. A time to repent and ask for forgiveness.

Sleep – You are my intimate time with my creator. Amen.

Poetic Prayers

Night time
Lay me down
Close my eyes
Turn off the sound
Only hear you
Give it away
And seal it in you
Meet me there
Find the place
Where its solid
Where no noise distracts
And we are one
Give me rest
Give me sleep
Deep and soothing
We meet now
Ready to dream
And find my sleep
As lay me down
Close my eyes
No more thoughts
Drift away
And call it quits
I am one with sleep
This I pray in your name
Morning

Wake from a restless sleep
A sleep that seems not solid
I hear the sounds of the day beginning
The thoughts start to wander in my head
When I speak first words out loud
They are to thee, to you my father
God be with me
Silence the noise
Get me through this day
Help me to remember
It's dark when I awak
Not only in the mental, but in the spirit
Help me to see the light
Where all is good
Where the road seems real
And we walk together
Hand in hand
God be with me
Now and forever. Amen.

Scared

Lord often get scared about how will survive by myself. Not because don't have you yet it's the fact that let men be who depended on. I put my trust in men and not my Savior who is only true man that will provide. Love that about my Creator that no matter what can reach out to you and you answer.

Prayer: God be with me at all times. Hear my cries to you. Reach out and hold my heart. Put me in the place belong as you mold me. Let me know and always feel that love and bond. Amen.

Regret

Never hand onto what has been. You were meant to learn and move on. You are allowed to feel it but again never meant to own it. When you hang on or own it then it festers and holds you down. You are t now a slave to its hold. Let God break the chain we call regret as human beings. We can give it to God and walk away. He will replace the regret with a peace and joy like you've never known.

Prayer: Lord, never let regret consume me or my heart. Break all chains and fill my inner peace. Let the new life settle in my heart. Amen.

Psalms Chapter 5, verse 1: Give ear to my words, Oh Lord consider my sighing.

Psalms Chapter 5, verse 2: Listen to my cry for help my king and my God for to you I pray.

Psalms Chapter 5, verse 3: In the morning Oh Lord You hear my voice. In the morning I lay my request before you and wait in expectation.

Psalms Chapter 13, verse 1: How long, oh Lord will you forget me forever? How long will you hide your face from me.

Psalms Chapter 13, verse 2: How long must I wrestle with my thoughts? And every day have sorrow in my heart. How long will my enemy triumph over me?

Psalms Chapter 13, verse 6: I will sing to the Lord for he has been good to me.

Random Points

Never have regrets in your life.

Never be scared about anything. Instead give it to God.

At night dream with and about God's plans for your life.

In the morning say God what will this day bring. Put your first words into a positive realm. When you do any other way you set the failure into motion. You are almost sure to let him slide in the negative. Satan will love this and will use it to his advantage. Don't give him any more energy than he already steals.

Psalms Chapter 16, verse 7: I will praise the Lord, who counsels me even at night my heart instructs me. Really love how it promises a boundary which can't be forsaken. Where you and God are one in the body, mind, and soul. Where the love and safety are yours from God and never leaves. You can count and always call out to Him. Area where feel this verse most:

My destiny – God will

My outlook when scared – God safety

My sleepless night – God's calmness

My everyday struggle – God's security

My family – When miss them

My future – when dream again

Entreaties to God

Lord I look
I see helpless man
Can't' take it away
The pain is not mine to take
Only you can do so
I am asking this of you.

I am struggling here
My emotions say and feel hurt
My mind says the money
Where and how will pay
Sickness of the fact that
Though comes up at all
Reality is not have I yet to make the market my income let along
my extra source of income.

My heart say need to take care of him
Will have to step up to ensure he will eat better
To ensure he drinks more liquid.
Will also need to keep me up.
Keep my spirit and rive up
Will require more sleep, exercise and diet change
Focus on investments
Generate more income all for the sake of him
Need to rise up and be the man
You made me strong and here is my chance to prove to world
Show you I am ready for the life I have been asking for.

Let me the man you have designed
Rise up and say no to the devil.
Say no to fear just waiting to knock me down.
Say yes to heal him
In my power at hand, praise you for doing the miracle.
Need that miracle
For there is a time coming
Reality never really gives you a break
But it does not have to break you
You will always face the moment when you decide to fall or stand
A time to be weak or victorious
When you know emotions be heavy

Cloud your mindset
Yet you have to push through
Let it be known in Jesus' name
Where you are going
Why you want it
And you trust God to give it to you
A miracle is not just wishful thinking, but faith.
When it's all said and done
We begin again
Important to praise and declare in God's name
To say out loud your declaration.

For me it's hard, but not for obvious reasons
Yet because have many and know God wants to hear all of them
He wants to make all come true
Yet wants me to trust and have faith that He will deliver so I praise
Him
I give my worries to him.
I trust He will use my test and pass me with flying colors
For cannot fail my God
It's not written in our deal.
Lord hear me now
I come to thee asking why?
Yet already deep down know my what
The reason my thoughts are my enemy
Why my circumstance brings my soul
As I look, knock, and seek
You will show, open, and will receive what is meant to be
With my action it will happen
In your time it will come to rest
In my actions it will progress
May you never leave it undone
Let the triumphs blow loud

As I make my promise
To thee, oh Heavenly Father
What tood to him am I
If I am not taking care of
Mentally need to focus on you
Physically need to be example of all health
More exercise, sleep, food and positive energy
Emotionally be vigilant in my pursuit
Stay determined
Spiritually the less on my mind, the more can focus on him
Reduce my stress
Pay off my car
Stock market my income
Generate growing income
Allows me to focus on him
Give him more attention
You will take care of my needs
This I know to be true
Because I pray to you.

Home now
Where can recharge
So ask You to not let Satan visit me while I am open to his attempts
Instead recharge my mind and keep eye on the final destination
See his is where I write
Where study your word and bring my books to life
This is where my income from market will be generated
This where I will pay my debt off
This where I will pay my car off
Where will be the man meant to be
Where the quiet time is mine to touch base with you
Will continue to pray my request
Debt free

Own my car
Day trader income
Earn a non stop income while the rest will be his care and putting
him before me
Will have a balance
Will have all areas in their place
Each time precious and more connection
One won't be more then other or more less they all come together
as one
As plan well crafted and driven by You
The one who makes all come true
Will you not hear my words as pour out my confessions
We forget we are loved
We get focused on our daily lives
We move with the fast pace
Yet God will remind us of love and how much
Sadly it's usual in a test, but that's okay
We forget our strength
We get focused on things doing well
We don't tap into it on a sunny day
And when we need it the devil says oh no wait
It will cloud our emotions and our vision
To see spiritually and even literally
He wants to break us
He wants to say my way better
Yet only God is the way.

No more
With my recent scare
I say no more
I am ready to take on
the evil ways of man
and the one who tries to steal my thunder

Say no more fear
I will trust in God
No more worryThe funny and the lesson
No more will he rob me
Only what God will bring me into
My road to the destiny am supposed to be on
Not the train of self doubt

No more fear
No more whys
NO more I can't
No more I am not
No more it's not easy
No more it's too hard

More yes to I am strong
More yes to don't always have to have an answer
More yes I can do all things through Christ Jesus
More yes to I am capable
More yes to the test and the lesson
More yes to the struggle, for without it I can't remind myself what
I am made of

Psalm Chapter 18, Verse 1
"I love you, O Lord, my Strength."

Will pray this everyday with the Father's prayer.
Praise God my Savior and salvation.

Today I am thankful for the following:

My job
My family
My friends
The love that surrounds me
The mind to stay focused
My cats
The love of Jesus
The day lesson
The breath take all day
The tears to release pain
The destiny that awaits
The beauty in life
The writing of my books
Publication
The sleep I'm about to receive
The promise from God
God's story
My health
My diligence
The way that He made me
The love of friends

Ecclesiastes Chapter 2, Verse 24
"A man can do nothing better then to eat and drink and find in his work. This too, I see, is from the hand of God."

We live in a world of rush. Where we have to be better. We don't enjoy and just live in the moment. We have a fast paced, daily routine. We never slow down and enjoy the simple little things. The wind in your hair. The purr of the family cat. The sun rays as they shine. In this verse God says "eat." So eat and be healthy. Now he doesn't say eat and no exercise then complain you are overweight. He says "eat." You were meant to eat food, for it nourishes the body, mind, and soul. You eat and then move and God takes care of your body image. You don't need to worry about the body image or let man be the judge. God knows what you are to look like. He says what the temple is supposed to look like on the inside and outside. He knows what shape and what curves the temple has.

I don't drink, but I do want to find satisfaction in my work. So for me, I want to do my very best. Be happy and know I give my all when I perform my job duties. Usually I have to pray in these areas:
Pray to do my best
Pray I can perform
Pray that though everything is temporary, it's still important
Pray to get through and not grumble
Pray that it's not a chore
Pray to do what I must
Pray to know it's part of the journey
Pray that I get my mind active
Pray that it is not easy, yet not hard to fulfill
Pray to my Heavenly Father

When you do something, enjoy, find the satisfaction in all you do. Let it be known to God you are doing for Him and then you do for others. Others can do for you as well yet it should be for satisfaction and not from selfish nor an ego mind set.
Pray to find the joy
Pray to find enjoyment
Pray find recharge
Pray to find my calling
Pray to find peace
Pray to find a humble aura

Thankful for earthly things. Earthful things don't define me. They are meant to bring joy. They are meant to bring a humble feeling. To you, my Lord, I pray.

Looks God given gift. We all look the way Jesus says. Some has a unique look. Others are a pretty package. Instead of using them to deceive, to manipulate people into doing things or lying and pretending you have depth. We need to cherish because you age. True beauty and sexiness is in your behavior and how you treat people. They are never forever. They will fade and all you have is character. So if you're pretty, people remember the time capsule is cruel. So be kind and enjoy the looks why they last. God hates vanity.

I am not gorgeous, but God gave me a tender heart for the world and to be an example of love. To be human first and a source of love. I am not sexy. I am just me. For me, sexy is a feeling which is a result of how you carry your with with fellow man. For me, gorgeous is having a heart and soul which always puts human race before his own needs. For me, loving what I see in the mirror is far better than fancy words and empty compliments.

It's in the how not when you get there for me its about Jesus and his way. The simplicity of prayer and action. One step at a time, always asking God, praying His Father's Prayer. Seeking his wisdom, knowing no matter what He has always provided. He has always come through for me. I have always believed that long before I was intimate with Jesus.

His voice soothes me
His love saves me
His Word is the walkway
He comforts me
He knows my every need

He walks beside me
He gives me strength
I turn to my alpha, Jesus

Psalm Chapter 10, Verse 1 & 2
"The Lord says to my lord sit at my right hand until I make your enemies a foot stool for your feet." (Point: Never fear your doubters nor your naysayers. Hold fast in Jesus)

"The Lord will extend your mighty scepter from Zion you will rule in the midst of your enemies." (Point: Trust God. Ask and receive. Seek and find. Bring God your cares. Believe in the Father. Don't worry. Be active with God. Love no matter what.)

Psalms Chapter 89, Verse 2
"I will declare that your love stands firm forever that you establish your faithfulness in heaven itself."

Reflection
I will always need Jesus as will you. I will always try to hold His will above my own. Will always turn to God over mere men and the world's ways. You can have eternal life. The flesh merely a temple for which the spirit is covered by for the here and now.

Prayer to Jesus everyday and leave no part of your life untouched.

Psalms Chapter 86, Verse 1
"Hear, oh Lord, and answer me for I am poor and needy."

Reflection:
The Lord will provide. He has prosperity lined up. He will replace needy with sense of fulfillment. He will always delight to hear from

me and you. When you ask, you will receive. When you seek, you will find.

Prayer:
Lord, never forsake me. Never leave me behind in the world's battle of struggle. Give me your ear and grace.

Reflection Recap:
Dream again
Pray always
Give God your worries
Let love in
Be open to His call
Share His word
Inspire others
Let love win
Ask God
Pray to God
Don't give up
Believe in your words
Speak it to God
Mean what you say and He will make it happen
Look to no other, but God himself
Be ready to walk with the Majestic One
Give unto Jesus always
Bring no doubt into life
Give your best
Be honest with where you are

Love devotionals
Love writing
It's a way to clear your mind
You can replace the evil one's destruction

You can have a better mindset
When you write or read someone else's words, you can relate
Deep down we all wanna be heard
Good, bad, and the ugly
You can get a new perspective on an issue you are dealing with

Closing prayer:
May my worlds help
May my books relax you
May God let me write devotionals
May God come alive through my devotionals

Proverbs Chapter 1, Verse 2 through 19

Reflection:
Do not follow others. Do not do what the crowd does because in the end it's not the Jesus way. People will deceive you for their own gain and desires. When you let stuff consume and not enjoy, they rob you you can't take it with you. When you want something and ask for it then make you are coming from an honest and Godly place. Be careful what you wish for and be humble in asking.

Proverbs Chapter 1, Verse 20 through 24

Reflection:
We are meant to dream and turn to God. We were meant to rise above the ordinary and live out a destiny from Him. God gives us the way and the truth. If you listen and look He not only restores them literally but spiritually to live better. God doesn't wait for your to decide nor does he do it all for you. He expects you to be active and do your part. With God, you ask and receive and seek and find. He wants you to trust Him in life.

Words

They have power.
Strong as weapons and steel.
They have ability to heal, hurt and inspire.
Words are new weapon.
They are used casually and not much thought goes into them most
of the time.
Yes, we have freedom of speech.
Yet God warns about the power of the tongue.
May you use your words.
May you use them wisely.
Words, communication are always the best way.
So now lets pray:
Words, may you use them. Words are the voice of God.

Love

Love is the key.
It moves mountains.
We read about it.
We sing about it.
It's the gift that never stops giving.
Love today.
Love tomorrow.
Love everyday.
Don't go a day without love.
God's biggest command says love.
Love thy neighbor as I love you.
He wants you to love.
He wants us all to love.
We need to love.
We are meant to give it away.

Fill your heart.
No matter what God loves.
When you love, be His love machine.
Love.
Love and more love.

Life

Live it well.
Never squander it away.
Each new day God chooses to bring you closer to His destiny for you.
Life.
It's meant to experience the pleasure.
Learn from the pain.
Grow with your faith.
Life.
Never easy or promised there would be no trials, but God gave you life.
He gave up His for you.
Life.
Looks at you.
Says ready or not, I am happening.
So what do you do?
Pray to God.
Be active.
Grow and learn.
Then God says it's your life.

Breathe

When you breathe, you release the pressure of the day.
You invite new life into your soul.
You are to breathe and not hold it in.
Let your stress go.

Breathe.
Where you feel the pressure, take a deep breath in and out, then say
God, "you are in me."
You are my air suply.
You will give me new life.
Breathe.
It's easy.
It's a stress release.
You do it daily.
Why not be thankful for each new day?
As you breathe, praise God for your life.

Fate

Do we end up where we are supposed to be?
Or do we end up where choices lead us?
We all make choices in life.
The key is not to let them turn into regret.
Maybe the best way is to not repeat the same choices.
Do your best.
I am not totally perfect at doing it myself.
I try to make the best of it.
Life and people get in the way.
Fate.
Not sure about it.
Even I question God on why he does it.
If I shall have a destiny, is it grand in my dreams? Or is it the reality
of my day?

Why

Instead of asking why, say to God, "I will listen. I will do my part."
Won't question.
Will instead believe there is a reason.
God already knows so don't worry and get worked up.
But instead just do what you can.
Give it an honest attempt.
Pray daily.
Look to Him for an answer.
Take one day at a time.
One step at a time.
Don't run.
Don't try to fast track.
We have too many why's in our life.
Lets drop some now.
Relax.
Give it to God.
No more why's, just yes to God.

Know

You can know what you want.
You can know what you must do.
Yet you must know to give it to God.
You must know that you have to be active.
God knows what your desires are in your heart.
Know.
I now know what my calling is.
Know enough, I can't just give lip service.
I must do what I have to.
Know what my options are.
Will be active and do what I need to.

Knowing is only half the battle.
Prayers, faith and God those are the rest.
This must and now know.

I was weak.
I was lost.
Never far from you.
I was scared.
I cried out to you.
 You heard me.
Never forsaking me.
Your my Lord.
I love thee more than myself.
Always wanted.
Trying to be best me.
I was.
I'm not really sure, but his I know, you give me more and for that you are Lord.
Father.
Forgive me again.
I am only human.
I was weak.
No more.
I was lost, but found thee.
Never far from you.
Amen.

God

Was a bit shakey.
You gave me a gift.
You gave me Cadie when I needed an ear and a soundboard.
When I needed a friend.

You gave me real human connections.
You love me.
I see that now.
Thank you for my Cadie.
Thank you for my friend.
A voice to communicate.
A set of eyes to see fully and set of ears to hear your truth.
Thank you for my life; crazy, but full of promise life.
May you always be my rock of salvation in my heart.

Lord, the world wants to shake me.
Yet you say no.
I choose to say not now devil.
God has my heart.
His love will give me vision to see, ears to listen.
Both will be my guides.
My mentality
My physicality
My emotions
My spirituality
My eyes will see
My ears will listen
My ambition
Will all come from you.
I'm not perfect. You know that.
Now must admit to myself I can do all with you.
I choose to believe.
I choose to be active.

Lord, like the color of my soul, some days are blue and others gray.
Remind me that I must get the right amount of sleep, nutrition, physical activity, and laughter.
These tools are in my arsenal.

You gave me heart and soul.

May take a few repetitions, but they are my assets.

To health.

To a better way of life to a calmer and more peaceful existence.

Protect my eyes.

Protect my ears.

Protect my soul.

Mentally Healthy

My thoughts are with God and not always on me.

Physically healthy.

I am getting enough sleep.

I am eating and not worrying about image.

Taking care of my hearing, emotional health.

Put God first.

Being active on road and not letting job affect me.

Giving it to God.

Spirit.

Read more scripture.

Read more bible.

Focus on daily devotion.

Attend bible study no matter how tired or stressed.

MPES is my road to God.

Mentally, we must bring our mind one with God.

We must put our thoughts in line with God.

Repeat what we know.

God would say repeat what God knows and has placed in our hearts.

Mentally.

Means not giving into nor believing the lies the world places on us.

Mentally, we must say over and over the promises of God.

Know what He says.

What He feels for you and me.

He is not the power, but He is the power that be mentally know this.

Emotional

My heart is on my sleeve.
I care too much yet I know God created me.
I always refer to it as my double-edged sword.
I can feel so much and get hurt.
Emotions are great and yet can be a burden.
I rather feel then not feel at all at least I know I am alive.
May not like the hurt or pain, yet emotions keep me going toward God and His love.
Emotions.
I have many and feel all of them with same intensity.
Emotions.
Many songs written and many feeling emotions.

Physical

Get enough sleep.
I try to get eight hours.
Used to be able to now not so much.
So much is on my mind, too much that I get mad at God.
Yet I know I was responsible for it.
You know my free will in all.
Physical.
All about balance.
All four have to be with one.
When you are mentally focused you are able to stay on track.
Then you get and eat regularly and you are emotionally at peace.
Finally you get a well balanced spirit.

Spirit

A lot of things calm it; my two cats, my music and singing, friends.
Yet when any of other factors of MPES are out of line, then my spirit is not so happy.
Then I must turn to God.
I sometimes yell more than once and though I do that, He is ready to help.
He may not be direct, but He has a divine way to make me see my faults.
Like he opens the reality, blinders.
Gives me clarity then a peace comes over me.
A full redemption of MPES.

My Prayer

God never forsake me.
I know I need you, always.
Even when I'm in a state of walking away, give me grace to come home to you.
No matter my words, I feel my heart and know my true emotions.
Let me see.
Let me hear.
See what I must do.
Hear your advice.
Physical and in all my MPES.
May the value of my worth be revealed through your love by which all I do is your will and pray for your wisdom.
My prayer for MPES.

I look in the mirror today, I see a broken man.
One who has done all right.
Always start from good intentions which is not always easy.

Has broken the temple and causes ugliness in his self image.
Has somehow lost his way.
Not just temporary, but way down in the soul.
A fearful man.
One whose emotions are all over the place.
You see a hurting man in need of simplicity.
A longing man in search of love and a way out, but not the kind you think.
A man who cries, yet never loses the hurt.
The man who once wanted to do so much and gave way too much of his heart and soul only to be beaten down by the game of life.
When I look in the mirror, I see a man who knows Jesus loves him, will never forsake him.
Restore his eyes and ears so he can be what God intended no matter how many times he wants to give up.
He won't take the easy way out.
Instead I will seek and dive into the covenant with God.

Accept

I did the damage.
No reversing the damage.
No so called miracle.
The products may do what supposed to if I wasn't so damaged.
I can't not eat or drink.

Changes

Eat better.
Less sugar.
More sleep.
No day dreaming.
Live in the moment.

Take it one day at a time.
Trust God completely and not half ass.
Give it to God and be done with the head games.
Listen to God and what He tells you.
Never do I try to give up.
So many times I have cried.
Not truly given up though I'd rather cry and have a moment.
Yet I need to remember Rome was not built in a day.
So neither will my mess which I take full responsibility for.
I will do my part and not let him do all the work.
I know and must see that.
He only does when you help yourself.
He is not home yet until then you must be smart.
Avoid, turn away, and not get caught up in man's world.

Where did my life go?
It's not where I wanted it to end up.
I was so ready to become someone, somebody, something.
Yet I think I got caught up in the game of comparing.
Trying to embody.
Live up to be just like in the meantime become.
Never satisfied.
Damaged.
Broken.
Hurt my MPES balance yet with God I know I can get back even if I can't change most.
Will have to accept what I can't change and change what I can.

This collection of my thoughts are based on dreaming and not giving up.
It's about hope and prayer, not feeling good about yourself.
Also finding strength and believing in God's timing.

So I dedicate the following:

Cadie Hockenbary

My Pastor Donna Fitchette

My step mom Cathy

May this be the first of many books published monthly.

Book one "Hello God, it's me, can we talk?"

CHAPTER 2 - CHRISTMAS

The snow fell
Was light and fluffy
It was so pure
Light rays of joy
They filled my eyes
My heart beat like a drum
To the rhythm
As fell the angels sing grace
They sang harmony
Song of jesus
Songs of saints

We need the light
The energy at its finest
The moments of joy
Daily reminder
The moments that keep us real
Where we are civil
Embrace the humanity

Was very well
Very special Times
When was innocent
Not filled with those things that mean so much more clearer than
ever before
You were always there with him
Now you walk alone

The color of my soul
It was driven by ego but it does not have a good idea
It won't happen again and again
I will be the man meant for you
I was not immediately clear
I see the light as the end of the table draws close

The lights
The color
The smells
The world and humanity
Both are in one day at a time
They are very essential to the point of view
Don't give it up

They won't break me
They won't hurt me
My time is with you
Christ the savior
The one who gives me strength
The house of god with all his glory

Bring memories
The candy
Grandma's house of love
Ribbon candy in a bowl
The scent of the gingerbread men

God
Warm my heart
It needs you
It's a union of kindred spirits
I Am upset
Forgive my heart

Soon
U be here
Cold days
Hot nights
Jolly sung around the world
The noise distracts the sad and lonely
Lights that light up your day
Your soul warmed from the heat

Ready for the destiny
The beauty of warm water
Rushing thru my veins
The power of his kiss
The scent of his manhood
The truth be told
His words will consume
The heat will ignite passion

The holiday
The season
Warm feeling towards him
The day he made
There are so many reasons
To believe
To become
To raise your life

Time to stop being mean
Reason to live for jesus
Reason to be human
Reason to be humble
You are the one that will change his chances
It's beautiful Prayers
It's joyous

Time to come home
Time to get back to work
Time to stop being so upset
Time to repent
Time to enjoy a great place

Tuesday lights
They are bright
Snow covers the streets
White envelope was found
The cold glimpse of his plan
The glitter
The radio playing frosty the snowman

Wanna sit under tree
The Christmas tree
Looking into his eyes
In.our pajamas
Drinking hot chocolate
Then kiss
We tell each other the words
I love you
Your my world
You make me so happy
We go to get up

You say to Me
Not yet
We need more time
Wanna be in this moment forever
I put my head down
You lift my chin
Kiss my forehead
Say i am your nicolas

Want to see the snow
Taste the cookies
Lots of hot chocolate
Chestnuts by a open fire
The carols Sung on the streets
The ribbon candy
The love of the ugly sweater

Want to spend holidays with you
Want to have that snowball fight
Swim in the ocean
Hold you
Make love on the beach
Travel to New places
Experience with your company
Tru new things

2024
Was very good
It's was with family
Friends and family will never be forgotten
The moments
The laughter of god with a confidence
You were always there

Sometimes not in front view
But in my heart

2024
Christmas was restored
Was relieved
My heart and soul was remembered
My inner strength and child was restored
I loved Christmas
I will bring it back
My words and perspective never fade

Christmas cookies
Christmas eggnog
Christmas cards
Christmas Songs
Christmas movies

This time of year very successful
The snow brings out the juice of creating
My spirit and my faith is driven to success and to make a difference
between the first and last minute thought
I gotta do this fight against the enemy
I can not repeat my own groove and then he delivers the same effect
on his behalfs

The snow was very pretty
It glowed thru the windows
It reminded shelia of the times with her husband
They walked and held hands
They loved the moments of love
The time spent
The time was precious

Each time sheila fell in love more with Tony
They planned future
The way they raise kids
The house they would live in
The street
The type of neighbors
It was all gone when night came

The holiday
It can be stressful
U are working hard and steady
You gotta relax and enjoy
Listen to God
Play some Christmas music
My spirit is free to do so much

Getting first snow fall today
It's so pretty
So wet
Christmas memories are a reflection of love and unity
They are the key to self image
The secret of god is a blessing

Christmas Love is key to a healthy spirit
You have to choose between the two part of your life
The reality and fantasy
True Christmas moment of impact
The secret It's a union of god and love

- Christmas memories and a sense of value in your heart..this one of my favorite things to celebrate….its not about the presents…it's the laughter and the joy I feel ….
- We had first snow fall

- It's breath taken
- It's got glow
- Very mystical loom
- love the first time
- Now it can go away
- No more snow

- First snow
- The light freeze on everything
- Its .majestic
- Hot chocolate
- Warm feeling towards him
- The egg nog under a blanket

- Last Christmas
- So many sung It
- It's hold is deep
- Good times And a end binded
- Both ends in a simplistic manner

- Christmas cards
- They are moments of love
- They bring people together
- They draw a lot of love
- So many ways to say
- I love you

- Christmas
- His birthday
- It's the real reason
- It's the holiday cheer
- The lights glow
- The community of hope

- Christmas List
- Lights
- Cookies
- Egg now
- Pretty paper
- Bows
- Tinsel

Wanna hear Christmas song
Wanna hear all night
Wanna see your face
Feel the pressure of god
Know his health
Love you too baby

Love Christmas
The time of gods birth
The tribute
The reason for your sake
The live story
The love story

Christmas music
Lifts me up
It warms the soul
It has depth of god's love
Angel's sing himself
They fill joyous sounds in the air

Christmas
Love the magic
The world and humanity
It's special times

It's filled with joy
It never hurts
Drink the egg now
Eat the cookies
Be merry

Christmas lights
The shiny lights
Holiday cheer
The egg now
The cookies
The family moments
The bow ties

Christmas and new years
Christmas and new roads
End of one year
New beginning
The best of all things
Shiny lights

Chapter 3 - Solution

The day after I got caught in a world of god I knew that his name was the result of trusting jesus...

I knew this was a truly beautiful sight from his eyes and his character was very beautiful

The day was filled with those two men and not just words that were hanging on to another day

- The social media
- The disgrace in huge numbers
- The world and humanity
- We let it go astronomical
- Not in good sense either
- It's gotten out of control

The only solutions are not going anywhere until you're ready

You must be smart and your love must be active in your hands as you mold your life and human connection

Just be real to yourself and admit you will see your life and human rights groups on same page

Solutions are the only confidence in their lives
They were going through a difficult situation
The day to improve my mind
The new man who wants more of you
The day to improve the situation and I will not let the enemy be

able to bring me into My path of time where I can't stay on my road

Solutions
You gotta get back on track
Don't have any questions about this one day
Your a very strong sense of pride
The people who never had a chance
Are my mission

Solution
Do your best
Give honest effort
Don't be fake
Be real
Be authentic
Your very best
It's good for god!!

Solution
Stay focused
Stay in tune
Do the work
Count on nobody
Give to your god
It's your very important gift

Solution
I know them
Must put into action
No more lips
No more utter
It's the destination

Solution
You are my savior
Your the real medicine
The real deal
The one thing not controlled by ego
More than once and when someone enters or leaves us
You are the basis.and christ will never have to do anything with your help
Just with your heart and soul

Solution
You are easy
You are not dumb
You are smarter
You not the fool
Don't be misled
His ways are not perfect

Solution
Ask God for it
Say you have the passion
Know the procedure and how much they need more time with their lives
Get the best thing ever
His word Inspire others to be honest

Solutions
Walk away
Not give up
Know your worth
Don't be afraid
Don't let them see you cry
They don't deserve those tears

Solution
Dump nicolas
Embrace nicolas 2
Go after Ken
Then ask god
To raise a child of your own
These men are boys

Nicolas
You are not ready
Your great salesman
You can sell
You can't commit to me
I don't know how much more can Play this charade
Love you and miss you too. Much

Nicolas
No regrets
I met you
You woke my inner strength
I was reminded
I am very desirable
You may not been sure
For me it was real
No doubt about my feelings

Nicolas
Need you to be real
I don't trust easy
You are too much
You drive me. Crazy

The solution
I must walk Away
I cant get caught up in this charade

Mr jeans
You are the temptation
I am the muse
Don't want to deny
Don't want to fight it
Know what I feel
From day one
Your my best source of love
It may not be returned but I will always feel it deeo within the soul

Find the satisfaction
Find your desire
Find your own groove
Find your favorite book of god
Find your Way around this time and place

Find your strength in god
Find your desire and love
Find your life
Find your own way and then you know how to give it away from
the enemy

Find your souls
Find your solutions
Be the one who leads us through the night
Be the best of all things
Be real admit fear is high and it rushes thru the windows
God bless the united nations

God is the solution
He is the only answer
Go now

My solution
No quitting
No looking back
Christmas memories and I am merely trying to make it count

The world is loved and need peace In their lives
They are not alone with their experiences
They just feel like a child of a burden
Let them know they are meant for pleasure and not just words

The solution
It's never one sided
It's two way street
Martha and I are going forward
We will be able to defend ourselves
The enemy is weak
God is my source

The solution is not perfect but it is worth the effort to keep it simple
and complex for a moment of impact
The very essence of this action is taken by a desire to make a difference
in your hands as he climaxes grabbing hold of my heart

The solution
I know it
Must act on it
Not up for questions
It's not your fault
You are blinded

By the enemy
My eyes are on god

The solution to every challenge is to change your mind and your life…

You will need to think differently

You will need to get rid of the enemy strong hold on your emotions

Face him and say go away You don't belong here

Your not my Savior who did the right thing by saying I didn't do anything until he was ready for new adventures

- The world is full of happiness and joy for all of us equally … .you just gotta keep on going to new heights…do the work and fight harder for you always refuse to believe in the world of darkness … .your light shines again and again…..
- The soul does have lots of love for the world and humanity
- It will happen again and again
- Your soulful way will find a solution to every problem
- You gotta find the soulful essence that leads to.your solutions
- The solution to every challenge is that I will never forget that he will restore all that money took away
- He is my point where you are Love devotionals and you reveal your heart to others thru god
- The very moment you give up and give into the doubt of your life and human connection with this new direction you move nowhere
- You must fight the urge to listen to man over god

- Louie and the alpha group will have a second chance of becoming more of who is the best way to live for jesus
- They won't let us go and get worked up in a way that is not perfect for us to remember It's dark is the starting point

Will find my solutions to the problem and the truth of our humanity is a very difficult situation with a lot of attention from people who never have a good reason why they are so called tightly drawn to a calmer environment

Find the joy of your dreams and hard times for you always come to a better way of thinking…your time is now in the process of submitting to god even though it was driven to success by seeing the world of beauty

Find the place Where its solid and a sense of value in your hands

The house is still available and if you are interested please let me know
Come to you
Always

Find the place
Find the the best way
Find the right direction
Find the satisfaction of your life
Find the most precious of all time just like the Angel's sent from god

Solution
I need it
I long to change it
It's in my reach
It's in heaven

It's the destiny
It's the destination for me and my faith

The World has gone mad ...we lost way of the humanity clause that says all life's matter and tearing down people has become normal....we need to get it back because without it the children of tomorrow have no chance .....they will not survive in this crazy world ....the world has beauty let's go with this one man invites himself into your thoughts and prayers....he will not lead you down wrong way ...do not confuse religion with relationship with the omega

- The solution is to go to god for he knows what we need and when we need it
- He will always provide
- Deliver his touch
- His love
- His wisdom
- Go now and believe

- The solution was the first time Tim had been known to commit crimes against muslims...the enemy used him to spread hate and fear ...what does the community think ?

- The solution always had to come out of the storm
- It's not the same thing that happened to them and all of us
- We have to find the simple bright spot for your sake
- I look to the challenge
- It's so intense that I will not leave the city until his death

- There is only one solution and his name is jesus
- He is the one thing that keeps me alive and feeling something real
- I never need a instant feel with him or a feeling like he opens up his own words into actual reality

- He does it continuously

- The very day lucinda and the alpha met she was not the same as anyone else's face…her very touch drove him very crazy and yet the man came back for more …he lived lucinda and her oral expertise

- You have one way to change your life is to go to god everyday and leave no part of your life as a secret from him

- I want to know how to achieve peace and serenity in my heart and know that I must study for my faith is not perfect but it does seem to find a depth of gods gifts

- I give you no more power over me or my destiny in your hands as I write my devotional journal prayer book for the world
- You are my mere men and I will never be sorry about that we face the challenges of being tired from being destroyed by the enemy
- Only you can stop the carnage
- God repairs your fight or flight

- There are always a new solution to overcome your problems with your own groove to make a difference between reality and your love of god
- I must find the solution to my problem and I will be in touch with the truth of this matter
- I know the issue does not go away anytime soon
- I am merely human being and I have no doubt that I am very happy about this new road led by my christ

The reason for your response is because you expect me to keep going toward him again and again...I need no reason why god doesn't have any questions about it nor does he want it to be a force of essence....his temp was so cute and I will never be sorry about my faith in mankind that we face a challenge to see if changed from our mistakes.....

The house of burden was filled on a day to day with no judgment and no exercise then complain about it nor does it say that I am very grateful...all said and done We begin again Important in our hearts due to this point of man and full of happiness in our hearts

House of burden
Lucinda was a great opportunity to work together with god and humanity
She only wanted to elaborate about how much we can do something real good that will only benefit us all
That's the only thing I can think about
Her very little sense of fear was nothing to her strong feelings about her destiny because of her husband

Don't step too far away from the heart of jesus
Go to the house of god
Look for the right direction
Get your physical connection felt thru sex and intimacy with your own groove
Let the same effect on your life so much that you continue your journey
Give it your all in all you have and do

The house
The love
The intimacy
The fights
It's all supports the home
It has a deep down know
You know god watches
He knows your broken
So let love in your house

The house
The walls
The warmth
It means nothing if you don't have someone to share it with
The best of all worlds help May my books relax you
May my mind find out what I mean to god for your life will never
be forgotten

The house is broken
It's full of noise
It's not calm
It's very important to us
The house is broken

The house of the broken down by his grace and sacrifice for humanity
is a very personal matter of saying that all of us equally need a new
normal life and human connection with this one man

The heart of my strength is christ and his Angel's will bring us closer
together and create the desired outcome of his plan to protect our
humanity from the enemy fears of our humanity....
The fears can't take over my life because I refuse to take a deep breath
and not just words to describe my emotions from all points of view

The Weight gave me no room for new and more efficient solutions for my faith is not perfect for any other way you deliver your love for the people who are struggling with this disease so they agreed to leave legacy of his plan and support from his glory in the house of god

The truth is my life went out of the human spirit and lights up your mind for yourself from a disaster zone that has been putting together some things you may want to know and some things you wanna buried here and now

The truth can't deny the reality of what you hide in the dark that will come out of the darkness into the light of day

Trust me with this one man who wants more of a burden of destruction when he says now is the only way that works for them because they know that they were talking about nothing but I merge with my words and perspective never fade away from god

The truth
It's honest
Not always welcomed
It's always real
It will return from his glory
Not everyone will have a good reason why
They may not believe or wanna hear it
Yet if you just be real it's contagious
So run to it
Not from it
The truth sets you free
It's a gift not all passes

The truth is people can't be real on social media because it's too easy to be fake ass punk…they use energy for the wrong sense and wonder why the life they got is bad yet take no responsibility for their bad behavior in their lives ..they waste time and energy on deceit and its really pathetic ….

My truth is not your truth and it's okay we have separate truths …it can be similar but it's not the same exact as it grows in a way that's going on a mission

The end result is you can be close in a similar experience with your own life and your love for god is great
We are very essential role for our value of humanity and our entire country is a blessing from his glory
People can't handle their own truth let alone yours but never be afraid to live yours out in the open

It's not going forward for the people who have had so many times in their life that I will not let it go to the point of mans view
See it's a very personal matter what I do Believe that you can dream but don't lose sight of your own way

The holy truth
It's lies on his tongue
It does not falter
You can dream anywhere and about anything you want
The very first thing to happen again and I think about it all begins with christ right now and then

Sam lied
He played me for fool
It's not over thou
I will hunt him down

Expose his fake ass
He won't know what hit him
Lucinda will get her revenge for a long lasting impact
His words will be the same as anyone else's life and human connection
He will beg her for help from the enemy yet she won't let him slide
and then get back to his house of lies

Hold Sam
He must be held accountable
His word often comes from within a certain level of interest to him
for a long time and place in a simplistic manner
He does not feel emotionless to be a force of essence
He just has no limits on what he says and what takes place in a world
where its not over till he says now

Hold Sam to a holy grail
His words are very deep within his mind
Does this mean he is playing me
I don't want to believe it
But today the red flags went up
I need to step back
Sam is going to get a lot more complicated and painful problems
with my decision I don't trust in god and love Sam for a moment
of impact

The holy grail of God We need to talk about everything big and
small and I will never be sorry about that
He is my best friend and will return the favor of his plan to make
sure that it doesn't happen again in a simplistic manner

The holy grail
It's vital
Sam Submerge and I am merely human beings who want a calm

river flow Where images of our sexual pleasure are in a way that's
going on with this new road
Your very sexy man and I will always need Jesus as well pulsate
with you again and again
Your my very own groove and full of comfort and joy in everyday
life will never be sorry

The holy truth
I need to give it to God
Give him my every concern and worry
My dilemmas
The sleepless night
Or the other times over there with me at my worst-case or so much
time worrying about image and stuff consume me or my looks based
on Hollywood standards
We never put biased thoughts on it because of it being about the
bottom line of understanding the world of beauty

The holy truth will come back here to dream about it before you
enter new beginning of time and honest effort then you know what
they say Life meant for pleasure and I will always try to hold His
hand in my heart

The holy truth is our world full of bad people and bad choices
We make them based on good intentions
We forget logic
Our emotions are all together for a new way
The day to day struggles
The very first thing I noticed is that we face a greater burden of
destruction

The holy truth is just as simple and complex as the snow is white and wet

It's depth for ever changing based on info it gets from the universe
The where you live is now the only one So far away from god deep into the light of jesus

The truth is that we are going forward with this new direction of our humanity in which god has been missing from for far too long

It's the destination of our humanity in which we start punishing the equality of all time just like rest is a means of survival for them both

You hold my hand
I hold tight
I don't give up easy
Your the anchor
I need my hail Mary
The two were physically healthy and I will never forget that
Your my Lord

Your working
Think of you
Your my Lord
Keep my head on my toes
Don't let the enemy win over your heart
Give me light on what I need to concentrate on

Sam
I love your words
The way you feel with your heart and soul
How much you wanna experience my body
We are connected
The day we met and now each day

Sam
I love you
Your a beautiful and wonderful person
Your in my thoughts always
My body aches 4 you
I want to taste the flesh
Feel the pulsate
Moan your ne loudly
Your physical pressed for a long lasting impact of climax sexuality

The holy man walked on water and in the heavens with no fear because he was raised from the dead to fulfill a destiny….now you must do the same effort in your daily life …its your responsibility

The holy truth is just as simple and complex to make sure you have a great place to begin with a confidence of jesus
The holy grail was a slow move by his own words into actual reality of his life will hold such power in the dark woods
They need not the answers but where are you going forward to knowing how much you are not alone

The holy waters washed his feet
The holy water purified
It clearly doesn't want you to think how much they need more help
The world and humanity are in need of a whole lot more complicated business than a couple of times
Its ready to be the one who decides what happens next

The holy truth is the most substance CONSUMING of any kind of impact on this journey through your life and human connection
The very essence is the best thing to happen with a single person who has been missing since early childhood but was product of the human spirit

The very essence and holy truth will never be sorry for any inconvenience caused by this situation here in the world of darkness God gives you a sense of value so use the essence of your life so much more clearer

The holy lie
The holy truth
The holy truth is just a little more peaceful existence and the alpha will be one of the human spirit
His words were very obvious to him
His word Inspire others to be able to defend ourselves
Where it starts at all Reality shows up and takes place on his behalfs

The holy grail
The holy house
The holy day
The holy angel
The holly and the alpha

The holy truth will never have patience for their actions from hurting others or others who don't know how deep they can scare you with their actions
The holy grail is what u like and cherish it in your heart because it's not just a thought of it but its rule of thumb is a great way for people to understand this and build their relationships together with god today and always the best of all things considered to have the same as the one thing that keeps your life will help others get better with you on your life and your love of god

The holy truth will never forget the struggle of this vision
The holy grail is what he says now is the only way to live for jesus
The holy water washes my sins from the world of man
The holy of our humanity is that we are not perfect but we will see

your face in our hearts

The holy are not perfect and we all. An be holy if we just follow one simple rule and that is love

Let your holiness shine bright in the world of darkness

The holy grail was not a physical connection felt thru and it rushes thru your head

You must be active in your life and your love of god

The holy truth

The holy grail

The holy of our humanity in which god knows how many days of new valleys we can get to

The holy grail was not immediately known until after the first time meeting with his angel of mercy

The holy grail of god with a new way for growth in our country is in your hands with a new generation of gods gifts

The soul is my point where I stand in my holy grail of a man who wants more of a champion in his name

The holy grail was a very personal level of emotion and courage to the Ukraine situation has changed dramatically since it began and they will reside in a dark place where they stand for their lives and they just want end to the noise and uncertainty of their lives..god they have no idea what they say about it or what they're doing with their experiences with each other in a time of darkness that feels like a weight on their shoulders

The holy grail of god is great and good for my family loved it because of my strength in seeing my life forever has been changed since my father in heavon is therefore a very strong sense of value in our country

The holy truth will not leave her alone with these things that mean so many depths to be in jesus and pray for the people of Islam and their lives are still being taken from a disaster zone and a purpose for being diligent in making a difference between reality and fantasy

The holy grail was not even a symbol of separations or even a few more questions about this new direction
It's in a box that travelled from one place to another and then it took over a hundred thousand years ago to get to know the better of a champion
The holy grail is what they search for jesus walks with a new normal...
they are draining their lives and their interests basically just like the Angel's sent from god deep down inside of your own groove
The Angel's sing his praise for his return from his perspective is a great way for growth to grow stronger than ever before daily and the Angel's sent from god and love that god created all of us equally will rise up the sky tonight

The holy truth will never be forgotten by god and he loves us imperfect and he loves us all the same
He plays no favorite
He will not leave you alone with these things that mean so much more to you than to others
He will restore all that you have lost with the enemy at hand
His grace is given to his message of hope and faith will keep going toward the light of jesus

The holy grail was a total sacrifice for humanity to Express freely through his work
The reason why god is great is that he will restore all of his plan and support his plan to protect our humanity
The sad part is we dont deserve it
We don't earn it

We waste our time and energy of course and the truth is that we face a very difficult situation with him in the future

The day she walk into god and love that he will restore all of her dreams that her life will never have gone away without a doubt and a sense of pride

The holy truth will never forget to pray for peace

The world is full of joy because you expect me to keep going forward

The very essence of your life is not perfect but it does seem like a good place to start new adventures and experiences with christ

The Ukraine situation has changed dramatically in recent days as it grows more rapidly than ever before

The holy grail was not total that I am very proud of my strength and confidence in my heart with a new way of thinking

The people of Islam and their families depend upon us for a long lasting impact of climax

The war rages against a man of faith and hope for humanity to Express freely in a way that's been done before and I'm gonna go far enough for the world to heal and change our culture

The holy grail of god with all your life will help others feel better about themselves and their lives...they need that very essence of the grail of god is great gift from a very personal level of emotion and courage to help others who are struggling with their experiences with each of their lives…

The holy truth is that I must follow my heart and soul even when I speak with my decision....god knows my cancer struggle is necessary for my life and my faith to keep going forward with this new direction of his plan

Where is he now from now on you know what you want me to do with your enemy and fears of our humanity is no longer a stumble block

The holy of our humanity in which god knows what you think of your life1

He knows the importance of our hearts due from his perspective and is thicker than we thought we would be

The day after being named in an effort by former actions of a man of faith by design and a purpose for being diligent in making a statement about how much they give each other a lot of attention from his glory

The holy grail was not immediately known until after he died
The grail was a truly beautiful sight from his glory days and he will not leave his family alone and helpless to get the better of his life in this world and humanity

The holy truth will never have been loved by any means of survival or anything else that would make it happen right now and see the light of christ

The holy truth was that he had to die and then come back to me while I still was alive and well within his time of life

The alive and well being in my heart is where I stand for humanity and our entire country

The strength of my dreams come from christ stronger than ever before I was going forward and clear the way to my family loved them

The other side of failure is success and it rushes thru your heart to others who will satisfy your message and your love shine on our nature of the human spirit

The holy truth will never forget the common sense of pride god gives to us and when we tarnish it in the very things that go against him

We do this daily and we go forward with no regard for our value is our savior and our entire country is in need of it

The very essence of the human spirit and mind that will change in this country where we care about our national security and our many enemies will go away from the fear that god is our savior

The truth about this new direction is that we face a greater burden of destruction when we talk in a simplistic manner as if it doesn't happen again and again

The truth of our humanity is we each must have faith in mankind and the truth of our jesus and pray for peace in our lives

Chapter 4 - Bold

Your not the answer
The enemy fears go ahead
The price of your own groove
The moments that mattered
The day to improve
All wrapped in the pleasure
Of being able to defend ourselves from his perspective
Perception , perspective , narrative is my source in ego and self awareness

Agree to disagree
Thing of the past
Humanity and it's down fall
The two will destroy each other's lives
It's so intense the cards
No fortune teller needed

Bold
To walk away
To raise your heart
To be honest with you
To be honest with myself
That this does not work for me

Bold
To say out loud
To say something real and victorious
To admit weakness
To raise your heart and soul

To raise my love of life
To get a new perspective

Bold
To go out into the world
The world of darkness and shine upon our humanity
The every corner of america
I will fight for the people
The ones who are struggling

Bold
To know who am
To know my place
To know my true emotions
To know the better part
To know what he wants
The god of my strength

Bold
To admit
To say no more
To climb the mountains
Do it up
Do it right

Bold
The way it is
It's the same as anyone else's
That we face a greater burden
We are going forward
I can't stop thinking about starting a day without love

Bold
I long to have her
I Want you to dream again
Don't worry about it before they speak out against him
You will be prepared
To stand
To deliver
In jesus name

Bold
To grow away
Bold
To admit
Bold
To raise the house of god
Bold
To be honest with you and your life
Bold
To know your words
Bold
To know your strength
Bold
To know your heart
Bold
To know his name
Bold
To raise your heart and soul

Bold to know
Ken Brad
Can be fake
He holds head up
He looks down

Love him so much
Bold to admit
Bold to cry
Bold to chase
Bold to create
Bold to say you'd be surprised if nicolas was not immediately available

Bold to myself
Bold to the world
Bolt to your calling
Bold to live my truth

Bold to admit
That I want him
That I desire his touch
Desire for your sake
Bring your truth
Nicolas your beauty

Bold enough to admit
You are the only person who can openly drive my fancy
You know your charm
You met your match
Don't tease if no deliver
This evergreen has the power

Nicolas is the only one So many wanna find
I found him
He just opened my eyes
Want to moan his name
Want him to say he has feelings

I can't stop thinking about starting a new way of doing life instead
of looking back at the spots where it matters less
Now it matters more

Bold to declare
Bold to my every move
Bold to know my truth
Bold to fight harder
Bold to will the battle

Bold
It's very important to know what you want
It's your time that you continue through your eyes and ears
Bold is very deep
It's essential

Bold To the point of time and place
Bold to your life so much more clearer
Be the boldest of all time and energy
Bold enough for me its temptation for a new normal
Bold has become us

Bold today and want to know how to achieve peace
Bold to know what I want
Bold to say that comment on this issue because it was driven to
success and to help others feel better

Bold
You are bold
Your a good man
You have soul

Bold to admit it not over until good says so ..I will push till I succeed….the day was filled with those who were in unity for their actions….iam a author and brand ….

I Am going to be bold enough to start saying what is the only one life I want that So many wanna find fault with
It's my time
It's my pleasure
It's gods plan
So beware of all things

Bold to say you'd be surprised
Bold to say what you mean by that certain level of emotion
Your words are bold
You are Bold to make a difference
You can't be bold enough for the challenge Find your desire and your life will never forget that he will restore

Bold enough to say yes
The hell to the no
It's the destination of our lives
We all have one
Stop trying to steal mine
You wont jump in to the inner thigh of your own way while chasing my life

Bold enough to stand my ground
Bold to say you'd be surprised if they push you back to the point of center of your body and sight of your own way
Bold to the point of view which means that I will never be sorry about my Creator and how much I keep my serenity even though it was tested

Be bold in your life and human connection
Be real admit fear of being a number of different types of the
human race
Your number one to call on the house of god
Be real admit to myself that you have the right direction of his plan

Set your sights higher
Don't let the storm get you down
You can rise up and get a good place to begin with an opportunity
for you
Bold enough to admit my life is not going the way I want and I will
change that !!
Be bold enough to know your true identity in your life
Be bold to never doubt the truth of our humanity
Be bold to make a decision about how much you love them both

I want to follow jesus
Bold
Can't wait
Bold
It's my time
Bold
I know I can get back even more wasted energy
Bold
For now on I will be done
Won't apologize
Will have what I want
Bold
It's my mistake
It's my pleasure
It's my fault
It's my favorite time of need
Bold

It's the destination of our hearts
I can't stop thinking about starting the second time of need to get
back the house of god
I will be done with this disease so that I can be open minded to make
a difference between reality and fantasy

Bold as you are ready for a few days and bad luck to discover his
glory in the house of god
It's always good for my faith
Will be bold
Enough to walk away
To stand against them both
Will be done by his grace
Will be bold to make a difference
Will be done with this one who gives me a sign that you continue
your journey

Bold enough
To do it in public
To not hide his love for men
He knew his sin
So does god
Not for man to judge
In end his boldness was his best asset

I am bold
Not weak
This haters gotta get a grip
U can come from christ stronger than ever before
Iam going to have it all

Bold bridges Was a tough guy
Wore tight jeans

Bulge that was obvious reasons why it would change your mind for a long lasting impact of climax
Bold knew no boundary
Bold came from my soul
It was driven to success with a confidence
The very day after he left
She knew his strength
His love for me
Boldness comes deep in the soul where you don't want to know about this one thing that keeps you alive until you get a well respected verst in your hands…you wanna reach out and touch the house and get stuck with it as you develop a little more concerned with a better day of hope ….

Bold and beautiful
Not often in same sentence
You are not alone
Bold gets better and better each day
You can dream anywhere

Bold Is sexy
Bold is essential
Bold can bring change
Bold does a lot to moments of change
Bold the first time Tim put his mouth on tom
Bold Tom wants him and his mans needs to feel love

Bold to know the power of the tongue and the truth of our hearts due from the beginning of time

You make me hard and wet at same time so now I must taste the house of sexuality

Let's not deny the fact God will always remain strong and powerful force of essence in self control

Be bold enough to admit the source of your negative thoughts are based upon your own groove that has followed the path of least growth

Your the best way he knows what shape you are in need of a champion…he will be your rock and your best friend and I'm gonna go far beyond what is meant to be

Be bold to admit the fact
You know where it hits most
The very first thing you need him to do is make a difference between reality and fantasy
You are the only person who has done this for

Be bold enough to calm waters and make your enemies look like a weight of their lives and how much Sadly it's usual in a test is not a problem for god

The very basic thing is that we face our humanity is a little longer than before but I merge all of us equally with each other better than ever before

The desire to walk ahead of the crowd who tries to conform me to the very limit of its own mind

I desire to fulfill her husband and chris holds on to another woman that will change the direction of my strength in seeing my god help me with this one man invites himself into a Frenzy of his own words

I desire to fulfill my goals for my future and my faith in my lord sit at my right hand

He holds his hand over my shoulder and his character was very well maintained image of the human spirit is a blessing from his glory

I desire my dreams
I desire fantasy becomes reality
I desire the house of god
I desire the best way he can handle it with affirmation of jesus
I desire to fulfill my goals and goals for myself in this world
I desire my career Always desire my god to heal your soul

Desires of our hearts
Desires of our humanity
Desire for pur soul
Desires are gems
They light our humanity
They give us a voice
Raise the roof
Bring the glory

Desire the power
Desire the ability
Desire the best for you
Desire always for the best way
Desire to do something soon enough
Desire for his wisdom and guidance
Desire the ability of god

Desire peace today god
Desire calm thoughts
Desire for the world and humanity to Express freely through his work
Desire the power of prayer for bob and I
Desire for a moment of silence
Desire the ability of god with all his glory

Desire to be the man who can stand on my own two feet ..i am a caregiver now ….this never ends and it takes so much out of me …but I know I will overcome …I cry lots and god knows this … don't trust my faith at times..I do Believe that I am very proud of myself for making money in a world where its a challenge Daily…..
Desire to fulfill her needs
Desire to do something soon and that was very helpful for us daily
Desires of Tim When he died
Desire to be in a way that's going on with his body sensation and his character is in your heart
Desire for your sake
Desire the breath you breath
Desire to fulfill your needs
Desire to do something for the world
Desire to be able and not just a thought

Desired activity for roger is a means to create an active environment in which we start punishing the equality and create the desired outcome of your business to achieve and provide a new outlook for the world and humanity

Desired outcome I would just like you would love to know that god wants me and my faith is not perfect for the house of god is great and I will never be forgotten by god

Where I will not leave her husband and chris holds on to another man that is not a good idea but I merge with my words and empty compliments of all time just to make a difference between reality and fantasy

The night is dark but his hands has no limits on how pretty good it could be if it was driven by ego and not just a thought of how long will it be known to us and we will see the beauty of this vision of my strength in seeing my beautiful eyes open to new heights

- The desire blinded me
- It took over
- It consumed
- It pulsated
- It did not wavier
- It dug in
- It took hold
- Not just once
- But a deceitful tongue crushes
- It lies to me
- It gives me sleepless nights
- How many more times ?

- Desire to fulfill her desires
- Desire to be in jesus
- Desire the house of god
- Desire the ability of god with a new way of thinking
- Desire for your diligence

- Weakness
- Men
- Hard body
- Lies
- Games
- They all.play
- The Ruby is a great gift for me
- It reminds me of your love
- Why can't it be so ?

- Look for real desires
- Toss old enemy out
- Get into Frenzy for more then once I know I can get back even more wasteD energy

Mean are thr weakness
The tight bodies
The smooth lines
The words dripped from a single spoken lying tongue
The essence of the beware I did not see
It's calling me but the flesh ignored the warning signs

Desire to do something soon and that was very helpful for us daily and keep her eyes open to the possibility of having a good place for them because they know not what they do

Desired the men on Facebook and then waiting for the next step to get to know what they want and desire for your sake protect yourself against the flesh of the human spirit which is dripping in deceit

Weakness of saying what happened and that was very narrow minded about how much we can do this fight for the house of god

I will never forget to thank God for help and support from the enemy because both of them were very good at staying on target for their actions were taken seriously by a few minutes of silence

The day is clear because iam not going to back down anymore ..Will use my gods strength for a better way of life and future with Seth

His body sensation and his character will bring me to my knees with such pleasure and not a problem at all Reality never forget to get rid of infection of the world and humanity

Dear Sam

You played me like a fiddle and I am merely trying not to dream about you or your life with me

You are lucky you are not the only one and the only difference is iam.not the victim you made me

I will be the man meant for pleasure and not just for you always come back to me with love and unity for you and me both are not going to be one unit

Sam
Desire no more
Desire
The old way
Sam
I LOVE YOU
Sam
You are my weakness
Sam
What the hell did you do

Sam
Desire our mirage
I desire you
Desire for your sake
Desire to fulfill the needs of your life
Desire the ability of god to heal your soul
Wanna be your friend and I'm gonna go far with you

Sam
I miss you
I want you
I love you
I can't stop
I won't stop

Sam
Desire your touch
Your manhood
Your lips caress me like a Map
You search ever corner to bring my moan to a boil
Sam
You are my intimate time with my words and your words
We will make it count on our hearts due to this cause of our hearts
We are going to make it

Sam
I desire his touch
His lips on my lips
His moans of my name
The pulse of his manhood
The look of his eyes looking into mine as he climaxes in ruthem to me
Desire this man's
Heart
Love
Body and future

Desires
We have em
We deny them
We act on them
They fill us up

They excited us
They burden us

Desire
What you wanna become
What you feel is your destiny
Feel free of Satan
Desire the ability of god
Desire the ability to dream of your own groove

Desire
His arms around me
As he pumps
As I pull in closer to my secret place
He moans my name
Breath in and out
Louder each pump

Desire
I desire my life
I desire my career
Always desire my god
Always got me a tender heart
Good reason to live for jesus

Desire my god
Desire truth
Desire to fulfill the challenges
Desire the ability of god with a new normal
Desire for your sake protect yourself against the enemy
Desire the ability of god to heal your heart and soul

They make wet
Make me happy
Make my heart pound
I Wanna cry
It's so intense
Could this be a new heartaches
Lord get me in clearview

The hard decisions make very hard questions because you are not torn between your desires and weaknesses ..they pull at you with such an amazing and amazing experience with your own groove

The desire for Sam is greatly appreciated and is going stronger every day and it's a very deep sensation…

Sam is a beautiful man who can openly Express intimacy and his character is the best thing ever for me

The very thought of Sam excites me all the time because he is in my bloodline..

When you desire you will be active and forget the wall that stands in your way…it's not the answer to how deep this is instead its how far can I go ?

I desire my own groove and I want to cry out for myself and to help them find a depth of gods gifts and what takes place in my heart

She desires her husband tonight…he had been gone to war for three years…he went on mission month after they were married …he was home and she knew he was here only a short time ….she was going to make use of the time

Weakness is not falling apart and I will never have patience for a long period of time and energy of my strength

Weakness and I am merely trying not to believe that I will never be sorry for my actions

I do the best I can with what I know in my moment of silence and despair of what is meant to be

The Weakness is not the same effect as being on a cold winter evening and it rushes thru her life and human rights

Desire 4 gods live
Desire for his wisdom
Desire for his return
Desire for your life
Desire your liver
Desire his touch
Desire the move In rhythm
Desire the flesh of hope
Desire gods words
Desire the ability of god
Desire the Angel's whisper

Desire for your sake protect yourself from the enemy and let your ambitions come to a higher level of emotion

Desire is not the same as the other emotions that have been through so much more and less than what they say is not perfect...dont let it come into play and you can do it together with your own groove

Desire is a great way to get your physical and emotional health to a certain level of climax

Desire for your sake protect yourself from a very important part of your own groove

Weakness is not perfect but it does seem to find a depth of gods love

Weakness of your heart and soul even when you are not alone is a real problem with a lot of question

The soul is the one thing u can see get a lot of attention from people who never had one

The soul is a little more complicated than ever before daily life is not perfect but it is worth more then ever before

The soul does have warmth and a purpose of being able to defend itself from a disaster zone and your own words that may or may not exist in your life

The soul will not give up even if it hears you say that comment you know deep down inside is just the weight of the world talking

The soul of this story is a means for you always come back here and now walk with him in his life
Your very best of all things considered by some kind of judgement is more than the actual judgment itself
Your very sexy man and full body shot you like a good man who wants more of you in a world of beauty in life
Your often wrote the story of what he does best in bed yet it's the same effect on your life when he gives you the opportunity for a moment of impact with ultimate goal of another climax

He is my friend and lover yet he becomes a man who fights alone ..he given into the fear and the disease ....he has been putting up *a lot more complicated than ever before daily life...his heart is strong but feels his mind has just accepted the disease and will not fight for us .....he wants to stay in the moment but won't let us pray for him and say things unless he's going to be in a way that's not going anywhere....god give him the strength to get rid of infection of the disease...*

Cancer takes

- *It robbed me of my strength in seeing the cover of the house of god*
- *I had my faith shaking up in my heart and soul*
- *I have had to do it for a long time and I am very concerned about delay in my mind*
- *I got to see what I was doing important things for my book success*
- *The cancer did nothing but it does make sense for me its temptation for a new day of hope is a means of survival*

Cancer reality

- *It's not pretty*
- *Weighs on everyone else in the family unit*
- *Its not a good place to be*
- *It does not mean anything but a lot of questions*
- *The day to day struggle with its effects are not perfect*
- *The disease has a swelled immune system that causes you to lose weight*
- *You are not alone with these things that you continue to face in the disease duration*

Cancer weakness

- *Hurts the body*
- *It stresses the importance of your own groove*
- *It gives you more than you thought you could answer*
- *The daily grind becomes a triumph of your life and your love of god*
- *The daily struggle with the disease has a hold on your emotions*
- *The nights get longer*
- *The days get heavier*
- *The mundane intensified*
- *The worth is like a weight on your shoulders*
- *The soul does not like when it comes to the reality of cancer*

I like that I will never forget that he will be a part of my strength and confidence in all that I do ....he will be in my prayers because cancer goes after good people and will ravage their bodies and emotions...it does such damage on a regular worries intensify the situation at a higher standard of living...if your heart and soul are in toon with each other you will get thru this ....cancer way taken over shelia and dick ...they were strong enough for the challenge

Find your desire and love your flaws as you can do this fight for the people of Islam

Find the simple bright spot for your response from a disaster zone and your love of god with a confidence that you have a great place for your sake

The weakness is not falling but the strong evidence of this particular issue is you are weak and not strong but if you keep plugging on your life you will be very awesome to have a second chance to share your thoughts and beliefs with everyone

The strength comes from your spirit and lights of our own angel of mercy because we have someone to watch over me and you when we are weak

The very first word or phrase is our savior of our humanity will you come to earth to show us what we are going forward with

Desire our life back
Cancer weaknesses are often associated with depression and anxiety
Desire for your life
Cancer will make you question your mind and your love of god
Desire to fulfill his lover
Cancer reality is that you have no sex and intimacy with your heart and soul
Your lover is too tired and out of it due to the cancer
Desires of the human spirit and lights up
Cancer puts you in the fog and a sense of loneliness that you have a mission to forge ahead ..you will with your body yet your heart and mind lag behind

Desire the simple bright spot for your sake
Desire for your response from your spirit and lights up your face
Desire the power of prayer for bob and I will never have patience with the truth
I have to choose between the reality of this vision and hearing from the enemy
Weakness is not perfect but it does seem to find a depth of gods gifts

Weakness in your life is not the only way to live for jesus and pray
for peace on earth
Weakness of a man is very deep within my imagination and is thicker
then anything else that they are doing here
Its okey to admit weakness but don't worry about the bottom line
of it but the strong evidence of a man who wants more of it is worth
more than anything else in this world

The boardroom
The two would spare off with heated words and perspective
Both heavy weights in their hearts again and again with respect for
the final countdown
The voices got louder than usual and they were going on with their
first ever showing of their soul
Neither would win and the alpha in them both would be great for
doing the right direction of our humanity
The conversation was not immediately clear yet whether they would
become good soldiers or a guide for modern man who wants more
of the world of beauty

The silence was louder then the sex was so deep that it matters most
in a way that's going away from each other ....its the disease And
nobody fault just the enemy fears of our enemies war he waged on
us...god sits by and wants to know your faith not lost forever ....its
shaken up and takes the time to come home from a very strong sense
of pride in your heart with god

- *No means no*
- *You owe no explanation of why you said no*
- *Once you say it there is no need to justify*
- *No need to feel guilty*
- *The no is not a problem for god*
- *He knows what you think and your honesty*

- *Tim's letter*
- *He read it by the fireplace*
- *It brought tears to his eyes and his face*
- *The words were inspiring and they were going through this process of being a very personal level of security*
- *The letter inside the white envelope was taken from his glory*
- *It brought tears from his glory in your eyes*

Tim and his weaknesses

- *He loves the body connection and his hands up your body*
- *The very essence of luke and Lucas being together*
- *He once lived for Lucas and now he was just single*
- *The word live for jesus because of his distance at moment in his life*
- *The smell of a man out of the shower and a sense of control over his body*
- *The days when sex is on over drive*

Desires of Tim

- *When the wind blows down the street of heavens and a warm day*
- *When the man is very deep within his body sensation only to repeat the pleasure*
- *When the two men reach the same conclusion as they fall into their hands and their bodies*
- *When the two men are in need of a good reason to live for a new day*
- *When you have to choose from our mistakes and not just words that were hanging on your lips*

The light on golden mist is a great thing to happen with your own life results and fast moving forward or call it a shot of your own groove is sometimes a great way to get a clue about what god says that he will restore....

The body of one person who was killed in a way that's been done before and then waiting for a warrant for this revival of his work in essential detail...the detective was not a physical presence in our hearts due to this point of view which was not immediately clear....

She did too much body shaming for her own self inflicted wounds.... she would have been through so many depths of experience with her emotions and his feelings for her ...she did not get his article done by his deadline for paperback....the articles on how pretty it looks to please society for his actions was written by her husband and chris holds her hand to his message....she does not do anything until he says its okey ...the depth of his hold over her is a burden that weighs on her mind ...she has thought of murder as a way to end the nightmare of her life with a lot of question.....she has Morales and would not kill anyone ..

The day before

The day before was very narrow minded day with no new information about her destiny in her mind...she was plugged into a Frenzy of criticism from her nightmare scenario in which she judges herself too much ...this would not give up on her life yeah just give her very little sense of value....she did things and tried to do it for her husband with slow and anguished emotions in her isolation ...she mentally and emotionally engaged mind would torment her but god was not a quitter or even quit working behind the scenes....the moments of tears are over and her strength was being uprooted to her spirit ....

December

*The disease has been putting out a lot of question from the heart of jesus...
he saw the world from heaven who was in a simplistic manner as if it
had been accepted by his grace ....man knew the wrong direction of his
plan yet the enemy was still trying to get the best possible outcome....
this would be a force of struggle to every man on! earth ....*

*The day after being diagnosed with cancer at age sixty six it would
change the new dynamic of their lives and their sexual relationships
This will make a difference between reality and reality of their own
hands on it because they have to choose from the enemy or the road
ahead with hope for a new day of hope with strong support for their lifes
The cancer was found on a time where they were going through a series of
events that would make them feel like a weight was placed on their hearts*

*The day to day will now come to a higher level of emotion and
courage to be in jesus name would now become more of a champion
in his name..the road to there will not be easy and the enemy will
use this to his advantage*

Nov

The man was laying down on his bed and held hands with his love
of a lifetime
They been together since they were going through a difficult situation
and they are not alone in this world
So many people do not wait until they get a clue from their sources
and end up alone
They start doing things that mean so much less then things that
mean so much
The world is full of couples who struggle and cope with every day life
and human connection with this disease scares they are seeing on tv

Nov

Desire for your life will help you understand what you want to do and experiences with christ are your best wishes
The weakness is not from your fate or faith it's from the enemy fears of our humanity in which we cannot survive without the truth of our humanity in the house of god
Desire for a moment of impact when they grow into their own lives and our lives are still alive in this country where we care about our national values
Weakness of your head and giving satin too much of your heart is where you find yourself at a risk of losing your child like innocence

We can learn from them and be active in your dreams or experience with your heart is where you find simplicity and happiness in the house of god

Nov

It's a new month for the world and same year for all
The light of christ has been missing since early morning
The day after he left office he entered the devil cave and was only in a simplistic position
The devil was in control now and not taking orders from him with a lot of question
Seriously the same thing happened when the world and humanity were so different from others and it rushes thru the windows and doors of my strength
The moment you know what you're doing with your life and human connection with this new direction of our country you will see your life in a whole new way

October

It's almost over
Its ending on a slow move from his perspective
The new month be here soon enough
The scope of my strength is christ and I am very grateful for this
revival
Both men were walking around with a lot of question from the enemy
The season was about to begin with a new way of life and human
connection with a lot of people
The journey is not perfect but it does seem to find a depth of gods
gifts and what takes place in a simplistic manner
The matter at hand was not immediately clear about his life with
god today and always has had a usually positive impact of climax
sexuality...the night becomes a great way to get a clue from his glory

October

She having a lot of attention from her body...its calling him out of
her dreams and hard times for her life with god today is shaky ...not
that she doesn't know what they are doing together but just little bit
in enemy lines....her days are long and difficult for her husband....
his health not the greatest and she watches him struggle daily ...she
Hopes he will have energy to give her a sexual climax....any way
they can be together be great even if she does all the work....

October

The reason lucinda has been putting up with a lot of people who
never want to grow stronger is a tribute to who she was
Her books were written by her own voice and she needs to stand
against them for their actions from hurting others will not be a force
of hurt will not be a part of this vision

The reason why she did what she does was to bring her back into reality with a new life mission and a sense of control over the devil

October

Lucinda remembers it well ...was a beautiful night by the sea side ...the stars danced on the water and it was very humid...she sits on beach with her husband and chris holds her hands....they were on the honeymoon of her third marriage ....but chris was a first time husband ....they were in love and unity with their emotions ....they wanted to make love on the beach ....they knew they were going through this same thing as they fall into place with a new baby..... that was just 9ne of the topics running thru her mind ..chris was thinking I want blow job on the beach ...

October

The harvest moon is high in the sky tonight ...its almost certainly a glow that will warm your heart ...you can smell the apple pie and apple crisp ...you see the leaves change color ...they will look bright and dark with rich color..the man of the limber and sexy fashion style will cover the magazines ...you want to roast marshmallows for smores .....then sit by a bonfire ...

October

Where you find a depth of gods gifts in your life will not be a weakness but it will be a part of the human spirit that soars into your thoughts and prayers....the strength of your soul from a new perspective is always there with him just trust in this time of need and desire for your life will never be forgotten by god.........the month started ou good and his character was in a way that's going to happen with a new day of hope and faith.....every day he wakes up he will be a part of the human spirit that we all need to connect with and cherish.....

Sept 25th

She knows her faith in mankind is very important for herself because she doesn't know where she sleeps calmly or when she's in a simplistic manner....the truth is just that because she's not going anywhere until she gets closer to her husband....no matter what and who they send her way she will be a force of life in her isolation of her dreams....she knows what matters in a marriage but if two people don't stay or fight for it or do what necessary to keep fresh then it's not going to last ....

- *She had a past of her life with drugs*
- *She was a truly classic lady of faith yet her divorce was not immediately clear*
- *She never looked at why it happened so much faster then she might have thought*
- *She was living in blinders and she needs to stand up for her life*
- *She has been putting together some more time with her emotions to admit what happened to the marriage*
- *Her voice is meant to give you new ideas about how much she enjoys him*
- *Even the sex was so hot yet it died as time moved on*

She was supposed to have her baby back and she needs more money before they start the process...they wanna see she can deal with a lot of things going on with her life and her thoughts on being a mother ...her drug use will destroy her life if she dont get it out of her life.... her faith is more important then ever before.....the drugs were not immediately clear yet whether they were in a full attack on her life was clear that they had a hold on her daily routine and life....she could beat the addiction if she only gave her faith the chance to share with her it's full capacity ....

She walked down the path.her usual walk and she was down tonight ..she may have found herself in over her head ....she sees a guy on a bike approaching but suddenly went into the woods ...she knew that she should turn around yet she did not care tonight....she had no spirit but it was the sleep that had deprived her tonight ....she really needed a big dick in her mouth ...that would be a great diversion from the pain....she is not a quitter or a idiot so she will have the right direction of her dreams and attitude..

Rick would not even know if he was ready for new advens... he will not be aware of the letter in the red envelope that he would bring into his future....it will later prove to be a force of god....it will bring him to new heights in a state of shock .....he will discover his own words and perspective never fade away from his perspective....if anything else it will work affordable for his actions are made by a new normal.....the red envelope fell into his place of course and then he will bring it to his message... .he will not even notice that red flag in form of red envelope that will be in his mailbox......

Rick got home and grabbed mail like all those times before....he took the mail put it on the stand next to doorway ....as he did a red envelope fell to the floor ....without realizing it he kicked it under the table ....he then went into his living room and sat on the couch ....he was tired from long day .....as he sat there the red envelope begin to illuminate a light on his legs....rick did not notice this light he was caught up in his program ....

- Rick was the **local meat manufacturer in the town of new haven**
- **He would commit himself to and be active in the gay rights movement**
- **He often crossed paths with the other guys from time to time**
- **In the gay community it was a regular thing to happen again and again**
- **Rick's lover committed suicide by being so upset about the affair rick had more then once**
- **Rick came home one day found himself in a state of shock**
- **There on his bed was leo who took a bottle of sleeping pills**
- **There was also a note that said you did this to me**
- **Rick never got over that**
- **So he spent rest of time us9ng temporary one night stands**
- **Sometimes more then once if guy was good**
- **But he never followed thru with a committed relationship between them both**
- **Rick was also very successful in his career**
- **He had lots of money and setbacks took place in his life but with help of god he would commit himself to a better way of life**
- **He was in middle of a champion because he saved money but did not lack for anything he needed or wanted**
- **He slept with Tim once**
- **He slept with Tony 3 times**
- **He slept with roger 4 times**
- **There was a string of serious events of sexual essence that had been accepted by both of the two men**
- **Rick could fall in love with roger but knew he had heart feelings towards another man**

- **Tony was very physical with his body**
- **Roger loved his sex**
- **Tim had no shame**
- **Tony could make his men cum a lot**
- **Roger loved his sex drive for tony**
- **Tim would sleep with both and had**
- **The three men were involved with a confidence of a threesome**
- **They all could enjoy each other better than ever before daily now that it's in the open where they all stand**

Tony loves roger and Tim loves tony...in a three way love there are really no winners....all will love and all will long for someone's touch and a final moment of pleasure ....the question they must ask is how long will they live in denial...they deserve better then a cliche or be just a number in a little black book ....

Tony desired activity for roger Ailes as well pulsate the man who can openly Express intimacy with his body sensation only gets better with time.....tim knew tim was a slut but he does not want to know how much he cares about his life with him....they so much as a lesson learned from his lips enter the same effect on his behalfs since his release from a disaster zone in Afghanistan.........so now tim loves tom openly ....he been known to have a threesomre with both tom and Roger.....all three men were addicted to sex....only god could break that down and keep them alive until they are not alone with their new active partner in a way that's been so great for them up to now ....gods timing is a blessing for them both for a new way of thinking about starting the second time of their lives are still being made by the omega ....

Tim and tony have been part of the human spirit of our humanity in the gay rights movement and our many enemies that attack the gay community....they will bring awesomeness and awareness to the heart of this vision of a new way of thinking about it.....they will not leave the city until his new book releases a series of stories that will help others feel safe and secure with their experiences in their hearts again and again with respect to their lives in the world..... tony the man but the Tim the future of life gets better with time for both of them....they will reside in Denver Colorado springs and make lots of love.....

Tim's weakness

- **When tony touches his crotch**
- **When tony sighs the first time Tim put his mouth on his body**
- **The rhythm in which tim glides back and forth between Tony's legs**
- **The breathing of tony as he grabs Tim's ass**
- **The sound of tony moaning**
- **The moment tony puts tom in his mouth**

Tony desires

- He long said he will restore his leadership in his life
- He will have that house of god with all his glory
- His man will be a force of sexuality and learn about his day
- He will be a very warm feeling towards him and his mans needs
- He will not leave you alone for his actions are made from heart of jesus
- He wants to mary his lover and live a good life
- They will reside in a simplistic manner for their lives and interest from other groups of men
- They will be for each other enough that no other man can do any harm

Tony Went to her space where she reminds herself that she will not leave her husband ...lucinda and tony are one mind ...they never realized it till now....tony has always loved the to share with tim all his pleasure for his package is very impressive...tim walk into a room and his crotch is full ..tony knows he is 9 inches ...if bulges and tony ready to drop to his knees and give tom a oral response and examine the situation of pulsating conditions that will change his chances for a long lasting impact of climax....they were great together with each other better and better each time they are intimate .....they had a usually done way for growth of his body sensation with another man in every moment of truth and honesty in his life ....one thing they never doubt is if they will cum when together but more of a question how much will be done by the climax that reaches a conclusion of heights that will change your love of intimacy

- He drives her crazy and goes out of his way through the night before they head out to god
- He loves god
- He wished tim would have been talking with him about it before they were going on with their divorce
- Tony wanted a man who can openly Express intimacy with his body sensation only gets a chance to get a new normal of hot intimate moments in sexual activity

Tony went to the market today ..he got the usual one of the flowers he loved ...he figured he go home and put them on table in the living room or in case on bedroom table by the window....he loved fresh flowers...the smell ....he remembers the time that roger bought him a dozen yellow Rose's.....

He gets to the flowers ...sees his old flam Andy...he was hot...he and tony lived together buy never made it to the point of time to share they were lovers ..more of a cat and mouse game of hearts

Tony and roger get along because they understand each other and their desires and weaknesses
They are in a simplistic position to make a great place for them both to be a force of love and example
The two men love sex and are good at it..they know where to please and when to submit the message to their please or to prevent it from happening in wrong moment

- Tony wants to hear roger moan
- Tony wants roger to get rid of the tension between his reality and fantasy
- Tony wants roger to get out of his way to live for a moment of impact
- Tony wants to rock Roger's world

The *reason why I am very proud of the human rights groups is that we face the challenges of their lives in a state of importance of the human spirit and lights up the mans in this case of a long period of research which we start with the truth of our lives better than ever before daily work to get the facts out of our minds free of traffic and noise*

1. Wants roger to go out into the light of the human spirit
2. Tony wants to hear from him with faith based on his behalfs since he was ready to go out into college with a confidence that they would become good enough to calm waters with a very strong sense of value
3. Tony desired activity for roger is a blessing from his glory days and bad luck with his love will not leave him alone in this time of need
4. Tony loves that moment he moans and breathes oh yeah I'm gonna get it right now and see how interested he might be

5. Tony loves it so much more clearer and better each time they are in the heat of seduction and then waiting for him to come home and watch him play with his body sensation

Tony desired activity is to cum
Roger weakness is the touch of tony
Tony desired activity is to make roger squirm
Tony desired activity for roger is to make him happy in bed
Roger loves when tony goes down on him
Tony desired activity is the moment his body pulsates and roger say shoot baby
Tony loves that moment he moans as he climaxes grabbing hold of roger by the ass and release the love juice

Tony and roger head to the local walmart in Israel ..as they do they listen to the radio and talk shop...tony loves getting worked up in the car and making roger squirm ....so he puts hand on Roger's knee....then slides up leg...and in to the inner thigh... the final part of the trill is grabbing Roger's cock ..he rubs it and firmly squeezes his head..he loves the bulge in Roger's pants...

Roger's replies keep doing that and your going to get a lot of juice..
Tony says oh yeah I'm gonna go down on you then....
They laugh at the moment of silence and they will have a good place to begin with once they head home .. ..

The day was a slow start for the week and tony and roger head to the Walmart door..
Roger grabs Tony's ass ..oh by the way will plow that later ..you started it you know what I do what I say so now u get something u like stud

Isaac was in the middle of nowhere because even though they didn't know how deep this was, it was easier to manage than to demand equal attention to detail….

Israel cry out for a moment of silence and despair of their soul in his name for jesus walks with them and they will have a good reason why they dragging their heads in their lives

They follow the same way they have been loved by the omega and in the time of need they will have to choose between the reality of their lives and how much they give to god daily

The battle between Israel and Afghanistan has become more of a burden of destruction and more violence against muslims is pouring into America with each day wanna go forward with this disease we face of hate

Where Israel was in a simplistic manner now it has a lot of question about whether or not they can start to turn into something real and victorious for a moment of truth in a very strong sense of value to be a force of god

Israel cry out for a new life mission with god's vision and peace with their lives. .
Isaac was in a way that's been the case for many people in this time of need for more information about how much they give to god

The world of darkness right now is the only thing that keeps the lives of Israelis in danger of losing their independence and peace

Where are you now cant wait to see you again and again iam sure goes thru the minds of Israel people among the noise

Iran supports terrism…

The battle between Israel and the Jewish people has reached a dangerously high level of emotion and violence is a common problem for the people of Islam society….

The day to day struggle with the world of darkness right now is a huge problem for the people of Islam

The Nigerian military has said that the whole process is a means of survival for them both

The identity crisis has become a reality for many people who are struggling with this new road led by the enemy

The Israeli media reported that they were in unity of how long the war will go on for the next generation of gods love is key to the point where they stand for their lives and economy for their Islamic heritage as a INDEPENDENT country….

The idea of being tired from being destroyed by the war is not a joke for these people ….they see it daily with the destruction in their street and they see it in their hearts … the emotions are so tightly controlled by their bodies into a Frenzy of violence in the streets….its a on going back and forth between the two part of the world and humanity……

The people have to live daily for the red alert alarm..they drive down the streets with no seat belts and windows rolled down...they listen for the alarm on the Gaza strip ...the routine they stop car or stop what they doing and lay on the ground so no shrapnel hits them…

Lord I cry out to you to come home to the Jewish state of Israel and Afghanistan..the people need you more then ever before ….this has to stop and think about what god says they are under his arms ….

Spiritual warfare basically when encounter opposite of gods teaching... how it effects you as a xhristian….to me its temptation ….seeks to destroy you from god and seperate you from god …..

Thoughts can come from your culture...its anything that will change or pull you from god ….
Temptation ….constant assumption of temptation...we see it is worth of people based on income and status of the world staus quo...money fame and good life …..

Today in Jerusalem and Palestinian leaders of israel are in need of a champion of peace and serenity in the house of god...he tries hard to prove it wasn't a good idea of being able to defend themselves against the enemy…..his regime in iraq where they stand for humanity and your love shine in this country where they have been through so much...the war wages on and its gotta get the best of all time just like rest of america we will pray for the people of iraq iseri and Palestine people….you are not alone here….

The bible talks about how we shall not murder ...when the angry monster Peeks its ugly head into the world and humanity from the enemy we can no longer exist in the world of democracy and our entire country…..we can let our bodies grow in a very difficult situation with a confidence that we face a greater burden. ….in this moment of time we forget the common sense of value in this country and we get tunnel vision……..then we start to turn into something real scary and we drift from god ….

The men were taken into custody after the shooting happened at the scene of a fatal crash involving two men...the suspects who allegedly killed two others in a car accident were reported to be a hit by the enemy….they were lost in their hearts and lost homes so they agreed to leave the church without a doubt…..when they did that last time they spend their money on drugs and alcohol in their lives….they were headed to the wrong direction of the world and humanity…. which now bring them to the day they met in a bar...got drunk and high that they saw gay couple driving by ...they recognized them from the neighborhood….

The men..the bodies that brought her to her knees more then once... she would get these visions of her man with other men drove her crazy...could not be because she did not know ...she was a physic after all...her man would get more action ….she was very competitive so if she lost or failed she was a total bitch in the purest sense of the matter….the visions were coming more frequently than before ….she liked her husband and her thoughts on this issue because she doesn't know where she sleeps in the room or a relationship between them…...she cant wait for her husband to make sure she doesn't want to go back up to the house of god…..she did it all begins with christ right there with her emotions from all walks of life…..

The men who played Lucinda would come in and out of her life ...they were reminders that her reality was not immediately clear about her needs…..she is the only one who gives the impression that she steps into her own voice and then waiting for her husband to make a move on her….she suffered this dislocated reality from her window of life…..the men and their lives were bound to get rid of their own lives and how much they need to talk with the truth of their lies ….

The men of the past mistakes are not going anywhere until you're ready to take the responsibility of your he

ad that lead you to come back here to stay calm….now once you calm you you can face truth and honesty for the next step and will get thru this one day of action and then you know what you are doing here right now just got to get to the house of god.

He was ready to go out into the world and humanity from his perspective he had much to say….the way he knows what you want to know about him he will reveal …the first time meeting with the house of god is a blessing from his glory…..the way to win his presidency and his character is in your hands as he does best to help you understand the importance of his plan…...

The army combat code..you protect your body and the world from the enemy...the system of a champion in the world of darkness right now has been all over the world...we face it daily and keep the devil on track and yet we don't rely on god as much as we speak of the enemy….he is right in front of us equally as god is but we ignore the fact that god created all these things that the devil uses as his seduction

The army has been a great way for growth in iraq and afghanistan….. its soul mission is the best way to live for jesus and his word often is not perfect for them because they know not what they are doing….. the matter or whether they're going on a plane or something that's just a thought about what they want to do should always be combated by their actions and answer god to heal them…..the army of god is great for them both for it is worth more then ever before and they will reside in a new world where they stand for their lives….

The men dressed in black jeans and white shirts were wearing their clothes on the way to the point of the end of mission...they wore she suede shoes with a new dress look....they wanted for the people to realize they were in a world where they stand for a moment of silence when we Mourn the president of the united states in his last hours...they fight to keep him and our humanity safe the enemy ....we take the enemy to war and destroy the enemy fears....the world of darkness right now has been on a upward scale of the human spirit..... the investigation into the parking space of a city street building that has vision and security forces will be done with this one man....that man is jesus and we must come together and create a world where its people are more willing to sacrifice their lives for others ...

The men were so quiet and they were talking about nothing more then ever so they had to climb into a fight against the enemy

They would become more comfortable with their experiences with christ who would never be fake or anything else but that in which they could have asked for

The men dressed in black and green clothes were found in each other and were treated for injuries and a sense of relief from their injuries would soon take over

The army has been a great way for growth in iraq and afghanistan to combat terrorism and the alpha group of soldiers will continue to do so much more clearer than they ever knew the duty of our troops will bring us thru the meadows of his plan

THE MEN OF THE ARMY CAN BE VISUALLY SUCCESSFUL AND VERY EYE CATCHING....THEY DO GODS GREAT WORK ...YET SOME ARE NOT ALWAYS REAL MEN BUT GAMERS AND PLAYAS ...THEY LIKE TO DECEIVE THE LUCINDAS OF THE WORLD ....THEY USE THEIR NAME AND THEIR LOOKS TO DRAW YOU IN ...THEN THEY SAY ALL RIGHT WORDS ...THE SAD THING IS THEY COULD USE ALL THAT WASTED ENERGY IN THE WORLD TO HEAL IT BUT WASTE ON DECEIT..

Today we saw a tragedy....it goes to show god is the only way... humanity was one reason why god doesn't want his children in a place where they will reside in the enemies...god wants us to talk with our christ in which we can do something soon enough that we face a challenge for our value in our hearts...

Why are they surprised with the truth does set you free and all things will change when you're in the house of god

When america comes to god then and only then can we face the challenges we face from the enemy on a day to day

Live for jesus and pray that you continue your journey through the house of god and never settle for less then your god will give you ...he knows how much you will see him again soon after you leave the village

The scope today cries out for a new way of doing life instead of looking at their past lives they must move up the volume of a champion for new heights
The president holds the highest level of respect for our value of life gets us through a variety of issues with our christ and society but when we come together for a new normal then and only then can

we get together in unity even if our own president has been a little more of a burden....

The president has a swelled head and giving the speech of some kind of judgement that is far from the truth
He owes it to people to realize that he wont be in the position and move on
The process was designed by the omega and natural progression of the people of the world vote and defend democracy
It's designed to help people with disabilities and their families find their way through the world
They were going through this difficult process of creating a new normal yet we can not let the enemy be able to bring us down to his message
The revival of his plan for my faith will keep going toward him again and again with respect for a moment of truth in his name

Tom wants to see the beauty in his eyes that god sees

He gets caught up on the image he sees in the mirror but not the man who stands before him designed from god
His promise is to change your opinion of your life and your image... yes we want great bodies and great sex...we want to know how much we are willing to pursuit what we started with god...he gave us a image that we must love...the physical connection felt thru sex is temporary....everybody deserves love ...in the end result physical beauty is tempting and temporary.......

Tom and chris been driving awhile now...they decided to take a look around this country where they were.....they had to get back to the city for work but wanted to get moment of relaxation for them both.... they were going out of their way but did not care....the daily grind took its tole....they had made it as far as Chicago......

Tom and chris been walking around the streets of Chicago for a while now….they looked at the color of the white flag FLOWING on the corner….they held each others hands as they walked through the night before they head back to work….they just want few moment of silence for their lifes…...the daily routine has become a major challenge for their own lives...

Tom was a catch
Chris was a player
Tim was a lover
Would these men know the love triangle that they were in unity for their lifes and interest in new position at a time when many people were not taken into account
They were in a way that works for them….they are to stand up for the world and humanity for their lifes of their soul mate was found in each other….they broke new ground in their own hands and they will be a force of life in this world…...they wanna go forward with this one together and create the desired outcome of their lives in Dearborn county…..they loved the whole process of creating a world where its not over till we unite the earth and eternity into this world….

Tom's heart was broken down by the enemy and fears of our humanity

Tom and chris are going forward with this new friendship and ultimate goal of this vision is to change our culture
Tom and chris been walking around in a world where its not over till god says that he will restore all of his plan

Tom would lose chris but meet tim years later ….he never knew about his life with god would be a force of life in a simplistic manner as he is the only one who leads us through a difficult situation

Tom prepared for his press conference…..he is very nervous about this ...its got so much attention from the heart…..tim wants to know what they say about the bottom line…..Tom walks in and says you ready for this ? Tom and tim have had a strong attraction to each other ….you look okey and know you will be great ….I am not physically okey tim ….funny tim replies you look okey...that bulge looks like it's doing just fine…….its been thinking of you ...hum he says let me get closer look ….as time gets closer he presses up against Tom...tim tells tom feels ready for anything…...tom says I gotta go to the meeting…. tim kisses tom and tom responds...tom crops to knees and pressed face to Tom's crotch…..tim don't have time for this thou want it … before he can say another word Tim has taken tom fully in his mouth ….tim starts working on Tom ….tom puts his head back while leaning on his desk…...suddenly knock on door comes ..tim walks in says you ready they are waiting…..?tom looks down and still hard but wet ….yeah I be right there ...tim let's talk later over drinks…..tim replies sure and by the way it was that good …...

Tim puts out his press release on the frontline of life and human rights….he knows god wants a better way ….jesus is a means of protection for me and you will see what happens when we come together…….for me god has been a great way for growth in our hearts due to this point of man is to view on how he lives his life……iam not only in his word but also his ability to see his beauty….I see his face in heaven for a few minutes before they speak....it is done with god today and always….I see him on a time of need and fear for his return from his glory is my point of truth in this life….he has the best time for real change in me and my faith in mankind…...my faith is driven by the grace of god with all his glory………

I ran thru the meadows...the tall flowers touched my fingers...they swayed in the wind ….I ran thru the meadows with a confidence that you my father in heaven for a new life mission is a means of freedom…...I ran

185

thru the meadows with the truth of our humanity in which god has been missing from us.....I ran thru the meadows of his grace in his name...I ran thru the meadows of the house of god with all his glory.....

Tim has been a member of Congress for several years now...he said in a statement from his office that he wont wavier from his perspective on this issue because he knows what christ says is a great way for growth in the world......Tom wants to hear from u about the future with your life and how he can handle the situation.....Tom and tim have been a secret for the past three years....they know what the enemy will say....they work for the people by the people....they know that God created all of us equally in his image....they love god even more then their careers....here on earth they love each other just as much.....they will never forget that he will restore all of us equally in this world.....he is the best way to get rid of infection of our hearts due to this disease we face in the world......

Tim has been a little bit different from this moment of silence....he seems to be in a bad place and can not turn off the world ...tim knows mark loves him....but tim feels so alone in this world....jesus is the only way he knows what he is doing in the world... .he calls out to him daily.....knows what he must do .....he calls out the dance of his life.....he looks to please god......all the time he struggles he has to believe god wont fail him .....he takes the time to stop being so angry about the future because he did it to himself....when he is honest with himself then and only then can the road be smoother than he knows it is now.....he will not give up the sky for a moment....his prayers for his forgiveness is of essence and time....his faith will continue until his death.......and his own skin will become more of a good result....all in the name of christ......

Tim has been missing from his life in the past mistakes that have made him more vulnerable to the world and humanity....the enemy was always at the door to make sure he was going through a difficult relationship…….the enemy situation in his own way of doing life instead of being able to talk to christ ….Tim knows where he sees fit to fill his life with god today…...the energy he gives to chasing temptation is not equivalent to the love that jesus will give him …..it only proves to be a temporary fix and lately not even that ….

Shelia comes home...she takes heals off and plops on the sofa…. her job is getting to her and has caused her stress….it drains the life out of her daily…

She knows you have plans for her life and she doing the right thing by you...lord give her the opportunity to make a decision to make it happen right now and see how things coming along with her husband and how they feel about the future of life….shelia lives for jesus and in this time of need you have the right direction of your life so that it can fill out the fire....rise for a new normal life to live for jesus.

shelia just not sure why you think of the world to heal the loneliness of her dreams yet again they have to choose from our perspective in this world in which god has a hold on her life…..

Shelia needs to feel love ...not just the spiritual….she needs to feel her husband in her isolation….they need to get back to bring one unit …..they need to feel each others skin..and the rythem of the dance …..the moments of pleasure ….they had a usually day at work and passion turns into something real with her husband that he will restore all the other times over the devil…….

The heart that beats for jesus is a heart that is alive
The heart that beats for jesus knows no more games or anything else that is not perfect
The heart of jesus is wide open to you today
The heart is where you find yourself in the house of god

The heart that burns for jesus also beats for jesus
The heart is where you find yourself in the house of god
The house of god is where your heart beats for 3
The house of god is the best way to get to know you better and be
active in your life

Day one
The scene set
Jack needs to get cross town
So puts ad in paper
Lexie needs the money
So she answer the ad
They talk on phone
They agree to meet next day at Dunkin
They will drive for few days
Will this work?
Will they discover more about life ?
They two strangers in a moment of need
They going on a trust that they have to choose between fear and hope
As night falls they both wonder
They were talking with u jesus
You answered the need and the solution
You will guide them and keep em safe
They both close their eyes
They will need the rest
This trip will take some twist and turns
No matter what christ is a means of protection as the road trip goes
ahead

Day two
The morning of the meet
Lexie gets there first
As she waits she watches people in and out of Dunkin

She sees singles
She sees couples
She sees guy couples
She sees female couples
After all she is in america
Suddenly a man approaches
He looks average
But sexy
He says hello iam jack
Hi iam lexie
Thank yous enter the air
They shake hands
So we ready to go jack
Yes lexie
They proceed to get into her lexis
Doors shut
And car starts
They pull away onto the road
Where it leads is only mystery that jesus will answer

The heart that beats for jesus is one that will be content in his own skin...the image of her dreams and hard work in essential detail for your sake protect her from harm .....christ does give her a sense of value in the world and humanity from his life in a simplistic mind to say that she steps into her new song from the house of god.....

Christ I look in the mirror...the image is blurred and I am very upset by this ....i can see two images...the one god loves and the one that the world sees everyday...the world is far from what god sees.... its effect on my heart and soul ways heavy on my mind.....its so tireing sometimes

Christ lives in me and my life….he is this force that says one more day ….I have much in store for you …..you are not to listen to the enemy…..my destiny and the plan has beauty all over it till the end of time …..you are the vision I created….see the light ….hear the beauty….i will restore the balance of perspective on gods change in you now…...

The reason I exist here is that I am a child of god with all his glory…. we all are the hope for our humanity...we can change the direction of our humanity in this time of need…..christ will be the best way you deliver your love for the world…...the world is very divided and we are in need to talk about everything big and small so we can do this right…..the world is full of joy it's full of promise…..we can be open minded to make a great place for the people of america…..the jesus we all hear about is ready to take a look at the end result of trusting jesus by making a decision to take the responsibility of our depression and the truth of our lifes…….when we do this …...not only will we be in better place ….we can heal the wounds we have started and built up …...the promise of tomorrow is now ….in jesus name I confess this is the most precious of all time just like the Angel's of mercy sent from god singing his new song from the house of god…….

Today was slow
It was driven by a large scale of distracted mind
All it could do was to have a good reason why I am so excited for this revival of my life
Iam here and now walk with god today and always by his grace
The scope of jesus in every moment of silence is nonthing personal and yet it is worth noting that there are some images for a new life mission that will change your mind for yourself and others will be amazed by how much you love him without any explanation
Christ bestow your soul in the world and humanity for its beauty will come back into our society and our children lifes will be better for it

Today I worry
Then have to remember
You are in control and you are the way
You will keep me safe from the enemy
Everything proceeding with you will work out
I know this isn't over till you say it is
You are my savior now and may I always have your strength in
your hands
You are the only person who has the power to make sure it gets better
with time and energy in the house of god

Jesus walk with me and my life forever has been a little more of
your life and your love for me ..I never want anything or anyone
else more then want you...you are my savior and I will never forget
that you have a mission in my heart to be a force of life in the world

I have to stop the carnage of our humanity and the world is in danger
of losing our hearts due to this disease we face

God all I do is for you always
Jesus is the best way to live for jesus
Christ bestow the journey of the human spirit
Let the angel sing new song from the hills of new release in spiritual
life
In.jesus I walk proud
In god I live in moment of truth
In christ I long for a MINISTRY
Angel of mercy shower me with love and joy

You are to dig deep with your FEET
You can not give into the doubt that holds you back
Set your mind on the christ in the heavens
He will get you a sense of value in your life

He will not fail you

The moment the enemy is working hard to prove it wasn't a good life you have to be ready with jesus and his grace

God loves the way you deliver your life and he will not let the enemy bring you down

Do what you set your mind to do

Then pray to god and let him hear you

Shout out loud to jesus

Say iam not afraid of the enemy in jesus name I will overcome

You are not perfect but you are the result of trusting jesus and his character

Where you find yourself in the world is full of happiness and joy in the house of god

The heart wants what it wants

The difference is knowing if its comeing from god

The reason you must know what they say about him because he has the comfort of being able to bring your best quality to your life

The reason why god doesn't make me feel bad instead he comforts my feelings and dreams of my life forever in the house of god

The heart holds all the secrets of the world and humanity for the house of god is the only way we can do it together with your help we will not be done with god and he is your best friend

Today just for moment the enemy tried to get hold of my worry

Then reminded the enemy how much jesus loves me

When did I was not haveing a effect from the enemy

The omega and I are a team

He restores

I believe in god and he loves me anyway

Today I am weary

Iam not confident

But know god worked his love for me
He made a way
He gives me a sign
He showed me the way
He was ready to go out into the light cf my strength
To brighten my darkness
To take my vision to my life
To raise the minimum for a new way
To be honest with the truth of this vision of my life
So pray to god and love the moment he will restore all that he will
restore in my heart
When in doubt dont give into your thoughts
Instead use them to reach out to the house of god
Go to christ and pray for god to heal your soul
He gives me peace in the storm
When the rain falls I'm dry
When the odds roll in the enemy favcr god just raises my mind to
say no more to the world and humanity for the enemy fears are not
going anywhere in this heart of mine

The heart that burns for god
The heart that burns for jesus
The heart that burns for christ

I been given a chance to help others thru my own experience in life
...iam ready to serve jesus and pray for the world to heal the loneliness
of your life and your family to have the right direction of his plan

We will never forget that you continue your work with the house of
god and love that god is great for your sake protect your child from
the enemy with the help of christ

Burn My heart burns for jesus the omega of all….its on fire for the christ who died for me and you…….

The hearts burns for the world and humanity in which god has been missing since the beginning of time….excuses and I will never have patience with the world if god is not in my life and my life forever has been changed for the better

Burn for jesus
Burn for god
Burn for christ
Burn for christ and pray for peace
Burn for jesus and his Angel's

Burning heart beat upon jesus today …let his live come to you free of any kind of judgement and you reveal your heart to others thru god   …burning soul keep the flames of red light burn with color in your eyes open for you always refuse to believe that you are not good enough

Today was a slow day …it just dragged on and on…..but the whole time thought about you god….how you gave my name and my future lineing up for the house of god with all the way to live for jesus…. you have put me in new road and will get thru this time of fear…you are using me as your witness and your love for me will shine on our hearts due from the beginning of the time

I will not sway from you
I will not leave the church
I will not let the enemy and fears set forth in my mind
I will never agree with the world of darkness
I will not be defined by my own limits
I will not be defined in any way other then by my christ

I willingly thought that I was going forward to knowing u were saying goodbye but I could not do anything for him…..I miss my dad I am very proud of your life so I stay away from the enemy and fears of our humanity
Christ will restore
Jesus will save my soul
God will revive my soul

Christ iam tired today ….iam on overload…….your the way to my salvation….look in mirror and dont like what see who become…..iam in a state of limbo….iam becoming more of who you want me to be …...you give me light to help me to keep going toward him……yet the scares are very deep and forever I can be open minded to the house of god…..have faith in what is your approach to this point I think…god knows iam strong enough to calm waters and I am very grateful for this revival of my strength…...so god will not let the storm get away with the chains that are so tightly bond to me and held by the enemy……

God release the chains that bind me
Jesus break the chains that hold me
Christ strip me of the world chains that the enemy has placed on me

Pray to god
Pray to jesus
Pray to christ
Prayers for the world and humanity for its sake is to change our lives and our children lifes

Lord I ache today ..I get in over my head trying to be all that can be….spread myself far and wide..oh lord help me slow down...help me up anytime u see me fallen….help me stop the insanity of fastracking my life...let me know what and see what christ has in store for me…

I pray to god
I pray to jesus
I pray to christ
I have faith in you creator of my essence
Just wanna write my books
Just wanna see your face in this world
Just wanna be with you

I look to higher heavens as a independent person who has been
missing since the beginning of my life

I look to god for a new normal...they are to be in jesus name and his
character is the best way you are to look forward and clear your head
of expectations that are not real or placed by gods design
God let's you speak
Humans wanna be in charge
God has plan for your life
Others wanna be your boss
I give my heart to god
I live for jesus
I look to christ

You cant change history
You can learn from it
You can teach your children new way and gods way
You are responsive and in charge of your role in the world
Never lose hope
Have hope always
Never forget to pray
Pray daily
Never forget to love
Live and love god
Love jesus

Love christ
Never lose faith
Have faith in all you do

We are the future
Pray to god
We are the answer to every challenge
Pray to jesus
We are the solution to every problem
Pray to christ
We are the connection to unity
Have faith in your god
Have faith christ will give you the right direction of his plan and his
character is the best way to get rid of infection that CAUSES you
pain and loss of heart

We are the change
Pray to god
We have the passion for them
Pray to jesus
We need the energy of the house of god
Pray to christ
We are a great team
Have faith in christ
We are in need of calm heads
Go to god
Have faith christ will give you the power to be a force of god
Pray to god
Have faith in mankind to understand what happened and what takes
place in the house of god
Have a mission to forge ahead in my life and human connection

Beauty lived in all of us
Its here and now
Its a challenge to see how things are happening
Its the best way to live for jesus
It's the same as what christ says about it before you enter the house
of god
Its a great way to get to know the better part of your family
Its the only way to live for jesus and his COMMANDS
Its the only thing that keeps me from getting into a messy situation

Beauty lives in all of us
Beauty is there any way you are ...you are gods creation and he will
restore all that you need...you are not meant to be like everyone
else....you are not to compare nor be compared to anyone else

Beauty is a means of blinders for mankind...we tend to judge the
person from the outside rather then in the heart....we look at the
surface and see what we wanna see...this sadness god because he
has the right creation and left his soul in the body of his children

Beauty is a design and a sense of value to gods heart and he loves us
inperfected for our value is not just on the outside....he knows that
this is all temporary yet true beauty is there in the depth of his temple

Beauty of his plan comes to us all
Beauty is the best thing ever for the world to see the light of jesus
in every corner of the human spirit
Beauty of this story is that we face a greater danger when we dont
follow god yet the beauty is he loves us no matter what
The scope of jesus is wide enough for me to keep going forward
with this new road
The reason for this is that we face the challenge of having the
opportunity to make a great place for the people of america

The strength they desire is in the house of god with all your will to be a force of god to heal the loneliness that we face daily

The revival is now in place until the world is full of happiness in our hearts due to this we must come together and create a new normal

My mission
You are in control of my life and your love for me is my best source to answer the question of whether or not I am very proud of your life so I stay away from the enemy and fears…….I really like this freindship going far and beyond here and now….so many times I feel comfort in my heart with peace of mind with jesus…..I dont ask for much my father….just that people love me like god…..that they will have the same effect on me for what they say about you is the only way to live for jesus….see for me it's about time I get to know u better and I am very proud of you makeing love to know what I mean to god....he knows about my faith in mankind and I am a little more concerned about the future of the world…..god in this country where we care about our lves and how they can start to get better soon after the trial of the enemies lies that satin is going to tell us…..we see it grow in the world and humanity for the sake of our humanity we will see your face in heavon and god will do what he does best in our best interests...we are in need of a calmer environment and the truth of this action will continue to share the value of your life…...god with your help we will see the beauty of the world and humanity from his glory and greatest sacrifice for humanity is that we have the house of god with us all in the spirit…..

Wonder
You have questions and thoughts daily ….you always question the world around you….you are to becau se if you dont then they will reside in your heart…..you never learn what god is telling you …..you have to choose from the heart of humanity and your life will

never be sorry…..you choose the house of god or the enemy…..you can never do anything else that you want until you choose god and faith in mankind

Tears

I cry them when happy and sad….they release the pain you feel and drain the negative…..they are road to your heart and ACCEPTANCE of your fellow man…..you are not weak when you cry...you are in need of the tears because they are the water of your heart….they relieved the build up of the world and its hurt inflicted to you…. cry to god….let god wipe your tears away ….its not just for your sake if you cant cry in front of the christ who died for you then who will you cry for?

Burning heart is where the love miracle comes from within our faith in mankind thru the house of god .when you give into gods ways and words your heart burns on the very level you slocombe to his truth

Burning heart is where the truth is just that because of my strength in seeing the world and humanity in the house of god and love the way we can talk about everything we need to know….that's gods greatest gift….he and the alpha will have the right direction to help us understand what we started…....

Burning heart and soul into the light of jesus is here and now we face a greater danger of life and death by our own lives than ever before if we deny that god created all of the world….a world where its citizens are now touched by his grace for all this time of need of the house of god is the only way that works for the world….stop ourselves in this world full of happiness is a blessing from god…..we must submit to god for your sake protect your soul from the enemy….

Burning heart is where you are to stand in the house of god with all his glory is my point of center….in my lord and god will come to me for what I am doing in my heart with joy in the house of god is the best way to live for jesus…...will walk to the house and the truth of our hearts due from the beginning of the world and we are going forward with this new road led by my father in heavon…….
May I always ask you jesus for my life is to change the direction of my life forever in the house of god
May I be in jesus name and his Angel's will bring me into such an safety net even when iam upset you will see the beauty

May I ask for your permission
 please help me with this new road led by my father
It begins with your heart and your life will be the best way he knows what I mean to god....he knows what I do to that point of view and I am very happy with his angel of mercy

May I come to you for physical contact...your love will be my energy and my blood that flows within me….my eyesight is the most important part of my strength in seeing you ...my hearing is the only thing that keeps me alive until we get together…..when god knows what I want it now is that I am very proud to speak out against the enemy and fears of the world……..god knows the pit stops and the truth about how much I keep my serenity in mind when it comes to the world and humanity…...he knows what I mean and use my restless nights to get my word on the way to live for jesus…...my words and perspective never fade away yet again they have been through the process of submitting to god even though the enemy is working hard to find me in this world and the alpha will protect us from getting into this mess of our humanity……

MY HEART BURNS ON THE WAY TO THE POINT WHERE YOU ARE THE BASIS.AND CHRIST IS THE ONLY WAY TO LIVE FOR JESUS...YOU ARE NOT PERFECT...DONT YOU KNOW WHAT THEY SAY ABOUT YOU AND YOUR LIFE WILL NEVER HAPPEN IN YOUR LIFE IF YOU'RE IN THE HOUSE OF GOD WITH ALL HIS GLORY IS MY BEST....SEEK IN MY HEART AND SOUL EVEN THOUGH I AM VERY GRATEFUL FOR YOUR LIFE AND YOUR LOVE FOR ME ITS GOD WHO WILL SATISFY YOUR NEEDS WITH YOUR HEART....

Burning heart is where you find yourself in the middle of nowhere and you reveal your heart is a blessing for your life...you only end up with you .....I have been talking to god and he agrees...he knows where u are meant to be
Christ bestow your touch....its in your heart and your life so much more THAN I ever thought about...u would have happened to me in my life and I am very grateful for your support and belief in me

There is a burning feeling...a battle within itself and the world..... long to give you my life and my heart.....I want to follow jesus in every corner of my life and I am very proud to speak it out loud.....I always say that you are not going anywhere until i treasure the moments of your life and your daily guidance in my affairs and my faith is in your hands........you are the rock that I need and desire to be the best way to live for jesus and walk thru the obstacles they throw out at me.....

The answer is they lost their heart and soul to the enemy and fears of the world...you can restore them in split second or end the way they are looking at the end of the human race.....

Sometimes feel my serenity is on trial...like the enemy loves when iam off my game...he loves it even better when you are in fear....

yet what he does not realize is that I have the power of christ on my side…..that god will get me thru the storm and back on the mountain ….no matter the situation god is my source of strength...he says he will restore all...its not just for us but we will see the beauty…... our children will have the opportunity to work together with god and humanity…..

May 9th and its snowing...now the sun is out and then...its crazy much like life the mood changes...god is the answer...we have christ to be the shelter...you have to choose between fear and hope that helps you get there with him and the alpha…..you and his COMMANDS are going forward with your heart you will see the beauty of this vision and hearing that you have god always with you.....I could do anything for the house of god with all his glory is my point where I belong to the house of god with the truth about how much we hurt and that he will restore all that we lost can only make you better person...

Sometimes I get overwhelmed by the fact that I will caught up in speed and getting there too fast…...then it effects my sleep and my mood...god help me slow down and keep my serenity in my life….. christ for more THAN once hope for the faith in mankind and my life to be simply calm and day to day...life is full of surprises yet still have time to stop and wonder what the beauty is…...see and smell the roses …..take it steady because not a race….when you live that way …..you create your life...gods way you deliver your life and your family happiness….want my life to be simple and enjoyable even when life test me….that's the normal part yet I dont wanna keep building or adding to my un easy and stress in my life

Sitting here watching tv..the sun warms me heart...it fills me with positivity about the day ahead ….no matter what comes my way…. the coffee is hot and wakes me up ….yet god is the true reason why iam awake….he has put in me a destiny and a mission to forge ahead in my life…..he wants to see me again and again to make it count for the world and humanity from the house of god .....god knows what is in my heart and my mind ...after all god put the right direction of his plan to make it happen again and again....he will continue his work in essential detail for me to keep going forward with this new road led by the omega and my faith......

The answer is the only way to live for jesus. By this mean that we can ask the question yet only answer is gods grace and sacrifice for humanity is the only answer.....no matter how many questions or how you ask the same question the answer you need to come up with is the house of God

The answer in time of fear is not to give into the world and humanity for its purpose is to change your mind for the better

You are to learn about your own way and then waiting for the house of god to heal the loneliness that you have

She walks up to the glass ...she wonders how she got here ...how did events turn to this...she did the right thing...she always tried to do the right thing....she never before did she even know what she was doing important for herself because she let the men and her image hurt her life....she put to much power in their hands and not enough of god in her heart ....where she fell short was the result of years of this story and its chain of events....how is not really a question anymore....now it's how she changes her lifestyle and habits that are more likely to happen in her isolation than her own life...see she wants to know what she was doing important for herself because she is the only one who gives her the chance to talk to her god.

God bless her and her image
 hurt bystanders with their lives were being destroyed by the enemy
..she and the world is full of happiness in the house of god with all

his love for the world..she only has to see what happens when you're in the house of god with all his glory ...when she truely is the only one who has to take the responsibility for her choices made by her feelings and not god being the driveing force…….I know what she feels….I have led by my feelings and temptations more then my heavonely fathers love...now more then ever closer to book comeing out few months do I know his love….all my life led to this point and that he will restore all that I have been through and lost ten times more then before lost it…...go to God and love him without any doubt about his life in this time of need and fear…..

God bless her future
May her future begin with her husband she will have and will get thru this time together…
May her future begin to grow stronger and better as she continues her career as a author….
May her investments have the right direction of the income needed to pay off all her debt and her life be more comfortable with her husband
May the days of counting as she puts groceries in the cart and haveing to have her husband or herself ask is this okey or say this is only x anount… may they buy the food they need …

May she have the passion for your life so that she will have the opportunity for her family to help her overcome her problems and make your life the best thing ever for her and her stability
May her investments be the best security in the here and now...may they provide for her family and children
May she never forget her husband that she will have...may the next day he is with her be the first one being held in the house of god with all his glory

May she never forget her name and his character is the most important part of her dreams and hard times for she will have the opportunity for her life to live for jesus

She walks along the boardwalk ...she listening to the sound of the ocean..the segal's in the air....so among many but feels so alone.... so reads the faces...she sees the couples..sees the Smiles in their faces....she is s screaming on the inside and nobody knows ....she walks along the board walk ......

Lord fill her with your heart and ACCEPTANCE of her dreams and your life will help her overcome the challenges of being tired from the enemy and fears that she will not find her way to live for jesus Help her to get back the way she is with you and her husband that she will have in the near future ...her children she longs for ....she sees the baby and the moms together in the neighborhood ...she sees the family on the boardwalk....take that longing she feels azad no wrap her In your gracd...let her feel the same way you feel about her....then let her rest in peace just like you would love her to ...stop thd torment she feels in her life .....the daily longing for you and life she thinks she will never have ....

The power of my prayers and strengths in faith..its that god is the safety net even when dont understand ....not meant to question his method or his work...
It is a on going thing ...its the world and humanity from the enemy fears god ...because if you are not afraid of the world and humanity in which the enemy uses you have a great outlook...in jesus name The power is in your hands god....you also gave me the brains and the wit to do what need to...you set it in my face and know that will do what I need to do....its not the money but it's the income that will allow me to build my ministry and write more books.....god your the muse to my art and the truth of why do what do in your

name....god you are the master of my strength and your the heart of my soul in as journey .....you will put the right direction in my life so can bring your glory to my life and my family....

The answer was yes but the strong part was that the world was not immediately clear about the bottom line

The answer is they lost their heart and soul to the world and humanity yet again they have to choose the house of god

They are the basis.and christ is the best way to live for jesus and pray for peace on earth that they have no effect on the ground floor of this vision

They were talking about their health and their lives were being treated as well as perspective on this issue of the disease

LOVE THE CHALLENGE
IT WILL BRING YOU MORE DEPTH
BRING YOU MORE THEN EVER CLOSER TO YOUR HEAVENLY FATHER
BRING YOU MORE DEPTH BEHIND THE SCENES AND THE TRUTH ABOUT HOW MUCH YOU CAN SEE THE DESTINY
Love the moments for what they are
Love god always
Love the way you deliver your own life
Love the storm
Love the aftermath
Love the moment

LOVE EASTER
THE CANDY
THE COLOR

NEW SEASON
FLOWERS POPPYING UP
WARMER DAYS
NEW HORIZENS
NEW MISSIONS
NEW BEGINING
DID I MENTION CHOCOATE BUNNYS

New days are always there for the world and humanity in the house
of god
New missions are underway for the people of america in this together
with your heart
New missions will have the passion for them because they are now
touched by god and he loves us
New missions will be available for the next generation of the human
spirit
New missions are underway for the world and humanity for its
beauty will come from the house of god
New missions will have the right direction of his plan and the alpha
will have the passion for your life

I often ask myself why
Why I put up the most walls
Or why afraid to go forward
Do you know how much this hurts me
God it's your time that will be the answer

Christ you are not away from me
You are the only confidence I need
You are my savior now and then
You were always there
Sometimes not in front view
But in my opinion the first one feeling

Had of why iam here
You were there even when go thru
The uncomfortable times
You are the voice in my head
You tell me to go out into the world
Make my life more THAN just a test to test way
Let me find peace today with the house of god
The reason for this time of sorrow
And pain
Are not only for us to remember what
You died for but what you
Are going to to do in us
Iam more then just a number in the world of man
Iam meant to heal and change world...god and the alpha will be
done with my decision....god is the only way that I feel comfort
God you have dad with you
He is watching over me
With your heart and soul heal his hurt
When he was here he had tough time
I know there was alot of damage done
But god will come down here and then he delivers his message to us
Dad and me never were great
We had our days
Being the first and a mommas boy
Did not help
He was in the navy
So the bonding years were
Not a bonding time for us
We were never close till it was too late
By then there was so much loss time
We had never said I love you
Like father and son should
So many times wondered what I did wrong

Why I was not good enough
What do I do to make him love me
When he died
I never got to opoligies
For my part
Communication is essential in any relationship
Yet was too busy blaming and shifted the responsibility

God forgive me
Was very narrow minded
Was very quiet in the truth
I did not see him for what he was
What his faults were
Treated mine like was better
Played the game of ego
So much I keep the wall up
I was part of the problem
Not part of the solution
God let me know when you are
With him
If I could only tell him how
Much love and miss him
Wish he was here to see my sucesses

Jesus and grandmother
She was my rock
She made me feel so spacial
Those lights we laughed
Watch tv late into the night
She would go to yard sales
Buy clothes for my stuffed bunny
Even washed them
Make mr my favorite dinner

Even thou she made dinner
She filled with love
We spent every weekend together
Miss her so much
She never doubted me
She was the first one to let me be me
So when grew up
The world was the enemy
 Built up the wall
 Built big persona
Wasted time and energy
Because what need is god
My life is empty without god
My weakness in mans view
Are actually strengths thru god wish
Iam very emotional
Very passionate
And feel with all my
Heart
Body
Soul
Mind

Jesus
The answer to fear
The answer to hope
The answer
The answer to all
The answer
The answer to how much you love
The answer to the question of whether you are afraid

Jesus is the answer
Take me home
Calm my emotions
LIKE SO MANY
WE ARE FIGHTING A BATTLE
WE ARE NOW
ACCEPTING A UNKNOWN FUTURE
THE WORLD HAD A NORMAL
NOW WE HAVE NEW REALITY
AS WE EAT OUR DINNER
WATCH OUR NEWS
BEING ISOLATED
ITS HAS A EFFECT
I HAVE TO DIVE INTO YOU
HAVE TO HAVE FAITH
WITH YOU CAN SEE THE LIGHT
WITH YOU I AM
NOT GOING TO LET THE STORM GET
ME INTO THE FEAR
FEAR OF THE WORLD
ITS A CHALLENGE FOR ME AND MY FAMILY
WE ARR SOCIAL CREATURES AND OUR CHILDREN ARE
IN NEED OF THE HOUSE OF GOD
The DISEASE HAS A HOLD
ON OUR NATURE
OUR DAILY ROUTINE
ITS NOT OVER TILL GOD SAYS THAT
BUT ITS DRAGGING OUT THE ENERGY
GOD REFUEL US
GOD BLESS THE HURTING
GOD SO MANY PEOPLE ARE MORE THAN THEY HAVE IN
weakness due to this disease
The reason for this isn't to be afraid

But question
What MATTERS
What is your approach to this
You are the basis.and the most substance CONSUMING of any kind
We are to follow you
Reach out to you
Call upon you
In this hour of need
Help me help someone who is in the wrong place mentally

Breathe in me
Restore in my hope
Give me the faith
You are never gone
Will always see
You will bring us our salvation
We will run yo you
Iam not the only one
So many wanna find you
May this time be the moment
The time to look at you
At the promise
In your eyes
That see the light
That open the view
That clears the fog
Jesus is the way to the
Heart of the sea
Heart of humanity
Heart of hope
Yes
I believe
I give my counsel

To his majesty
To his message
No left or right
But to the house of god
GOD

DON5 KNOW WHY THEY PLAY THE GAMES
YOU WOULD NEVER DO THAT
TO THEM ITS BUSINESS
YOU ARD ABOUT PEOPLE
YOU ARe THE PRINCE OF PEACE
THE MAJESTIC ONE
You put hearts
You put value
You put human life before money
Why cant they
They know not what they do
Dont forsake
I know now must not judge harshly
Questioning human nature is natural
But you deal the punishments

In the moment
I struggled to stay positive
Seems face back lash
As you did when you wanted us hear the good news
It's still worth it to me
Can not let the devil
Hold me in doom and gloom
He has taken hold of so many
In these times
We will be in jesus
We are to trust him now

We are to get hin in our country
God is where I feel safe
In the house of god
Where is the most important part of your life and your family will
be the one thing that keeps you alive and well
When does it count for the world and humanity in this together we
will see your face and your grace
Lord help us to meet the people who never have been loved and
need peace
In their hearts
They long
They desire
They are on edge
You soldiers now
Are to step up
Answer the call
To heal the loneliness
To restore your hope
To testify against the enemy
To bring your best quality to the house of
God
We need you in the world and humanity to get rid of infection
The revival of his plan is what he does best
The reason for this is that the whole country needs to stand up to
the inevitable
Revive your life
Revive your day
Revive the joy
Revive the world
Revive the energy
Revive the news

Revive yourself in the house of god
Revive your life and your family
Revive the news and you reveal your heart

God I need you…my life is in termoil….i started great new career …iam a author….my job is like wolf hanging on to my mind….miss my freinds who cant be with all of them…i can only use technology and isolated is my new normal ….I wanna feel good about future…. if I look at all the man made stuff there is no hope….the house of god is where draw my strength….its the place where I go….to find solitude and new hope….

God …they fight over the details….they put the human population….in the mean time people are dying from a disease….. its in need of you….your the real medicine….your the the reason we stay in hope…..your the why in any question we have

God …we need you to come home…we need jesus to be the one who gives the world a sense of hope….we need to realize you are the basis.and the world is loved by all of the house of god

God…..iam in need of you….iam a strong person…. human nature is disappointing me right now…we are not comeing together in places we need to….we are in time crunch….we are in a race to solve a answer to the people ….not the big answer that is you we are failing as a whole in man world…..

Mary
 sits at her table
Sips on her fresh poured coffee
And ponders
The world
The news

Is in chaos
We are running scared
We dont know facts
She has to reminded about god
And her faith
To make sense of the whole thing
She prays
She cries
She really just unleash the tears
She knows it's a short fix
But god says do so
It does
Help

Mark
Sits on his porch
He looks at quiet streets
He hears the silence of the scare
He knows god is there
But this moment says why
He wants the answer
He has none of his own
He simply but wants the depth
So he just sighs
He just wished
He knew the answer

Cadie

She walks her route
She delivers her mail
She knows the people
Who usually great her

Are now behind a door
Or in a window
She waves
She smiles
She feels the heartache
She feels the loneliness

Rick
Just saw his new son
Breifly into this world
He wonders
What future will he have
He will do alot of wonder
His son is his first child
From marriage
Of 30 years
They were so happy
But now wonder the new year
Will he know
Will he play ball
What new world will he know
But he is healthy
And prays to god
Saying thank you
I trust
In you my father

Jodi
She drives cab daily
She usually has busy day
She meets new people hourly
She laughs
She shutters

She smirks
She lives helping go from point
A to b
Now she watching news
She wonders when it will return
The days of the going to work
And the days of the sun in her face
She wont see the world
Just so loneliness
Yet her god
Is there
It's not going down

Carrie
Wants to go to school
She misses her freinds
She loved her classmates
She like her teachers
And the recess time

I believe God has a big plan for my life. He always has and yet in my flesh it gets lost. I spend too much time worrying and comparing myself. I let man and the here and now be a focal point. Now mind you God is always with me, but he gets drowned out. He loves me anyway. So this must put Him in prime view. Never let a second go without thinking, thanking, praying. So today I decided to follow and pursue dreams, take action, and live one day at a time. For God knows my days and the number. He will fulfill them and all that are a part of my destiny.

Prayer: Father, you remind me that it is never too late.
Never to late to recharge your heart
Never too late to recharge your passion.

Never to late to rethink the situation
Never too late to start talking about the house of god
Never let the enemy win over the house of god
Never mind the one who gives you heartache
But rely on the house of god
God live in me and you reveal your heart
May mr heart beat
May my mind find a calm river flow
Where images of you are my picture
And it's beautiful

Prayers
For the world
For the human spirit
For our neighbor
For our brother and sisters
For the enemy we are facing now to subside
For the health of all to receive the benefit of the house of god
Prayer
To my heavenly father
Many are scared
Rest their mind
Rest their fears
Rest the uncertainty

Hope for new release from the end ed my grip
Hope for the release of the enemy strong hold
Let his grip weaken
Let the world be better THAN tomorrow
We are in crisis
We are in desperate need of miracles

Love
Give it freely
Seek it
Appreciate it
Love one another
Spread it in the dark places
Count n it
Live for it

Realization..what do I?
Iam okey
Not going to fall
Not going to be weakened
Not going to break
Have god
Have god and my faith
Have my family and freinds
Have inner strength that is un broken
Have a sense of urgency
We are one with god

Prayers….that I never stop fighting for life
….that I keep my sense of the power of the prayer needed daily..
that I can be strong
Prayers…..that people never stop rely on you …that they see you
as the answer for the life they want…

Prayers …..we see the hope …that we see the sun and clouds precious
even in the dark times

Prayers….that we move forward as a team….that we stay united
and together….we stay hopeful

Prayers …..we yrust you
We love you
We listen to you
We look to you
We get in touch and stay focused on you
We look to faith
We think as brothers and sisters in christ

Realization

In my human flesh I am so easily ready to place blame. To point a finger. Now mind you, I was one who put myself in the problem. I spent too much or went overboard, letting the enjoyment of stuff become more important than common sense. Instead of enjoying and using what I already have, I would just get more. Now I have more books then I've read, more CDs than I can listen to, more scarfs than I can wear, and more DVDs then I can watch. Now I am not saying you can't have these things or can't enjoy them. Yet it's the enjoyment and the use that's more important than the number. They are meant for pleasure and not the Assumption. There are many who would love a third of what I have in these man made pleasures. I am thankful for them.

Prayer: Lord, may You remind me that enjoyment over assumption is the way to go.
Thought: Read one book before moving on to another. Watch DVDs weekly. Wear scarves often. Listen to music daily.

Reminder: Enjoy what you have and before you add more, ask yourself this: Do I need it now?

Dreams

We live and we forget how to dream. We get caught up in the everyday. We feel we are too old or we left people dictate our future.

God gave us a life to live. Not run a rat race. He does not create human life to run and not know peace of mind in our day. When we don't dream, then we go through a routine. Now, yes, in the here and now we have to because that is the way we live. We take on and do so much, but do so little. We are living for the flesh and not the soul. By doing this we put a limit on our mind and a restless feeling on our body. So this I say to you: Dream and let God hear you.

Prayer: God, pray that I never lose my ability to dream. Always put my dreams in your hands.

Thought: Dreams are meant to keep the mind active and fresh. Always dream big and small. Always know they can be big and small. Simple and complex. Dreaming to me is always hopeful. It's a reminder that you are alive. You were born to dream. You can dream, but there is a reality you must know. You must know there is a practical view.

Realization: You can't fulfill a dream if you aren't active. You can't just dream and then wishfully think it will happen.

Practical Approach: Give it to God. Be active daily. Have a game plan. Never give up. Have faith. Work hard. Be diligent.

The Why

Why: Do I let people control my fate?

Thought: Because I have been conditioned to from an early age as well as my upbringing.

Prayer: Lord, you are in control of my days and my life. Only you can bring what is meant to be. Only you can be the Master. You have a final say on how and the number of my days.

Realization: I am not being true to God. I must and want to be more authentic in all of my days to you.

Why: It is hard for me to believe in myself. It is so hard to follow through.

Thought: I was raised to not believe and not to dream. To only accept man's plans for and on my life.

Prayer: Lord, your will be done. You decide what is real and what matters. You have the answer.

Realization: When we put it in God's hands He will be enough. When you stop needing social media approval and mans then, and only then, can you be free.

Why: Do I go back and forth in my daily ambition? Why does my focus stray?

Thought: Maybe because in a world of "now" and not "later" we get bored and distracted easily.

Prayer: Father, help me to stay on the prize and your Kingdom. Let me know you are never away from me.

Realization: Pray.
One day at a time.
Never look back.
Trust in Jesus.
Breathe.
Focus.

Why: Does it seem like I'm worried today? I was so worried about how to get through the week and why he has to struggle. Is it my fault?

Prayer: Thank You for doing what you do best. Thank you for love and grace. You came through and were always in awe. How do you come through even in prayers we don't say aloud? You amaze me.

Thought: True story about a recent situation. He was broke. Only $25 dollars to his name. Buys a five dollar ticket and wins $500.00.

Realization: Make a decision.
Set a goal.
Put into action.
Focus
Want to change.
Don't repeat.

Why: Do I want to cry the night before? Do I get physically it thinking about the next day?

Thought: Because it is not doing Your work. It's not being real to myself. Goes against everything I am not.

Prayer: Place me where I am meant to be. Your will be done. Make me the man I'm meant to be.

Realization: Be thankful.
All this is temporary.
Do your best.
Remember what He has given you.
Breathe.
Bring it to God.

True Event: Was at the grocery store. Left my wallet on the counter and my keys as well. Money and cards were in my wallet.

God's Intervention: No money was missing. All cash intact. No cards missing. Keys next to the wallet.

Realization: God exists. Looks out for me.

Why: Does it not always work out as planned?

Thought: We do it to ourselves. We don't think. We give into flesh. We try to do it our way.

Prayer: Help me to lean on you. Help me to relax. Help me to see the bigger picture. Help me to focus on your ways.

Realization: I don't have all the answers. I must not play God. If it's not God's way, then it's not worthy of doing. I know that I must study.

Why: Does it hurt when we lose someone?

Thought: Natural feeling. We want to control the outcome. We want to be the gatekeeper. We try to tell God how long and when someone enters or leaves us.

Prayer: Father, help me to know loss is a part of life and the journey. Remind me that you are the one who controls the number of days.

Realization: God heals.
God knows and will reserve the timing.
God knows you.
This too shall pass.
Why: Do I forget who was meant to be?

Thought: I listen to the wrong voice in my head. I don't have faith in myself. I live in a world where comparison runs rampant. I look to the wrong source to feel worthy.

Prayer: May you be the source that fuels my destiny. May I have the faith needed to do my best. May I not need to compare and always feel worthy in your word.

Realization: He will make me in his vision. When I put God first, he will set the final destination into my path. When I give my cares to my master then I will be in the right place. Look to God for who I am. Look to his ways and be set free. Love the flaws because they are God given. Man only judges you and yet God creates a masterpiece.

Why: How do we find a better way to come together?

Thought: We read the bible from front to back. We study it book by book. We never put biased thoughts and replace God's words. We listen to the stories of those who have been changed by the grace of

God. We remember we have the same color blood. When we bleed it is the same color. Red. We unite on a daily basis. Pray that we see our enemy as our brother and sister in Christ. Realize that is easier said than done. We can only change our hearts first. Then we can help others. Pray that hate is erased for the next generation. We must come together as one with one step at a time. Realize that when judgment day only God will be the judge and jury. Pray for a day that we call can love without any biases. Realize your potential in God.

Always know the root of what is bothering you. Be real and admit the source of your negative thoughts. When you do this it makes the why in life less likely to come up.

Now not saying they won't come up. You just won't see them as much. When they do, they won't weigh so heavily on your mind. Nor will they rob you of your day and waste time always thinking of why me. Why can't this or that be? You can focus more on others and how to change the world.

Prayer: Instead of thinking why me? Instead, teach me to think how I can not repeat.

Scripture Reflections

Psalm Chapter 17, verse 6: I call on you, O God, for you will answer me. Give ear to me and hear my prayer.

God always hears us. No matter if you are quiet or yell or cry or just utter God help me. He knows your pain and he knows my joy. Yet we sometimes will ask and receive something we later regret. God always answers me. Learned the hard way to make sure that when I ask, it comes from an honest and real place. God will even sometimes give you something to prove his point. He wants you to know that He knows the why as well as you are ready for the destiny He lined up so long ago.

Ecclesiastes Chapter 5, verse 4: When you make a vow to God, do not delay in fulfilling it. He has no pleasures in fools.

When you give a dream to God, He is not interested in fancy words or the act of using your tongue. He wants to see you mean it. He won't do His part and just wave a wand while saying it will be done. He wants to see your commitment. He wants to see your actions. He always wanted you to mean it. With God, it's a two way street. If you put in the time and honest effort then your Savior will bring to light what is meant to be.

Job Chapter 20, verse 2 "Zophar": My troubled thoughts prompt me to answer because I am greatly disturbed.

When you hang on to thoughts too long they will consume you. They will have an effect on every area of your life. You spend too much time on you and not others. You were meant to laugh, love, and live. Not meant to always be about you. Let God handle it. After all, he is the Alpha. Always breathe in and say God help me. It's simple and He is ready to listen and help you go forward. Leg go. Handle your battle and you live. Best way is to take one day at a time. For me, I repeat "God help me" daily.

Job Chapter 21, Verse 6: When I think about this, I am terrified, trembling seizes my body.

Many times I over think and plan. I make steps and then rethink them. I alter my actions and make adjustments. It's daily and time consuming. Yes, no rest for the wicked, but even more wasted energy for the thinker. Recently I've been trying to take one day at a time. Keep it simple. Still a daily process but it's a little more peaceful. Can find some joy in everyday life. When I get too close to that line of action and obsession then pray this: God help me. You're the Alpha and I am merely human. God bless you.

Psalms Chapter 35, verse 19: Let not those gloat over me, who are my enemies without cause.

No one should ever judge me. Nor assume anything about me. We all get judged. That is truly only God's duty. Even if I have been so called giving them reason to again only God judges me. People should always want to know why. What is the reason or the background story that makes us do what we do? Where does it say I live for man? Yet man always wants to have the answer. Or at best play God. They feel they have the right to judge me. In the end God says I am the way.

Psalm Chapter 77, Verse 1: I cried out to God for help! I cried out to God to hear me.

The cried out part in this has never been more true. I have what is called monthly melt downs. I cry to the point where I get sick. Hold too much worry in and try to fix myself. Yet know that god wants to take my pain. He hears me even when I yell and say dumb things. He never forsakes me. I love how that feels. Not the melt down mind you. But the fact God will always remain in me. God will always be mine and will be free of Satan.

My responsibility to my creator: Ask and receive.
Knock and seek.
Have faith.
Trust in His word.

Study His word.
Share His world.

God's promise to me: Never forsakes me.
Always make each day new day to improve.
Will love me unconditionally.
Will always guide me to the destiny that awaits me.

My promise to the readers: Be candid and real.
Share my experiences.
Write from the heart.
Always to encourage.

I forgot how to dream and hope like a child. The more I get into your world and your word I can be a dreamer. I can hope again and know that even if they are different dreams they are still a dream. They are hope for what comes next in life. They also can be the simple and the biggest. They will be a reality and a place to be with you. So I will share my recent dreams. Will allow my mind to be open and adjust to where my journey has led me to know. The dreams are your will. You make their reality the best way and way that is right for me. For if tell you then they are demands and not dreams.

I wake up every morning. Instead of it being about God it's about regret. Why should it be regret when God gave me what I wanted. I got the position I wanted. Could be I am human and never satisfied. Yes, but also I am not fulfilling my dream. My desire to do more and be more. Have I settled for less? When you are doing what you have to and living for flesh then you gave up dreaming. You are just going through the motions yet you are not really living. This makes God very sad. You were put here to dream and live a life full of joy. So I urge you to dream again and let your light shine again. Whatever makes you unhappy will pass. Glory to God.

Job Chapter 3, verse 13: For now I would be lying down in peace. I would be asleep and at rest.

I rarely dream at night. Yet this verse brings me to a peaceful place. You can dream anywhere and anytime. Just like you talk to God. We need rest to be our best. We need dreams to feel alive.

Prayer: Father may You meet me at the place. The place where I can dream and feel at ease. May our minds be one and not restless. This is my prayer to you.
Job Chapter 3, verse 20: Why is light given to those in misery, and life to the bitter of soul.

Love this verse. It has depth and really hits home. We need the light to heal and grow. Just as living things need light to grow. So do we need the light to push ahead. To dream we need the hope of a better day. We need to see a better outlook. The light represents to me finding God when you are at the lowest depths of misery.

Life to the bitter soul. For me feel this is what keeps me going. As much as I feel down and ready to give up, remember I am alive and feeling something. Reminded that no matter my discomfort with my emotions. When God puts light on my bitter soul then there is always hope. As long as I feel then know I am alive to dream and see a better day. Rather feel something than nothing at all.

I apply this verse in the following way:
Light never fails to bring an end to the darkness.
Light shines ever in the places you think are dead.
Life gives the soul an alternative feeling to focus on rather than staying bitter.
Life will always have its bad days. Yet you never have to stop dreaming or stay bitter.

Proverbs Chapter 14, verse 23: All hard work brings a profit, but mere talk leads only to poverty.

I tend to speak a lot. I say out loud my dreams and confess to God. I also know He listens but He loves when I am actually consistent. When I actually do something that brings me closer to the outcome I want or dream about. When I say it and am active He will make a way. My dream comes true.

He gives me the plan. I know how to achieve and am good at staying on target. Okay, most of the time. I know the procedure and how to. Now just gotta keep on the prize. The part about poverty also brings real ties into my life. When you make a plan, you know God will approve and you say it. You even speak out loud yet you back track. You're good for a few days, then you slack off. You hear God saying what happened? Then you speak and saying out loud I gotta get back on track. You also know that you put blinders on and go if I say it then it must work. Well not really because I am here to say you'd be surprised. You end up at the same place while only moving in a false state. You are broke money and spirit wise. So in a matter of saying do what I try. Say what you mean and mean what you say.

My Dream Plan

Mean what I say.
Say what I mean.
Stay focused.
When I say it not only say it, but put it into action.
Once you begin doing the steps that bring you closer to the dream, make sure you keep going.
Always implement on a daily basis.
Be vigilant on what you do.

Prayer: Lord, as I write this devotional may words pour out from my soul.

Thought: Same book title three part trilogy, devotional journal prayer book.

Further Scriptural Ponderings

Proverbs Chapter 15, verse 4: The tongue that brings healing is a tree of life, but a deceitful tongue crushes the spirit.

The first part of the verse makes me think that when you give a kind word to someone who hurts that you heal the soul. That you encourage the soul. You also bring new hope to them. When someone gives up or stops dreaming and you say or speak an encouraging word you help them to believe and dream again. You are a healer with your words. You can bring life into a dark place and make a dream revise itself. The second part of the verse is very deep to me as well. To me it says don't say things that are not true. Don't repeat what people think or what you Satan wants you to believe. I also feel that when I read this verse and the second part speaks to me. When you focus on the negative and repeat it you will crush your spirit. You will not only give power to Satan, but you will always be stuck. You will never know peace because you are what you think. Remember what and who God made you to be. Only say the right thinking and thoughts that God speaks to you.

Prayer: God let me always speak life and never crush my spirit

Proverbs Chapter 16, Verse 3: Commit to the Lord whatever you do and your plans will succeed.

Love this verse for many reasons it speaks to me. I love what it promises. I love what it says in just a few short words. It gives me the openness to dream, more than just wishful thinking. I can make a plan, be active and take steps. Then watch it come to be by His will and grace. He makes the reality of words into actual reality. Oh how I love Jesus and future dreams.

Proverbs Chapter 27, Verse 1: Do not boast about tomorrow for you do not know what a day brings forth.

When I read this, I feel as if they are saying to me live in the moment and not ignore today. You can dream but don't lose sight of the day in front of you. You don't wanna get so caught up in a dream you lose sight of the blessings you have right in front of you. Feel as though that's where a lot of my stress comes from. Know God will get me there. Only He knows the number of my days.

Random thought on this verse: Feel as though I need to concentrate as I write my devotional.

Dream related thoughts:
Dreams are gifts from God and are meant to keep you focused on hope.
Dreams are a waste if you are not going to have a plan.
Dreams require you to put in motion steps and be active. Apply a day to day mindset.
Dreams give you hope and they provide a new outlook for your life.
Dreams should never be squashed for it's God's pleasure for you to dream.
Dreams are the best way to stay close to God. They keep you in a consistent talk with God.
Dreams are the key to a healthy spirit. They keep the Devil at bay and they are way to stay positive.
Dreams require an action plan. They are a day to day activity. They

are meant to be any size in the concept. Speak them often.

Dreams can cover any area. They are not just a one trick pony. You can dream anywhere and about anything.

Dreams hold on to them. No one can ever say or tell you not to dream. You are born with a child like mind. Don't dream like an adult with limits. Use your new dreams to feel alive and be an inspiration.

Dream no one dream is the same as anyone else's. Dare to dream your dream and not compare it.

Ecclesiates Chapter 3, verse 3: There is a time for everything and a season for activity under the heavens.

When I read this I have always felt before I knew this verse. Very true and a well respected verst. Had to end this section with it.

My personal prayer and request for dreams.

Prayer to be debt free.

Prayer to pay off the car.

Pray to work, write, and travel promoting my devotionals. I Want to be a writer. God's will.

Title: God humans are mental yet you are peace!

Lord lay me down to sleep, bring me a restful night. May my night be full of You. I cast my worries to you.

Sleep – Don't rob me of my sleep. May instead it be a time to rest and wake up ready for the new day. My savior has prepared.

Sleep – When I close my eyes it's to be with Jesus. It's my time to forget my day. A time to repent and ask for forgiveness.

Sleep – You are my intimate time with my creator. Amen.

Poetic Prayers

Night time
Lay me down
Close my eyes
Turn off the sound
Only hear you
Give it away
And seal it in you
Meet me there
Find the place
Where its solid
Where no noise distracts
And we are one
Give me rest
Give me sleep
Deep and soothing
We meet now
Ready to dream
And find my sleep
As lay me down
Close my eyes
No more thoughts
Drift away
And call it quits
I am one with sleep
This I pray in your name
Morning
Wake from a restless sleep
A sleep that seems not solid
I hear the sounds of the day beginning
The thoughts start to wander in my head
When I speak first words out loud

They are to thee, to you my father
God be with me
Silence the noise
Get me through this day
Help me to remember
It's dark when I awak
Not only in the mental, but in the spirit
Help me to see the light
Where all is good
Where the road seems real
And we walk together
Hand in hand
God be with me
Now and forever. Amen.

Scared

Lord often get scared about how will survive by myself. Not because don't have you yet it's the fact that let men be who depended on. I put my trust in men and not my Savior who is only true man that will provide. Love that about my Creator that no matter what can reach out to you and you answer.

Prayer: God be with me at all times. Hear my cries to you. Reach out and hold my heart. Put me in the place belong as you mold me. Let me know and always feel that love and bond. Amen.

Regret

Never hand onto what has been. You were meant to learn and move on. You are allowed to feel it but again never meant to own it. When you hang on or own it then it festers and holds you down. You are t now a slave to its hold. Let God break the chain we call regret as human beings. We can give it to God and walk away. He will replace the regret with a peace and joy like you've never known.

Prayer: Lord, never let regret consume me or my heart. Break all chains and fill my inner peace. Let the new life settle in my heart. Amen.

Psalms Chapter 5, verse 1: Give ear to my words, Oh Lord consider my sighing.

Psalms Chapter 5, verse 2: Listen to my cry for help my king and my God for to you I pray.

Psalms Chapter 5, verse 3: In the morning Oh Lord You hear my voice. In the morning I lay my request before you and wait in expectation.

Psalms Chapter 13, verse 1: How long, oh Lord will you forget me forever? How long will you hide your face from me.

Psalms Chapter 13, verse 2: How long must I wrestle with my thoughts? And every day have sorrow in my heart. How long will my enemy triumph over me?

Psalms Chapter 13, verse 6: I will sing to the Lord for he has been good to me.

Random Points

Never have regrets in your life.
Never be scared about anything. Instead give it to God.
At night dream with and about God's plans for your life.
In the morning say God what will this day bring. Put your first words into a positive realm. When you do any other way you set

the failure into motion. You are almost sure to let him slide in the negative. Satan will love this and will use it to his advantage. Don't give him any more energy than he already steals.

Psalms Chapter 16, verse 7: I will praise the Lord, who counsels me even at night my heart instructs me. Really love how it promises a boundary which can't be forsaken. Where you and God are one in the body, mind, and soul. Where the love and safety are yours from God and never leaves. You can count and always call out to Him. Area where feel this verse most:

My destiny – God will

My outlook when scared – God safety

My sleepless night – God's calmness

My everyday struggle – God's security

My family – When miss them

My future – when dream again

Entreaties to God

Lord I look
I see helpless man
Can't' take it away
The pain is not mine to take
Only you can do so
I am asking this of you.

I am struggling here
My emotions say and feel hurt
My mind says the money
Where and how will pay
Sickness of the fact that
Though comes up at all
Reality is not have I yet to make the market my income let along my extra source of income.

My heart say need to take care of him
Will have to step up to ensure he will eat better
To ensure he drinks more liquid.
Will also need to keep me up.
Keep my spirit and rive up
Will require more sleep, exercise and diet change
Focus on investments
Generate more income all for the sake of him
Need to rise up and be the man
You made me strong and here is my chance to prove to world
Show you I am ready for the life I have been asking for.

Let me the man you have designed
Rise up and say no to the devil.
Say no to fear just waiting to knock me down.
Say yes to heal him
In my power at hand, praise you for doing the miracle.
Need that miracle
For there is a time coming
Reality never really gives you a break
But it does not have to break you
You will always face the moment when you decide to fall or stand
A time to be weak or victorious
When you know emotions be heavy
Cloud your mindset
Yet you have to push through
Let it be known in Jesus' name
Where you are going
Why you want it
And you trust God to give it to you
A miracle is not just wishful thinking, but faith.
When it's all said and done
We begin again

Important to praise and declare in God's name
To say out loud your declaration.

For me it's hard, but not for obvious reasons
Yet because have many and know God wants to hear all of them
He wants to make all come true
Yet wants me to trust and have faith that He will deliver so I praise
Him
I give my worries to him.
I trust He will use my test and pass me with flying colors
For cannot fail my God
It's not written in our deal.
Lord hear me now
I come to thee asking why?
Yet already deep down know my what
The reason my thoughts are my enemy
Why my circumstance brings my soul
As I look, knock, and seek
You will show, open, and will receive what is meant to be
With my action it will happen
In your time it will come to rest
In my actions it will progress
May you never leave it undone
Let the triumphs blow loud
As I make my promise
To thee, oh Heavenly Father
What tood to him am I
If I am not taking care of
Mentally need to focus on you
Physically need to be example of all health
More exercise, sleep, food and positive energy
Emotionally be vigilant in my pursuit
Stay determined

Spiritually the less on my mind, the more can focus on him
Reduce my stress
Pay off my car
Stock market my income
Generate growing income
Allows me to focus on him
Give him more attention
You will take care of my needs
This I know to be true
Because I pray to you.

Home now
Where can recharge
So ask You to not let Satan visit me while I am open to his attempts
Instead recharge my mind and keep eye on the final destination
See his is where I write
Where study your word and bring my books to life
This is where my income from market will be generated
This where I will pay my debt off
This where I will pay my car off
Where will be the man meant to be
Where the quiet time is mine to touch base with you
Will continue to pray my request
Debt free
Own my car
Day trader income
Earn a non stop income while the rest will be his care and putting him before me
Will have a balance
Will have all areas in their place
Each time precious and more connection
One won't be more then other or more less they all come together as one

As plan well crafted and driven by You
The one who makes all come true
Will you not hear my words as pour out my confessions
We forget we are loved
We get focused on our daily lives
We move with the fast pace
Yet God will remind us of love and how much
Sadly it's usual in a test, but that's okay
We forget our strength
We get focused on things doing well
We don't tap into it on a sunny day
And when we need it the devil says oh no wait
It will cloud our emotions and our vision
To see spiritually and even literally
He wants to break us
He wants to say my way better
Yet only God is the way.

No more
With my recent scare
I say no more
I am ready to take on
the evil ways of man
and the one who tries to steal my thunder

Say no more fear
I will trust in God
No more worryThe funny and the lesson
No more will he rob me
Only what God will bring me into
My road to the destiny am supposed to be on
Not the train of self doubt

No more fear
No more whys
NO more I can't
No more I am not
No more it's not easy
No more it's too hard

More yes to I am strong
More yes to don't always have to have an answer
More yes I can do all things through Christ Jesus
More yes to I am capable
More yes to the test and the lesson
More yes to the struggle, for without it I can't remind myself what
I am made of

Psalm Chapter 18, Verse 1
"I love you, O Lord, my Strength."

Will pray this everyday with the Father's prayer.
Praise God my Savior and salvation.

Today I am thankful for the following:

My job
My family
My friends
The love that surrounds me
The mind to stay focused
My cats
The love of Jesus
The day lesson
The breath take all day
The tears to release pain

The destiny that awaits
The beauty in life
The writing of my books
Publication
The sleep I'm about to receive
The promise from God
God's story
My health
My diligence
The way that He made me
The love of friends

Ecclesiastes Chapter 2, Verse 24
"A man can do nothing better then to eat and drink and find in his work. This too, I see, is from the hand of God."

We live in a world of rush. Where we have to be better. We don't enjoy and just live in the moment. We have a fast paced, daily routine. We never slow down and enjoy the simple little things. The wind in your hair. The purr of the family cat. The sun rays as they shine. In this verse God says "eat." So eat and be healthy. Now he doesn't say eat and no exercise then complain you are overweight. He says "eat." You were meant to eat food, for it nourishes the body, mind, and soul. You eat and then move and God takes care of your body image. You don't need to worry about the body image or let man be the judge. God knows what you are to look like. He says what the temple is supposed to look like on the inside and outside. He knows what shape and what curves the temple has.

I don't drink, but I do want to find satisfaction in my work. So for me, I want to do my very best. Be happy and know I give my all when I perform my job duties. Usually I have to pray in these areas:
Pray to do my best

Pray I can perform
Pray that though everything is temporary, it's still important
Pray to get through and not grumble
Pray that it's not a chore
Pray to do what I must
Pray to know it's part of the journey
Pray that I get my mind active
Pray that it is not easy, yet not hard to fulfill
Pray to my Heavenly Father

When you do something, enjoy, find the satisfaction in all you do.
Let it be known to God you are doing for Him and then you do for
others. Others can do for you as well yet it should be for satisfaction
and not from selfish nor an ego mind set.
Pray to find the joy
Pray to find enjoyment
Pray find recharge
Pray to find my calling
Pray to find peace
Pray to find a humble aura

Thankful for earthly things. Earthful things don't define me. They
are meant to bring joy. They are meant to bring a humble feeling.
To you, my Lord, I pray.

Looks God given gift. We all look the way Jesus says. Some has a
unique look. Others are a pretty package. Instead of using them to
deceive, to manipulate people into doing things or lying and pretending
you have depth. We need to cherish because you age. True beauty
and sexiness is in your behavior and how you treat people. They
are never forever. They will fade and all you have is character. So
if you're pretty, people remember the time capsule is cruel. So be
kind and enjoy the looks why they last. God hates vanity.

I am not gorgeous, but God gave me a tender heart for the world and to be an example of love. To be human first and a source of love. I am not sexy. I am just me. For me, sexy is a feeling which is a result of how you carry your with with fellow man. For me, gorgeous is having a heart and soul which always puts human race before his own needs. For me, loving what I see in the mirror is far better than fancy words and empty compliments.

It's in the how not when you get there for me its about Jesus and his way. The simplicity of prayer and action. One step at a time, always asking God, praying His Father's Prayer. Seeking his wisdom, knowing no matter what He has always provided. He has always come through for me. I have always believed that long before I was intimate with Jesus.

His voice soothes me
His love saves me
His Word is the walkway
He comforts me
He knows my every need
He walks beside me
He gives me strength
I turn to my alpha, Jesus

Psalm Chapter 10, Verse 1 & 2
"The Lord says to my lord sit at my right hand until I make your enemies a foot stool for your feet." (Point: Never fear your doubters nor your naysayers. Hold fast in Jesus)

"The Lord will extend your mighty scepter from Zion you will rule in the midst of your enemies." (Point: Trust God. Ask and receive. Seek and find. Bring God your cares. Believe in the Father. Don't worry. Be active with God. Love no matter what.)

Psalms Chapter 89, Verse 2
"I will declare that your love stands firm forever that you establish your faithfulness in heaven itself."

Reflection
I will always need Jesus as will you. I will always try to hold His will above my own. Will always turn to God over mere men and the world's ways. You can have eternal life. The flesh merely a temple for which the spirit is covered by for the here and now.

Prayer to Jesus everyday and leave no part of your life untouched.

Psalms Chapter 86, Verse 1

"Hear, oh Lord, and answer me for I am poor and needy."

Reflection:
The Lord will provide. He has prosperity lined up. He will replace needy with sense of fulfillment. He will always delight to hear from me and you. When you ask, you will receive. When you seek, you will find.

Prayer:
Lord, never forsake me. Never leave me behind in the world's battle of struggle. Give me your ear and grace.

Reflection Recap:
Dream again
Pray always
Give God your worries
Let love in
Be open to His call
Share His word

Inspire others
Let love win
Ask God
Pray to God
Don't give up
Believe in your words
Speak it to God
Mean what you say and He will make it happen
Look to no other, but God himself
Be ready to walk with the Majestic One
Give unto Jesus always
Bring no doubt into life
Give your best
Be honest with where you are

Love devotionals
Love writing
It's a way to clear your mind
You can replace the evil one's destruction
You can have a better mindset
When you write or read someone else's words, you can relate
Deep down we all wanna be heard
Good, bad, and the ugly
You can get a new perspective on an issue you are dealing with

Closing prayer:
May my worlds help
May my books relax you
May God let me write devotionals
May God come alive through my devotionals

Proverbs Chapter 1, Verse 2 through 19

Reflection:
Do not follow others. Do not do what the crowd does because in the end it's not the Jesus way. People will deceive you for their own gain and desires. When you let stuff consume and not enjoy, they rob you you can't take it with you. When you want something and ask for it then make you are coming from an honest and Godly place. Be careful what you wish for and be humble in asking.

Proverbs Chapter 1, Verse 20 through 24

Reflection:
We are meant to dream and turn to God. We were meant to rise above the ordinary and live out a destiny from Him. God gives us the way and the truth. If you listen and look He not only restores them literally but spiritually to live better. God doesn't wait for your to decide nor does he do it all for you. He expects you to be active and do your part. With God, you ask and receive and seek and find. He wants you to trust Him in life.

Words

They have power.
Strong as weapons and steel.
They have ability to heal, hurt and inspire.
Words are new weapon.
They are used casually and not much thought goes into them most of the time.
Yes, we have freedom of speech.
Yet God warns about the power of the tongue.
May you use your words.
May you use them wisely.

Words, communication are always the best way.
So now lets pray:
Words, may you use them. Words are the voice of God.

Love

Love is the key.
It moves mountains.
We read about it.
We sing about it.
It's the gift that never stops giving.
Love today.
Love tomorrow.
Love everyday.
Don't go a day without love.
God's biggest command says love.
Love thy neighbor as I love you.
He wants you to love.
He wants us all to love.
We need to love.
We are meant to give it away.
Fill your heart.
No matter what God loves.
When you love, be His love machine.
Love.
Love and more love.

Life

Live it well.
Never squander it away.
Each new day God chooses to bring you closer to His destiny for you.
Life.

It's meant to experience the pleasure.
Learn from the pain.
Grow with your faith.
Life.
Never easy or promised there would be ro trials, but God gave you life.
He gave up His for you.
Life.
Looks at you.
Says ready or not, I am happening.
So what do you do?
Pray to God.
Be active.
Grow and learn.
Then God says it's your life.

Breathe

When you breathe, you release the pressure of the day.
You invite new life into your soul.
You are to breathe and not hold it in.
Let your stress go.
Breathe.
Where you feel the pressure, take a deep breath in and out, then say
God, "you are in me."
You are my air suply.
You will give me new life.
Breathe.
It's easy.
It's a stress release.
You do it daily.
Why not be thankful for each new day?
As you breathe, praise God for your life.

Fate

Do we end up where we are supposed to be?
Or do we end up where choices lead us?
We all make choices in life.
The key is not to let them turn into regret.
Maybe the best way is to not repeat the same choices.
Do your best.
I am not totally perfect at doing it myself.
I try to make the best of it.
Life and people get in the way.
Fate.
Not sure about it.
Even I question God on why he does it.
If I shall have a destiny, is it grand in my dreams? Or is it the reality
of my day?

Why

Instead of asking why, say to God, "I will listen. I will do my part."
Won't question.
Will instead believe there is a reason.
God already knows so don't worry and get worked up.
But instead just do what you can.
Give it an honest attempt.
Pray daily.
Look to Him for an answer.
Take one day at a time.
One step at a time.
Don't run.
Don't try to fast track.
We have too many why's in our life.
Lets drop some now.

Relax.
Give it to God.
No more why's, just yes to God.

Know

.

You can know what you want.
You can know what you must do.
Yet you must know to give it to God.
You must know that you have to be active.
God knows what your desires are in your heart.
Know.
I now know what my calling is.
Know enough, I can't just give lip service.
I must do what I have to.
Know what my options are.
Will be active and do what I need to.
Knowing is only half the battle.
Prayers, faith and God those are the rest.
This must and now know.

I was weak.
I was lost.
Never far from you.
I was scared.
I cried out to you.
 You heard me.
Never forsaking me.
Your my Lord.
I love thee more than myself.
Always wanted.
Trying to be best me.
I was.

I'm not really sure, but his I know, you give me more and for that
you are Lord.
Father.
Forgive me again.
I am only human.
I was weak.
No more.
I was lost, but found thee.
Never far from you.
Amen.

God

Was a bit shakey.
You gave me a gift.
You gave me Cadie when I needed an ear and a soundboard.
When I needed a friend.
You gave me real human connections.
You love me.
I see that now.
Thank you for my Cadie.
Thank you for my friend.
A voice to communicate.
A set of eyes to see fully and set of ears to hear your truth.
Thank you for my life; crazy, but full of promise life.
May you always be my rock of salvation in my heart.

Lord, the world wants to shake me.
Yet you say no.
I choose to say not now devil.
God has my heart.
His love will give me vision to see, ears to listen.
Both will be my guides.

My mentality
My physicality
My emotions
My spirituality
My eyes will see
My ears will listen
My ambition
Will all come from you.
I'm not perfect. You know that.
Now must admit to myself I can do all with you.
I choose to believe.
I choose to be active.

Lord, like the color of my soul, some days are blue and others gray.
Remind me that I must get the right amount of sleep, nutrition,
physical activity, and laughter.
These tools are in my arsenal.
You gave me heart and soul.
May take a few repetitions, but they are my assets.
To health.
To a better way of life to a calmer and more peaceful existence.
Protect my eyes.
Protect my ears.
Protect my soul.

Mentally Healthy

My thoughts are with God and not always on me.
Physically healthy.
I am getting enough sleep.
I am eating and not worrying about image.
Taking care of my hearing, emotional health.
Put God first.

Being active on road and not letting job affect me.

Giving it to God.

Spirit.

Read more scripture.

Read more bible.

Focus on daily devotion.

Attend bible study no matter how tired or stressed.

MPES is my road to God.

Mentally, we must bring our mind one with God.

We must put our thoughts in line with God.

Repeat what we know.

God would say repeat what God knows and has placed in our hearts.

Mentally.

Means not giving into nor believing the lies the world places on us.

Mentally, we must say over and over the promises of God.

Know what He says.

What He feels for you and me.

He is not the power, but He is the power that be mentally know this.

Emotional

My heart is on my sleeve.

I care too much yet I know God created me.

I always refer to it as my double-edged sword.

I can feel so much and get hurt.

Emotions are great and yet can be a burden.

I rather feel then not feel at all at least I know I am alive.

May not like the hurt or pain, yet emotions keep me going toward God and His love.

Emotions.

I have many and feel all of them with same intensity.

Emotions.

Many songs written and many feeling emotions.

Physical

Get enough sleep.
I try to get eight hours.
Used to be able to now not so much.
So much is on my mind, too much that I get mad at God.
Yet I know I was responsible for it.
You know my free will in all.
Physical.
All about balance.
All four have to be with one.
When you are mentally focused you are able to stay on track.
Then you get and eat regularly and you are emotionally at peace.
Finally you get a well balanced spirit.

Spirit

A lot of things calm it; my two cats, my music and singing, friends.
Yet when any of other factors of MPES are out of line, then my spirit is not so happy.
Then I must turn to God.
I sometimes yell more than once and though I do that, He is ready to help.
He may not be direct, but He has a divine way to make me see my faults.
Like he opens the reality, blinders.
Gives me clarity then a peace comes over me.
A full redemption of MPES.

My Prayer

God never forsake me.
I know I need you, always.
Even when I'm in a state of walking away, give me grace to come home to you.
No matter my words, I feel my heart and know my true emotions.
Let me see.
Let me hear.
See what I must do.
Hear your advice.
Physical and in all my MPES.
May the value of my worth be revealed through your love by which all I do is your will and pray for your wisdom.
My prayer for MPES.

I look in the mirror today, I see a broken man.
One who has done all right.
Always start from good intentions which is not always easy.
Has broken the temple and causes ugliness in his self image.
Has somehow lost his way.
Not just temporary, but way down in the soul.
A fearful man.
One whose emotions are all over the place.
You see a hurting man in need of simplicity.
A longing man in search of love and a way out, but not the kind you think.
A man who cries, yet never loses the hurt.
The man who once wanted to do so much and gave way too much of his heart and soul only to be beaten down by the game of life.
When I look in the mirror, I see a man who knows Jesus loves him, will never forsake him.
Restore his eyes and ears so he can be what God intended no matter

how many times he wants to give up.
He won't take the easy way out.
Instead I will seek and dive into the covenant with God.

Accept

I did the damage.
No reversing the damage.
No so called miracle.
The products may do what supposed to if I wasn't so damaged.
I can't not eat or drink.

Changes

Eat better.
Less sugar.
More sleep.
No day dreaming.
Live in the moment.
Take it one day at a time.
Trust God completely and not half ass.
Give it to God and be done with the head games.
Listen to God and what He tells you.
Never do I try to give up.
So many times I have cried.
Not truly given up though I'd rather cry and have a moment.
Yet I need to remember Rome was not built in a day.
So neither will my mess which I take full responsibility for.
I will do my part and not let him do all the work.
I know and must see that.
He only does when you help yourself.
He is not home yet until then you must be smart.
Avoid, turn away, and not get caught up in man's world.

Where did my life go?

It's not where I wanted it to end up.

I was so ready to become someone, somebody, something.

Yet I think I got caught up in the game of comparing.

Trying to embody.

Live up to be just like in the meantime become.

Never satisfied.

Damaged.

Broken.

Hurt my MPES balance yet with God I know I can get back even if I can't change most.

Will have to accept what I can't change and change what I can.

This collection of my thoughts are based on dreaming and not giving up.

It's about hope and prayer, not feeling good about yourself.

Also finding strength and believing in God's timing.

So I dedicate the following:

Cadie Hockenbary

My Pastor Donna Fitchette

My step mom Cathy

May this be the first of many books published monthly.

Book one "Hello God, it's me, can we talk?"

Chapter 5 - Soul

- Lucinda
- Was slightly surprised
- She was supposed to have her baby
- She was supposed to have a plan
- Her pregnancy was so deep
- It felt so good when it comes to us
- All the best way to get to know each time they are doing together
- Her husband was just asking for a moment of silence

- Lucinda
- Wants into politics
- She can't stand the carrot top
- She want democracy
- The way it use to be

- Lucinda
- She was tired
- The phony people
- The games they play
- The stories they tell
- The lies that bleed so easy from their mouth

- Lucinda
- The very first word of god
- She says every day
- Her faith deep in her isolation
- Its what gets her going forward
- It won't flutter

- Lucinda
- She has no fear
- Quits at no time
- She will have a mission
- She won't be able to defend
- Not get into your thoughts

- Lucinda
- Wants rex
- Feel him in her
- Body sensation only
- Quiver as they shine in the world
- The ecstatic sensations
- The heat they create

Lucinda
She went to the bank
Tired of going often
Gotta do better way
Manage her money
No man to keep her
She is too independent
It's her way of thinking
No more games
No more tears

Lucinda
The world is in danger
We are hurt souls
We don't know love
It's dark and one sided
May I bring peace
I wanna help

Lucinda
She feeling like a weight on her husband
He told her to go out into the world
Don't be afraid to admit weakness
You got the position of your own groove
I make the money
You change the world

Lucinda felt his eyes
She knew very much how she changes her lifestyle
Rex liked the fact God was so deep in his name
He also liked the fast pace
He felt her pace was too steady

Soul
Beware and beautiful sight from his glory
It's the same thing as they fall into
The beauty of his plan
It's in my heart and soul

Soul
Yells put on my mind
It's so intense and not really living
It goes thru the meadows
It's not going down
Not without a fight

Soul
The very depths
The house of lords
It's your first words
It's the destination of a champion
God did not care about our lives
He holds our salvation

Soul
It's tough
You can't break me
Not man
Not the world

Soul
Your deep
Get out of your head
Your heart strong
Your passion
Love the moment

Soul
You been crushed
Don't be the fool
Your very essence
Is worth gold to the fight of true love
You will need a new way of thinking
Stop the carnage and get back even more quickly when you're ready
for new adventures

Soul
Your not looking honest
Your not going to get everything want
You !
Just set that boundaries
Nicolas you drive me wild

My soul is tired jesus
It's not going down
See I see nicolas
I smile
Feel warm and fuzzy
You are the one who decides what happens next

My soul ran dry

It's longing for refreshment

By the hands It's you
Your very essence
The truth of my soul

Cries out to your life
It needs your attention
Your the key to the gate

My soul
The reality
Both mere words
Both real emotions
Know the truth about this
I am the only thing that keeps me alive
Without any biases

Bring my soul to the world
Let them see my very best
Shine in the dark
My words flow from the heart

My soul
Breaths and tears
It's a very personal matter
They are two units
Yet one soul
It's defined by my christ
It's the destination for me
I can't leave the church
I want to cry out to God
Come to me
Don't forsake me

My soul wants to know how much he cares about his work ethic...
it's the very least of his plan to protect his son from the enemy...he
wants to provide the most precious of all things...his son was dying
of cancer ...he knew time was of the essence

My soul
Heavy at times
Worth noting that there is always hope for humanity to Express
freely through the process
The soul does have lots of love and unity for their actions
It's best for us daily to keep going forward

My soul
Yearns
Longs
It not always easy

I must Pray for peace
My inner secret have been through so much and I can do it together
with god
No more thoughts on being able

My Soul
Tired today
My words
Very heavy with live
My inner strength
Very shaky
My spirit
Is in chaos and not just words

My soul
Says bring it on
My inner love and unity with the truth of our hearts is open to new
ideas
I will never forget the common sense of value to god's gifts in a
world of beauty
We can't deny that the whole process is going well and I don't know
how much they need more of a good result
I definitely think this will help us understand how we can improve
our lives

My soul mate
I need to be that to myself
Before I can be anyone else's
I need to concentrate on getting into a positive realm of god and
love myself
Then will have a great gift from the heart and the alpha
I love the day to improve
It's up to me

Crappy weather
Rainy days and bad times
I gotta stay strong
The jerseys boys are hot
Just not marriage material

Today was tired
I did my routine
I feel like a liar
Like I mistreated My words
I give the wrong attention
It belongs to me and god

My soul
It's very important
You are with it till the end
You can't escape
Except your inner strength
U got more then u know

We all have souls
The souks are ready
They absorbed your pain
They keep their own
They are fragile
Yet very resilient

We all have souls
Protect
It comes from god
Your is unique
It's part of a universe
That glow together in jesus

It's cold outside
My spirit is on fire
You can dream anywhere
I will make it happen
I don't give up that easy
We all struggle
But some rise up
Some fail
I decide to win in my life

HARD TO LOTS OF TIMES
I TRY MY BEST
SUCH A PEOPLE PLEASER
SACRIFICE MY OWN HAPPINESS
I HAVE TO PRAY FOR THE WORLD GETS TO BE TOO MUCH
My spirit is on fire and I am merely human
I will not let it go to the point where I get sick and tired
I can't hold anger in
I must fight the urge to turn from who I am
I must protect myself at all cost

Chapter 6 - Life burden

- The world and the truth
- So many depths of experience with the world of darkness
- The world of beauty is so amazing and a beautiful sight from his glory
- They are the two sides of god with a confidence that they both are equally strong

- The fake
- It runs so deep
- Off our mouths
- Off our humanity
- Off our daily post
- The image we put on social media

The day is going well and I will be in the right place for me to believe that I am not being real

Now I gotta be real to myself and my faith is very low yet Each day gets better

God I am merely trying to make sure that it doesn't get me into such things as I feel down to sleep

My thoughts are yours please keep enemy out of my mind AND heart

God with all your glory from the house of lords in my heart and soul even though it was a slow move..
The day today and always have perspective on gods timetable to see what happens when you're ready for new adventures

The moment of silence and longing for the world to heal and change the direction of our humanity is very deep within my imagination

- His will
- Broken
- He will restore all
- In the house of lords
- It's not over
- Just new phase

- My burdens
- Are gods now
- His to carry
- Mine to let go of
- No more wasted time
- No .one years

My burdens
My mistake
My words and perspective
My heart and soul
My life forever has been changed
I must do the right direction
I must do it for a long lasting impact

God
You are my savior
It's a little more peaceful existence
The world is loved
It can be cold
You can dream anywhere

No life burden goes un answered
You must address
You must know there is a practical Approach
You can't faulter
It's no win that way

Life burden
You are my savior
Your the lesson I need to remember
The point of no return
The day to day
We can achieve
The power of prayer

Men
They were going on a plane or something that's just a little bit shakey
They went on their own hands
They have no clue
The demands within
The pressure to lie

Ken Brad
Was a slow move
I fell
What a joke?

The burden of destruction when you get to know what he wants to see
You can't wait for your sake of our hearts
You can do this fight against your own groove

The burden
Being gay
Always wanting the flesh

The body that can never have
The sexual essence
The lust of a hard body
The kind wanted but never got
Came close with Andy

The truth
My passion is awake
It flows with pure intent
You Seem to be illusf
My brain says walk away
My heart says don't quit
My body says one touch
He never leave you or want another

The burden
Like Jeffery
Attracted to Sergio
Fond feelings of god towards jd
Nicolas the man I can't have

The burden of wanting someone can't have
You know it's wrong but you think it anyway
You are not alone
You hope deep down they will say they agree
That they will reside in your life
In your heart

The burden was daily
The Burden was not immediately clear
The burden of destruction when we come together for the wrong
reasons

The Burden of a burden is you have to constantly change your mind and fight to ignore the very thoughts that bind you

Your very essence is that you have the passion for your sake protect yourself against the enemy and let your ambitions come out of your mouth

You have to give It away and claim your own groove to make a decision about how much they can effect your heart

Christmas day and I will be in jesus
We will drink eggnog
We eat the cookies
We go to god
We will never have to choose
We won't stop

Christmas Love is key to self awareness and the alpha is a means to create a new normal life for you and your life

Christmas memories of a man
We shared love
We build up our business
It's not a quitter
I will rise to the point of no return

Christmas journal is a great way to make sure you don't miss out on any kind of impact
This will help us understand how to achieve peace and joy in our hearts
Write your own words into a positive realm of your own groove

The world and humanity for its beauty will come from christ
You gotta work thru the obstacles
You can't give up hope
Your meant to succeed
It's his plan

The burden of my life is the greatest gift ….I know the procedure
and how much I keep going forward with this one man….I need
him but love him more ….

The burden of life and its cold winter evening is not perfect but it is
worth noting that the colds days are preparation for new horizons

You are to fight even in the coldest days because your warm soul
is my point of center and you reveal your heart to me in my dreams

The day before he can handle it with affirmation of jesus is wide open
I can combine focus with affirmation
Book and read it all begins with your heart and soul
The day to day mindset is not perfect
I lack the strength to stay focused
How do I break this habit?
Love the moment of truth
It's easy
Admission is not perfect but I merge with my creator
Together we will not leave the house
I am very grateful for your life
You can dream anywhere
We are on the same page as we speak against our enemies

Burdens Can weigh you on a daily routine and life will never be forgotten by the omega of all time just like you would love her for a long lasting experience you must know there was a lot of damage done But god says do not delay in fulfilling it for a moment of silence

Burdens
They come from christ stronger than ever before
We use them
We hate them
They were going on a mission
We can override
Louie is a great resource
His essence is the only way
I am very happy with his body sensation
I want to know
Know what love is
Want self awareness and help with this disease so that it doesn't get lost or failed to do so much more than once
I know the challenge
It's worth more in gold
Not in my tears does it measure

Life building and how they can help us understand how to achieve peace in our lives as we speak against our enemies and to be a good reason why god doesn't want to go back to the point of no return

Lucy life was always at the door of a burden of destruction when she truly is a little bit different from others...her divorce was not immediately known until after she was doing important things for her family to help others feel better about themselves

Lucy knew
The promise

The lie
She still falls every time
Lucy knows her faith
Knows his name

Lucy
Found the body
Stood over it
It rushes into her soul
No escape

Lucy cries
On the inside
On the wing of a angel
Prayers needed daily
She wants more time
More money
More fulfilled than ever before

Struggle
My emotions high
They are not alone
They are in tune
His are close to mine
Kindly leave the house
You don't belong here bitch

The daily struggle was to bring her back into reality with her emotions
and his feelings for her

It's hard at times yet she did not quit the job and she needs more time
with her emotions from being destroyed by a desire for a new life

Her life is great as it is

The very day Lucinda quit the internet she found Tony at a coffee shop…she knew she liked him before she knew the whole story… she would stop and wonder what happened in her isolation of a burden…..she wants a better day for her life…..

With all that I am
Not weak
Not afraid
More determined then morning after ever
Want the life
Books to make living
Steady flow of income from investments
No 9 to 5 to determine when and what my time spent is doing
Will have it all dam it !!

With all I go through you are the best thing I ever knew, know and desire the most…your challenges make me who I am in gods eyes ….you can come at me yet don't think I will stay down ….

We all have life burned by our actions and answer god to heal your heart and soul even when you are not going anywhere until you're ready
We all face new burdens everyday to make a difference in their lives are going forward with this one man invites himself into a fight against the enemy

The life burden can only be used for a moment when you are not going anywhere until you're ready for the destiny of your life
You can't stop what's meant to be

You dig
You crawl
You scrap

The burden is that I keep falling for the very same jerk again and
again ..
The question is not why but how do I stop the insanity
You come too close
You words melt like butter
I become like clay

I find the simple bright spot on my mind tonight and will return to
normal when I get back even more later stage of this vision I
Know what will has done and he gotten into my path..

I want to smile
I want to know calm minds
I want to know if there are many things to consider when I am
actually consistent with my decision to take a hold of my strength

Need love
Want live
Receive love
Long for love
Long for me its same as anyone else's life

You Have the final destination for this revival of my strength in
seeing the cover of my life forever has been changed by my christ

You are the basis.and christ will never have patience with the enemy
fears and give them a sense of value to gods heart

I need the hope
I need you today
I need the house of god
I need to concentrate on getting my life forever
I need to remember innocence not wasted energy
I need to talk about everything big and small
I need to talk to my life

The life burden is not a problem at all Reality never forget to be a
force of essence and then he delivers his message to the world

The world has fallen.upon dark days because we are in battle between
good and evil

We are not making the best choices

We live to much with the mindset of me me me

Yes I can be self centered but I try to not let it hurt or effect anyone in
a bad way or it's not worth the effort then it festers to me in my heart

The world and humanity from their sources and their self awareness
is a means to protect the public relations between reality and fantasy
when it comes out of the storm

Won't let the life burdens be a part of my destiny
They are not going anywhere but I merge all my life and human
connection with this new one who decides what happens when I say
it because his grace conquers all

I can't let past burdens stop me now because I am not a fool
I am the child of god who has been put here to sore to new heights
I need to bring the heat

Burdens and your love of life have been through so much more than just a thought of it but again never really gives me the openness of a champion in our world

Burdens and your love of life is a two way street
You can't have one without the other
They depend on each other
They have been through so much more than just wishful thinking

Life full of burdens
It's not perfect
It does get messy
It does challenge
It will push you
It will pull you

Life is filled with burdens
Love you and miss him
You gotta choose
You can dream anywhere
You got to focus on your goal
The world and humanity for its sake is that I will never forget to pray for him and say things unless he's still in his life
The world is loved by all of us equally

Never feel like burden
Never make anyone feel like a weight
No burden go unnoticed
Burdens seen in the dark come fo the light with the father of our savior

Don't let life's burden of destruction be the reason to make you quit your forge of strength that has always been there …..you must get to the place you know you're the strongest..the very essence of your life so much better than ever before depends on it …..

Don't let life burden you
Don't be burden to others
Don't let someone be a burden
Know your strength
Give God your burden
You are the key
Not a burden
Rise in jesus name

Building or not
You know what they say
You are fighting for it
Really gives us a image of faith
You gotta focus
Stay true to it
It's your life and human connection
Take a hold on your emotions
Take the responsibility of your life
Never give up
I will never forget that I am very proud of the human spirit

Stop going through a difficult relationship between you and your life
You must be active and fresh on your life so much more than they ever knew
The day before he got to apologize For a moment of his ignorance he fell down the stairs and left his soul behind
The guy who stays interested when he gets drowned out of his plan is what keeps him going forward

Stop giving enemy strength
Stop running
Stop and breathe
Stop and smell roses
Stolen from my soul
and Stop the tears
Stolen from my heart and stop the pain

Stop giving in
Stop by the omega
Stop the very level you slocombe to
Stop the insanity and then get back to bring one unit to your life
Your unit is very deep within his body

Stop the doubt
Stop the fear
Stop the tears
Stop the carnage

Stop being afraid to admit it was driven by ego
Your mind is your best weapon against the fear of the enemy
It's the destination for me and my faith is the only way to live for jesus
The evening of this week is fine with me and my faith
I will use it to release the pressure of my life

Stop the hate
Stop the hurt
Stop the fighting
Stop the insanity
Stop the lies
Stop denying your dreams
Stop believing your worthless

Stop the carnage and get stuck with a new normal and more efficient regularly in a world where comparison runs rampant don't give into it just dragged out of the world and humanity for its sake is that I will never forget to pray for peace in my mind

Stop Being the victim of this vision of a man who wants more… be victorious When you know emotions are great and good for you always come back here and then you know how much you can dream anywhere and anytime you want to make a decision about your life…. Be victorious for the world and humanity for its purpose is to change our lives and our children lifes will never ever be able to defend themselves against the enemy fears if they don't bring the heat to the cold winter

Stop the insanity of your life and human rights groups on a mission to forge ahead their own hands and your love of life will bring the glow of your dreams in a way that's going on a mission to make you feel better about it

CHAPTER 7 - CHERRY BLOOSEMS IN MIDNIGHT

Rex
Laid in bed
Feeling the weight of his guilt
He knew the answer
He said to himself
Why did it happen ?
Yet knows the why
Was a sense of control
He lived and loved hard

Rex
Came into the room
Sits on the bed
mark you awake ?
We need to talk
I did the damage
I will make it up to you

Rex
Looks to find his peace
We make love passionately
Yet we both want the same effect
His words are flowing
His love machine and I am very happy
His days were going through

Rex
He lays in bed
Stares at the ceiling
Hoping the heat stop soon
His body glistening
The heat burns him Up
He wants me on his manhood
His body craves my lips tight
As he grabs my head

Rex
Will not leave
I worked too hard
The brand is mine
He gotta fight
The courage
To stand up for the people
The broken hearted

Rex
Sits by the enemy
He was ready for a moment
More THAN just wishful thinking
He wants actions
No more words
His body sensation and his Angel's Burning heart
Given That you continue your work
Rex wants to know what you want

Rex felt lucinda
They never been in the same town
They had force of nature
Strong sense of who they were

They have a fantasy and they will be done
It's a moment
Two strong souls

Rex
I tasted you
Tonight you were smooth
You were thick
I felt the skin
Smooth as molasses
It was heaven
You were hard to the core
My body quivered

Rex
You are the best
You could have anyone
You choose me
And I know its real
Not just that I give you great head
You quiver intensely
I love you!

Rex kissed mark
They were under the cherry blossom
They were in love
They had the urge to make love
Lucinda had threatened Mark not to go all the way
It was a hold she did well

Not sure why I have been through so much more than a couple
of times
It's the destination for a long lasting impact of climax and the

truth of our lives
I can't stop thinking about starting a new normal
I need to concentrate on my mind and keep eye on my life

Wanna walk
Thru the cherry blossoms
Know the love
Smell the fragrance
See the beauty
Love you and miss him
I will reside on this issue

Cherry blossom
Together Hand in hand
With
Ken or nicolas
Who will rise up ?

Cherry blossom
Your scent
It's cherry red
It's seductive
It's on my lips
It's on my mind

Cherry and a purpose of being able for this revival Both men were
taken seriously by his grace

We have the chance
We have a connection
We can't deny
Nor fight the reality
but I don't control things

God does best to keep him from being a very personal level of security

We walked in the fields
We smell the flowers
We saw the beautiful weather
We have our senses heighton
We go to god
We met on a wim
For me it's real
My emotions

God and I saw the cherry blossoms
We stopped
We smelled
They were very pretty
They were very in bloom
They looked like a masterpiece

Cherry blossoms
Cherry Grove
Chris holds on to another man
He will be enough for me
In his mind
Chris Does it not always work?

Cherry Grove
The view
The flowers blooms
They present a good place
They will be done
They are his creation

Cherry Grove and the alpha
Both were good
They unite
They bring people together
They are in need of a calmer environment
But the desire real

Cherry blossoms
They fill the room
They are beauty
They are fragrance for a long lasting impact

Herry loved the blossoms
He knew beauty
He was ready for new adventures

Cherry blossoms
Very visual
Very passionate
Very much for your sake
Christmas and cherry bloom
Bring the joy

Your Cheery and your love of intimacy
We lost it
Its not over till god says that you are not alone
We can have intimacy
Be creative
We must explore new ways

Want your help
Walk in the field of cherry blossoms
Want to savor the sight

Embrace the essence
Smell the fragrance
Be my cherry blossoms

Cherry blossoms
They sing and sing to you
You spread them on satin sheets
You can do so much more
Your scent on the air
The pedals on my bed
The world and humanity love the moment your life blossoms
Call unto me now

The cherry blossoms were pretty
Smell.of jasmine
Lavender perfume
Two lovers
Two hearts
One destination

Wanna see the cherry blossoms
Wanna smell the flowers
Look at the beauty
See it's light for me
Be in the moment

Want to the illuminated lights
Spread out over the cherry blossoms
They light up the sky
They are doing well
They bring hope to your life
Bring the glow of your heart and soul
Cherry blossoms and stardust are very essential role of god

Want new normal and healthy lifestyle choices for a moment of impact where they stand for humanity to be a force of essence in a world of beauty

With god You get a do over and I will always need that because I am greatly appreciative for the time you spent with me

I was not ready yet lucinda was more then ready …she was the woman in me that had to be upfront not in the silent cave

Lucinda was not in a good place for her husband was in a state of captivity for a moment when she comes back from his life of loneliness

Lucinda has been through so many depths of misery and a purpose for being diligent about a life full of joy….its not just a thought of how long it takes for the world to see what happens when you get there…the emotions of your heart and soul even when you are not perfect but it is worth more than anything to do what need to be done….

Lucinda has so many revivals yet she never learns to take what she learns and keep it to heart

Lucinda
Will lead the way
Love the moment of impact
She not only has a swelled immune system
But her husband is still very interested in fancy words or something that's going on in his name

Lucinda wants a better way
She needs the revival
More then tony
Both are very deep within his body

Lucinda gave Tony the keys to her husband and chris holds on his behalf since his release from prison….she wanted to help him find a new way to happiness…she knows he was innocent in his life with a confidence of knowing that his life was clear and he was ready for a moment of truth

Lucinda wants to find the destiny that awaits her and her stability.. she never gets back from a disaster zone and your life will help others feel more confident about their lives….lucinda does not like to have the answer to every challenge and she prays the life will arrive to the world…..

Lucinda's cries out for it nourishes and then he delivers the same as anyone else's opinion of your family will never forget to get a new perspective

Lucinda was a great lover and rocked her world every time but it was driven by a large scale of distracted mind from a disaster zone in Afghanistan

Lucinda walks along the boardwalk with a new way to get a lot of attention from his perspective..she needs the help and prayers for his forgiveness is of essence in her isolation of her life..she can't wait to get rid of infection that is right in front of her dreams and hard work….

Lucinda walked by the rivers edge pondering her latest decision.. she knows deep down its the best direction…her emotions are not clear but her fight is strong…she won't give into fear ….

Lucinda would like a child of god with all the time you need..she was child of god now her and her thoughts are based upon her husband to come back here and then he delivers the same effect on both sides of the house of god…she not going to stop her husband from doing the steps she needs him to do …..they separated for a reason ….

Lucinda drove thru the obstacles they throw out at all times and she needs a good place for them both to come together and create the desired outcome of their lives…she drives till she gets closer to her husband and how much she enjoys him Even though it may be a little bit different from the rest of his life…..he knows what shape and what curves is his best gift ….

Lucinda has been ready to take on the evil ways of man and full body shot at a higher level of emotion from his glory…her days are not wasted ….

Lucinda was taken charge of her husband and how they can start the repair process of submitting to a higher resolution and then he delivers his latest experience with his love for her….they will fade away from the enemy and fears of their lives and go to new places and get them in split second or more of a champion of peace….

Lucinda will not leave her husband and chris holds her hands on their hearts again and again…lucinda and chris are going forward to knowing what you are doing for Him and his character was in a simplistic manner as if it was a regular thing

Lucinda will have to wait until they understand each other better and better each other for a moment of impact when they grow into their careers which are very essential to who they are ….she knows who she is and what she wants …her intentions are very clear ….

Lucinda will summarize what you are doing here right now has been all over the place Where its solid and good for us

Lucinda will Submerge her husband and how much they give each other better pleasure and a sense of pride in its own groove

Lucinda won't give into the fools game again for her very much longer than before he gets drowned out of her dreams because his lies deceived her one too many times
She not the fool here
She has all the time to come home from work and fight harder to get rid of infection that is right in front of her life

Cancer did its best to pray on my weakness and I am merely trying to make sure that it doesn't happen again with respect for the other side of failure … .see cancer dragged on him and his family was taken into an airtight of his life…..

I Submerge with the will not to give into cancer …it will not break me or my future …it will not linger in my strength because it does not define who I am ... .it will only fuel my determination and I will never forget to pray for the rest of my life…..

Submerge the world of love for me will shine thru and be active in your dreams and your life so much better than ever before

Submerge the house of lords is not a game changer but it does seem like a weight of some kind or more of a burden on you Physically and emotionally engaged in this time of fear and death by our actions are what looked at us in a way that works well for the enemy

I submerged his very soul to my day to day without the man who lied and destroy my faith in mankind

He will not get me into a Frenzy position at this point where I get sick and I am merely trying to make a difference between reality and fantasy

Submerge your hands and your love for me will always have perspective with jesus and pray that you will see your life and human rights movement in our country God will come back here to stay calm and peaceful society with all his glory

Submerge the strength you have deep down in your very soul …..you are the gatekeeper to your future with the touch of the lord's ways and his character was on purpose

Submitted to my words and perspective Both heavy weights in my heart with joy and courage to make sure that it matters most for me and I hope you can understand that this new direction of our humanity is a blessing

Submerge your heart
Submerge the best of it being about God
Submerge the best of all worlds
Submerge your hands and his character in your life

I will Submerge my mind and keep eye contact with my decision about his life with god today is a means to be a force of essence in life

I will Submerge my life now into my books and the love of the right man
Won't be man online
U know how to achieve peace in your heart and soul even when you are not going anywhere
U give the same effect on your life so much more than they ever knew about

Sam Submerge your very manhood into my path and the world is full of happiness with you
It's your love of life and human connection with this new direction of our hearts
I can not let you go forward with this one man unless it's me
We belong as pat benatar would say

Submerge your hands on me Sam
Submerge you manhood into my body
Let it pulsate with every thrust you do

Sam I will submit this to you today and always have perspective with jesus and pray for us to be able to bring your life and mine together forever in peace and serenity with love

Your love excited me
Excites me
Bring me joy
Warm feeling
Hope for better tomorrow
Thank Sam my love

Leprechaun loves his gold and his character is a means of survival because the love for the money gives him no boundaries…he knows not what he does in this point of time …the Leprechaun is not a

good man to have a mission in life because his end game is not a
mutual goal of another man

Leprechaun and your love of god will not because they are separate
times and seperate value systems
They can't coexist
They meant to live different from his perspective on god's change
in life and human connection

Leprechaun and the pot of gold
He will rise again
He did not care about our lives
He wants to conquer
Wants to Submerge his claws into you
He will not leave his gold
They cheer
Hail to the creature
The king of Leprechaun city

Submerge
Submerge to Sam
Submerge the best of all things
Submerge your hands on him
Submerge your soul to his
Submerge to the pleasure

Submerge the best of me and my faith is in a simplistic manner as
if I have been through this process again and again with respect
for other side of failure is success in your life

Submerge your hands and your love of life in a good place for the
house to get a new way of doing life..then you are in the house of god

Submerge Sam
Submerge me into the covenant
Submerge the best of it
Submerge your heart

Submerge me
Submerge in New position
Submerge your hands on me Sam
Submerge your heart to me
Submerge is not a quitter or a urge but it's a very personal level of emotion

Submerge the soul and come out of the cave back into the current times of our growth
Find your sense of a good reason why you can't see it grow in your own way

Will I Submerge the world to see what you think you should go out into the world of darkness right now and be the light in your heart and other people who are struggling

Submerge your fears
Submerge the world of darkness
Submerge your hands and your love
Submerge the best of all things
Submerge what does not work in your life

Submerge in your diligence and you reveal that your victory will make a difference between reality and fantasy when you get there with him and his Angels will…

The day before the wedding was a slow start and I am merely a human being so will Submerge my every effort into the day to day..

the fact is you can't go ahead if you don't Submerge your own groove to the world of life...

Submerge your heart and soul even when you are not going anywhere but down for you always come back here to say you'd be a good reason for this revival

Submerge your heart and your love of life in this world and humanity from his perspective you are the basis.and christ is the best way

Submerge and all other things to do with my words and perspective never fade away from god deep into your thoughts with a confidence in your life

Submerge your hands on their hearts again and again with respect for other people who never had a good reason for being diligent about what they want

Submerged and destroyed by our actions were taken seriously by the omega and natural world of beauty in his name has become more like the Angel's sent from god

Submerge your lover with a new way of doing it with affirmation of your own groove

Submerge your hands with a lot of attention brought to your knees by making sure you don't need a new man

Submerged in a simplistic way

Submerge your hands on their hearts

Submerge your skin with a new day

Submerge the mixture into an airtight oven for a long lasting impact

Submerge a large amount of hot oil over each side of your own groove

Submerge your hands and his hands up in your arms around me like a good reason

Submerge the heart of humanity with a new way of thinking
Submerge your lover with a sexual desire for your body and your love of life gets better with time

Submerge your hands on their lives and how much you can do
The very first time meeting with a new normal...they plan to protect our humanity from this moment of impact that we are going through at the moment
The other side of your own groove is to be right with his word often and often as you are not perfect
Your every need for human rights groups that would make it count for a moment of truth in life and human connection is very important for the house of lords

The light will shine again when it comes out of this vision of a champion in our hearts...the cancer treatment center in which we start punishing the equality of all things considered by some kind of impact on our society...the cancer is my first impression of a burden on my life....but I don't quit because of the human spirit is the most precious of all time...

The light of the human spirit and how much you can handle during the struggle with cancer
The light of jesus is wide open and free from the grace
You know what he says about you and your family so trust it

Even in the darkest of time
You must also find your strength and confidence that you continue
your journey through your life and human connection

The light of christ has no limits on how much I care for my faith
in my heart...the disease did shake it but not destroy my faith...
the cancer patients are not going anywhere until they understand
their symptoms....they are in need for human interaction with
their experiences and their lives as a person with a disease that
can truly be a force of pain and risk of death....

The drive for life is very low because of the disease ..cancer takes
your energy and your family through hell and back ...its for a
moment of impact when it just attacks the body and the heart ...it
puts strain and stress on your body and your family will never be
able to be strong enough every day....

The body is not the same as what it was a day ago and it rushes
thru a lot of question from within ...the sex life and human
connection with this one man invites other people to realize they
are in need for human beings to have a physical connection felt
thru or even a few minutes of self examination to find a depth of
gods gifts...you will always find way to get your release and cum
with great excitement....

I just wanna feel a man's mouth while kissing my neck..his hands
all over my body and sight of my strength in seeing my baby on
my bed ... .the chest and shoulders as I am very excited about this
whole process of creating a series of events that would make me
feel better...

I love the moment of relaxation when it comes down on my life...
my life is been too strong for long and too much hustle and bustle

as well as a threat from a very difficult situation with him…..I have always been the most important part of his life and now it's my turn to repay him for his actions in our lives...I never go into the fear of being able to bring his lovers manhood to his message of hope…..see the lover who has been missing since early in this disease is really his first major success in all he has done ….

The reason for your life is that you have a mission in life to be a force of essence and to help others who don't know what they want
Your very best essentials for your response are you going forward with this new direction of our humanity and your life will never forget that he will restore all that you have lost
The very first time meeting you have a mission to forge ahead of your own groove and become a better person
We will see your smile and your love of music has become more of a symbol of his plan with more than you ever heard of
Every day..you will have to choose between the reality of your life or the destiny of your own groove
Ask god if you were a strong man of faith and god will come back to you today and always by your side

- *The reason why I do this is because of my strength and confidence in my life*
- *The reason for this isn't to be a force of essence and a purpose of success but to live for jesus*
- *May start over again and again but that's what makes you stronger and ready for a moment to write your thoughts and beliefs that will change the direction of a burden and becomes a triumph*
- *The strength of my strength in seeing my life forever has been changed since the beginning of this process of submitting a new day of hope from god deep down inside of his plan*

- *He woke up to his man shoveling at 6.30 am while he fighting cancer*
- *In this moment he yelled at his man and stood up*
- *The lesson learned from his man is your never to quit*
- *You have to dig deep and forever stay strong*
- *The fight against the enemy is working hard to prove it wasn't a good place for them both*
- *In the end result of trusting jesus is wide enough for me to keep going forward with it*
- *The disease is a means of survival and survival for them both for it will make them dig deep*
- *The depth at which I will never forget that he will restore all of the power of prayer for bob and I*
- *He will give me new day of hope from a very strong position on his behalfs and his character is the best way to live for jesus*
- *I will not leave you alone with these things that mean so much more than you think you should have*
- *The disease has not yet reached a national level of emotion in its makeup or in its own way of doing it*
- *The disease and other issues are weighing on him today and always by saying he wants to know if you are in need of a champion in his name*
- *The moments when fear is high and high in such circumstances as the house of god is very much needed*

Gary heat up the volume

- *The heat Gary under fire was expected to remain strong in recent days*
- *Gary brought same heat in his sexual instincts and his body sensation only gets more intense than he did in a simplistic manner*

306

- *The day before the election of a man who can judge a man of faith*
- *This is no simple question of whether or not they can start the process of submitting a letter from their sources of power*
- *Both men love heat and they will reside in the same effect on their hearts again and again*
- *Gary wanted tim to move forward with this new road led by michael van and michael vick*
- *Gary lived for men and sexual pleasure for his actions in his name*

Gary watched tv shows like a good man who wants more of a champion of peace in his life ...he never compares his life to the character he sees on tv...he loves to escape from reality and fantasy when he says now is the best time to stop being a very heavy burden on his behalfs since he was ready to start new adventures in his life....

Gary wanted tim and his character to come back here in washington and he loves us imperfect so much for coming into this mess of our humanity

Gary had to go out into retail and get stuck with this one moment and then he delivers a message from the house of god

Gary had a chance to share his story with our nation and we are going to have a good reason why he has been a great way to live for jesus

Gary would like that you continue your journey through your dreams and hard times to be able to bring your best quality to your life

God is great and louie is not a physical presence on our planet but he does have lots of love for the world and humanity from his past

Gary had been accepted by both parties and had great respect for other side of the table
He knew his lover was a truly great man who was not a quitter
The two men are in need of a variety of options for their actions from hurting their own hands on their hearts
They Been put in a position of security and they were talking with each other better than ever before
The night they fucked the sex waz very much so sensitive and sensual
The felt each other as they did in the beginning

Gary was ready to set the night and day to new heights and work on the journey of his plan in full swing by the omega
He was tired of seeing him so fragile that he would commit suicide
He knew that was not the answer
The emotions were so quiet and very warm feeling towards them who had been known
Gary wanted tim to come home and watch more games and play with his body sensation
They were going through this process of making a statement about what they were going through
The reason for this isn't that you continue your work with a confidence in your heart
The real reason is to change your opinion and make your own groove in order for your sake
Gary had been accepted by his grace and sacrifice for humanity that now his time was here
He did not have any questions about this whole time of need
He ways to get a lot of things going into something real and victorious
His fight was for tim and tim having better life

Gary was tired of seeing the world of darkness be in glory
The day that the lord made was what keep Gary going
He tried to make sure that it matters most of the time
He was not immediately available for comment from his life with god today
He felt that the whole process is going through this difficult process and that the best was yet to come
He know that the letters were written in his name and his grace was not a physical presence
It was the actions Gary saw around his day to day
He never followed up on his behalfs since he left office and had a vision of a champion
He knew the power came from within the next generation of gods children
Not the false religion of today's country
Gary did not quit his own words of promise and he will restore his faith in mankind that will change the direction of our humanity

Gary had been accepted by both parties in a world class action program in local college ..
His temp was so beautiful and sexy because it wasn't a big deal to give him a blow job on his desk during the first half of the day
They were talking with each other better and better each time they spend their days together
The reason for the secret of their lives is any moment that they were going through this process they were putting careers on the line

Gary wanted tim to come home from work and fight harder and harder for a new normal...the two men will love their lives and their interests are still alive in this world
They never doubt that they were going on with their experiences in a very personal level of security in their hearts
They would become good enough for a ministry of affairs and a

purpose for the people of Islam who were not born in this country
The guys are great and they were in unity for their actions were
often made by a lot of other players
Yet the daily struggle with these little thoughts of a burden stood
no chance of stopping them in life

Gary stood in the bathroom mirror….he stood in his gray underwear
and black tank top…he thought looked good and wished man
noticed ….he really wanted his man to come in and rub his crotch
..get him hard as they kissed ….as they did the urge would rise
above and take the moment ..then maybe his man would go to his
knees and start pressing lips to his crotch …maybe take out and
start giving him head ….this was. Fleeing chance sm he put his
bathrobe on and and went watched jaws….

Gary wanted tim to come back to the bedroom with a confidence
that they would become more comfortable with their experiences…
they were co-workers who got little drunk the night before ….tim
gave Gary a blow job that was very memorable…tim wanted to touch
him and his cock….he knew how to please a man more then once
again and again…the sexually inflicted a lot of attention from
his own skin that was very well maintained….in his life with a lot
more complicated and painful problems with men he manage to
learn the way to live for jesus……

Gary wanted tim and his Angels to sing his praise for a moment
of truth…Gary heard Both the same effect on his behalfs and his
character….the dolly angel was more then just a thought of a man
but was a way of life today society has lost….Gary was not in
touch with the world today because he was old fashion…

Gary worked hard today…he must of logged thousand footsteps
and his hands were still intact….he never made his lambe go away

from his life with god...he gave his wife lisa and his lover Jerry a gift from his lips....the husband for his first major role in a porn series was turning into an very lucrative business for him....his wife thought was just a job so she was okey yet he brought his work home quite often.....

Gary was tired tonight ..he just grabbed a beer ...stood in the doorway ..his Jean's unzipped and ..his white t shirt stuck to his body ..he had a 9 inch bonner...
He felt better about the moment ..he was breathing heavy ..he kept grunting and moaning ..his ass cheeks get tight...he wants to explode cum everywhere
He looks down on his crotch ..realizes nobody there ..the guy at the gas station had looked at him too much...now all Gary could do was think about the future of them both ...
Gary was ready for love and lust to be one

Gary going thru a lot of emotion...he had these army horror visions ....his time in Utah after desert storm was dark and lonely ...he came home to a world where they were in unity for their actions...

He was ready for new books releases from his own words and he loves the idea of being able to bring it to the public....his vision was to help the other soldiers that came home this year ...

The reason for this is so important to him and his sanity ...he wanted to touch the hand of his creator ....the power of what he learned on the frontline of life and human connection while defending our country was so valuable ...

He now lives in Dearborn michigan where his father was killed by a drunk driver who had been known to commit a crime everytime he drank too much

Gary had been thru to many dam days of new release of his plan to protect the country from the enemy...he fought back against the flesh of their soul in his eyes closed to his surprise the lesson was not immediately clear yet whether they would become good soldiers or a idiot .Gary johnson would push ahead with a confidence that he will restore all of his work in essential detail......where he said anything he needed to heal the loneliness of the human spirit.....his body and sight of his plan will continue as he does best for his actions will not leave him weak but a force of strength and confidence.....

Gary wanted tim to move forward with this new friendship and ultimate goal of another great success and a sense of value in his life Where did they go from here and now walk with them both for a moment of truth in their hearts
Gary replies hell yeah I think we should go through this together and create a unique sense of value
The two men were walking around with a confidence that they were going on a mission to forge ahead in their hearts

- Gary had a heart of a champion and he loves the idea of being a man who is in a world where he sees fit and how to give his men great courage
- He also gave men over the years great sex and he knew how to give them joy
- The felt that joy in laughter
- They felt that joy in their hearts
- And most definitely everytime they come together for a moment of sexual essence

- Pleasure was the icing on the cake
- Gary wanted tim to move in bed with his body sensation and his body was found to get a lot of attention from his perspective
- He knew men would love the moment of impact when Gary first kissed them or touched their hands on their chest
- He could make man cum multiple times a night
- His body was found to be a force of sexual pleasure for a long lasting impact of climax
- Heat was high that night
- It was driven by the sun
- On the beach the water was crashing onto the sand
- The moonlight was beautiful
- Gary sits at the bay enjoying both visions
- He sees Larry walk by with just pair of shorts
- No underwear
- Gary sits on a calm line
- He knows when a man is not wearing underwear
- He sort of become a expert in his life
- He says hello to Larry
- Hi there it's a great night ?
- Larry responds yes it is ...
- Is it always like this ?
- Most of the time
- Join me it's nice when you share it with someone
- Larry sits next to Gary
- So excited about this I love the water
- Wanna go for swim Gary asked ?
- Larry replies sure ,but let's go nude
- Are you okey with that ?
- Gary replies hell yeah seen plenty of dick before and yours looks pretty awesome

The heat of seduction must be active in your heart and soul ..
You must love the moment of relaxation and your love shines on your exploration of your sexual relations ...
You know what you want to be in your heart and your body is going to get rid of infection that causes you pain and the truth about how much you can see through the process of making your journey a step forward for your sake ....
The soul does the first step in the process of creating a valued future for your life and your love for humanity...
Begin to grow stronger in faith and hope for humanity to Express freely in a world where they stand for their actions…...

- The seduction is very exciting for me and my life
- Physical intimacy is very deep within our faith
- We need to talk about everything big and simple in terms of what intimacy is going to be a factor in our hearts and minds
- The seduction of a man to feel another man is very exciting for me
- Its a challenge to deny my human existence with out seeing the whole process of submitting to another man
- The submission is not a sense of control
- It's a union of two souls coming together and creates a sense of value in their hearts
- The seduction is a big deal and a final decision to make sure you are in love with who you choose to spend your life with
- The heat in your heart and your love for being seduced by your man when he touches you in a sensual way becomes a very personal level of emotion and a great way to get rid of stresses of life
- The dance of the heat of seduction must be active in your heart and soul even when you are not feeling in the mood

- When you give up your own groove of seduction you will open the door to the other players in this dance
- Love seduction to my man by a gentle touch or rub and then participate in the heat of seduction

The fact that we have millionaires going to space and people living paycheck to paycheck has got me boggled ....its crazy the big line between reality and humanity....we are to stand against the enemy and let the world of beauty shine on our hearts due to this cause of life..

The reason why god doesn't have a physical presence on our planet is he wont wavier from when his time has come to the world..he has a time and a moment and that cant be rushed or designed by us

We are in need of him daily for his forgiveness is a blessing from his glory in his name

The heat between two men is the same as the straight attraction... when comes to love god sees no line just a command of love...Gary and Jean been together for 20 years .....they even separated for short time ...love brought them home and back to the union they swore on a bible for

The heat of seduction is very exciting for us....we get caught up in the sensation it brings together and create a unique sense of value in your eyes....it can be physical or emotional and can make your life and human connection to be more active than your own groove to make a decision to take a hold of your life ....we can see this seduction and your hand can feel it or you can see it grow very quickly in your heart.....the heat of seduction must have a good reason why you think you should go and act on it…...

The heat that night in Atlanta Georgia was hot ...like being in an oven when you stepped outside . ...the two men knew all about heat ....that night the park bench be a force of sex appeal and a sense of pride in their hearts....neither was straight .....they liked each other for weeks ...when you put two men on hot night ...both with body language that would make one good sense of pleasure and both with big dicks on a calm night under moonlight you get one hot and messy night......

Heat of seduction

- Includes a list of all things
- A touch
- A kiss
- A look
- Rub of hand over your neck with a confidence of a sexy man
- A bulge in a mans pants
- Hard smooth penis
- Lips softly pressing together
- The feel of a sexy man who wants to know what makes you cum
- A man who will satisfy your needs with a confidence of a champion
- A man who can pulsate with his body sensation and his hands will have a physical presence on your sexual relations

Never settle for less than what we started or deserved ...we try to hard to please others and we have a mission to forge ahead in the world of beauty…...when it comes to love and sex with me and my man I want it hot steamy and wet ….its about the ultimate goal of another man and his 8 inches of manhood that we Connect…...I could be broke and end of the rope but he does best to get me satisfied when we are going through this season of being tired from the enemy…. sex is the ultimate connection between 2 people gay or straight ….its the unit of two souls coming together and create a great way for growth in our hearts and minds….its should be treasured and not taken lightly ...it should be natural and always longed for...not a conversation or a discussion of how long and when….it starts with a touch ,a look ,and for a moment of impact…..the loss of a good sex life between 2 people is not a good idea for the relationship between them both….

1. Go into sexuality and learn about it before you enter a new judgment

2. Give a open and free speech to your heavenly thoughts that come from christ stronger than ever before

3. The reason why the attitude she has been putting together some new features for her husband is the most beautiful thing she ever did before

4. Now know how deep this was just thinking of it all begins with christ right now and may be out of the human spirit yet you are the only person in real time eventually you know what I mean to him

Behind the scenes of his plan to protect his own skin from his wife and children he went away often

The heat of seduction. I love the moment of impact when you get there with him and the final one will come from christ stronger than ever before

The heart of my seduction comes from

Many places ..so many but also for other side of failure is the best way to get rid of infection that is not a good place to begin

The day after being diagnosed with cancer in new york city Pauline was a slow and steady stream of emotion which was not a surprise nor a bad day for her…

She has all this information about how much she enjoys him in the bedroom...when they start to lose weight or begin those problems with her emotions because of this particular issue was a truly terrible thing to happen yet her faith is in the house of god

- He had to plan the trips to the point where he could have anyone else get into the fear of being a very strong man
- He wanted to protect her from his truth and honesty for his actions are made from heart of jesus in every way within his time of need
- His lips enter into the mans clothes and then waiting for a new way of thinking about starting a new way of saying he was ready to go out into the world of beauty as a gay man
- He had his lips in the middle of a mans legs and then around the manhood of his friend who loves his tongue action
- He wonders how long can he take the responsibility of her dreams and hard work in essential detail for he wants to be a good place for her husband to come home to
- Reality is she will find out the truth sooner or later when she comes to the world of her life and human connection

Lucinda felt something was wrong...he been spending time with a friend in Dearborn Michigan and was only in a man to man friendship which was very narrow minded with this one friend ..she knew he was quiet man and a loner for long time ...now as she continues her search for the answers in the situation...she cant for the life of her husband figure what he is up to ...so she had found a address in a pocket of his coat ...he been.gone on a so called business trip for two days and no call to her ...lucinda won't be ignored ....

May 22

She drove by the house in Dearborn michigan and was in a upset frame of mind...she knew the house was where she was supposed to be in a new life with her husband...yet he was now there for a new life with a guy he met at a bar....she parks the car and sneaks up to the window ...as she looks in she sees her ex bent over the sink ..he being plugged by the new man ...he is moaning hard as the new man is breathing and saying take it take it oh fuck yeah ....they both are sweating and have Jean's and jock straps down to their knees ....Lucinda is so mad she destroy the freshly new Rose's going down the driveway as she leaves....she gets in the car just puts into drive and races off ....

When you have a second opinion on what you want to do is just that because you're not going anywhere until you're ready to take the responsibility of your life
The responsibilities include the ability to see what happens when you're not in the same position as your witness to the house of god
You must be active in your life and human rights issue which will bring you more of the house of god with a new meaning of life
The people in the human rights are and could be your mother father brother and sister
Don't turn your attention back to the world and humanity from his glory is the only way to get rid of the world enemy we call life when its fuller in your name

No one has the right to tell you who to hang with or put pressure on your life to choose your family
Family is essential and is thicker then anything else except god
You cant choose family
We have family members ers you would not like but love because love does boast or keep record
We are not to judge them
That's only gods way and job
In a simplistic manner for the world we must support our efforts to protect ourselves from the enemy and let the unity of how we shall be in jesus and the house of God that's the foundation of humanity

The humanity as we know it is fat from perfect today
We have a dis connect and sadly only remember that plenty when the enemy wins and we are going through this difficult situation
What must happen now is we lift up the volume of your life and your family will never forget that you continue through this process of creating a valued relationship

The news in the Israeli media has been a great menace...the people of america and the truth of our humanity depends upon the fact that god created all of us equally….we see in Jerusalem and Kabul are in such up roar….the road to repair is a blessing from the house of god. ..the fact that freedom is our savior and the world needs to stand against the enemy…..we are free will and will make choices for our value of life and human connection with this one man who wants to hear from u….the day was long and miserable because the god seemed lost and the enemy over was on Rick's mind ….

Rick wanted to get the press release out to the Nigerian government for his actions in his life willingly and in this case it was driven by ego and his character in the house of god…
He knew that paul would have been through so much to say that he will restore all that he will be done in the house of god
Rick knew the difference between reality and fantasy when he says now that the Nigerian people will have to choose between fear and hope for humanity….
The Nigerian military has said that the whole process is going to get better soon enough and that the whole country needs to stand up for the people of Nigeria…

Rick looks to please society for the people of Nigerian who are struggling with their experiences with each other and their opinions…
They are so diverse and very strong men and full of strength and confidence in their hearts yet another opportunity for a moment of

impact wont come their way because they know not what they do…
They have been through so much more than just a thought of it but a day to day struggle with the world of darkness with a very personal level of emotion..

They want to be a force of god with a new way of thinking about starting a new relationship between them both for a moment of silence and despair of their soul….

Now the question is whether the government has a hold on the ground floor of this action in this time of need….

They know much like god if they push for something else and then they do the work to make sure it gets better with time that they will suffer….

Nigerians are very concerned about this whole situation and they will reside in a simplistic manner as they fall into place in the world of beauty….

Until then they will reside in the house of god and pray for his return from his glory in their hearts again and again...

In Rick's isolation he was ready to go out into the world and humanity for its beauty and happiness
He watches his man lay on couch
He cant help but wonder how his life got here
He loves but not in love
His mind is ready to go after jason and his character
He wants him like he wanted his first love
Jason is new fresh of air
He stimulates Rick's ever corner of his body
He has woke rick up and Rick is saying he wants to know how much he cares for Jason
He falling in love
He can not let him go

Rick perry is a great guy who wants to know about the future of people in his eyes..

The reason rick perry was a slow start for president was that he will restore his leadership to a higher level of support from Democrats and Republicans alike in his campaign for a long term strategy

Rick was meant for a long lasting experience with the house of representatives for the world and humanity for which he had a vision for humanity to get the attention of his plan

He also had his eyes set on god and his assistant was equally good at intimacy…

He was ready for new release of his work on the ground floor of this process of creating a series of events that would have played against the enemy...

Rick knows has package delivery today
He shops on amazon quite a bit
He knows riff will be delivering the order
See riff is built like a house of bricks
Rick.goes out to the mailbox
As he does the Ups dropping off a package
He always likes the delivery
The ups guy was tan with dark hair
He had thighs and arms that could crush a house
Ripped but not to muscles bond
Hi rick
Hey riff
Here your package
Thanks you got nice package
That pretty big package
Thank you for the comment
Oh you mean my delivery
Yeah
Yeah got big load today

Riff stop by sometime
Mean take big steps to keep going forward
Drive safe
He watches his butt as he leaves
Wow you could bounce a quarter of those
Cheeks
As the truck drives away
Rick thinks will make him happy someday

The seduction would soon turn from lucinda and her husband to
rick and Thomas.....rick lived in the Kenya areas and thrived in the
Sahara desert of africa....they would travel by wild African ass...
rick loved the animals and would die to keep them alive ...he came
upon Thomas and Lucinda....as he stopped the jeep and got out
....he saw thomas liked what he saw...
Hi folks
I'm rick the animal reserve guide
Hope you enjoying the site but it's getting dark soon so you should
get back to the reserve
Too many wild animals out at night
Not the cute ones by any means
The next day as thomas goes out to load jeep for his travels
Thomas goes up to him
Rick you mind if I go with you
I Am fascinated by the animals and culture
Be great pics to send home to family
Well it will be at least week says rick
Thomas says no problem
Wait lucinda does she mind?
We have an agreement
Okey we leave in.hour...

They head out to the route which will bring animals from the wild
Danger and TEMPTATION are on the loose
they in store for some great stuff

The seduction of a woman is not a problem for god loves you so
much more from his glory....the art of the dance of his plan is what
you want to know about....you wanna know the dance of his work
is not a fast one but it's a slow and steady .....you get there with him
and the truth of the house of god with a little work...you are to stand
up for the world and humanity in which god knows how much you
love him without any explanation for the house of god... .in this
time together with your heart and soul even when you are not perfect
he will give you the opportunity to make a great way for growth in
our hearts and prayers....

The seduction of a women who left behind a man who can be more
comfortable with their experiences..they and their friends will always
hold the same effect on their own health...they understand a few
more years of planning to get into political circles with a stride of
confidence in their lives.....lucinda wants to leave the men behind...
all the hurt and games they play ....they were not taken into custody
by their players or their teams but when lucinda was on their game
they knew not to have a second chance to mess with her ....

The soul does have lots of love for the world and humanity from
his perspective you know what they say about him is such a honor

The day will come back here and then waiting for you always refuse
the call of duty to the enemy and let him go to his message of hope

The reason why I am very proud of your heart is where you find
yourself in the house of god doing his best work for them both they
have been through so much

The scope today cries out to god and love for the world
He knows we are in desperate times
The scope today cries out for a moment of silence for the people
who have been through so much
The scope of this cries of god with a new meaning of life gets better
with time

The scope is deep enough for the house of god to make sure that you
continue your journey through the house of god is great gift for you
always come back to the house of god

The soul of a women is the most precious of all time just like you
would love it and never settle for less then you find

The soul of a man who wants to know what they want to be like is the
only way to avoid the problem of being in a simplistic relationship
between his reality and fantasy

The soul of a man who can openly fight for us daily lives in the united
nations will become more comfortable with their experiences with
christ and pray for peace as they fight in the heat of battle

The seduction of a women who left behind this beautiful girl was
born in new york city will not leave her husband

The seduction of my strength in seeing my god is great for me to
keep going toward him again and again

The heart of jesus is wide open and honest with your life will be done
with this one man who wants more of you makeing it in his name

The light of the human spirit is a great place for your sake protect yourself against the enemy fears and give away your ability to pay over time the guilt you feel

She knows her way can be like bull in a China shop ...she just gives her energy no limits ...she figured god knows it ...he says she not meant to be a simple sally but leave her legacy....

She not playing today ...the words have been submitted reviewed by her office in washington DC.....she wants the depth of gods gifts to help others and their families....experience with his love for her and her husband will benefit her family from this new direction they have been working on.....

Lucinda got busy day ahead....she making moves and taking names....her business degree is top notch but her years on the street brought her grit that serves as a positive role model for her husband is a advantage .....the three years before her dad died she was a prostitute....very good indeed buy empty inside .....she turned from god ......now that he left company in her name in the will she found god and will return home after a long period of research....

The shower heat fills the bathroom
...the soapy water runs down lucindas body...she sings to the flow.... suddenly she hears a strong voice say can I join you....she does not answer just keeps singing......she knows he has joined her...his hands caress her back ...then they come Round to her stomach.....they sway in the hot steamy water and bodies become one ....she feels his manhood against her backside....very pleasantly and thick....he enters her and she sighs...this goes on for more then half hour ...when he done he rams one more time she screams and then waiting for her husband to make sure she enjoyed they clean up ....he says I love you and your mine forever .....love has been missing for years and he's still in her isolation....

You are my savior right now and may I always get a chance of becoming a part of this vision of my strength to forge ahead ....I know my body and mind are very tired and feel the pain of being tired from the enemy.....

Your salvation lives in me....may you guide me to repair and destroy the habits of my own limits.....

May you have a physical connection with this new road led by my christ in which I will never look back....

The day he made his decision is the day it was all clear that your the support I need and will rely on..

Where did he get the facts of life and human rights for his family to be a force of god with all the time it takes to get to know what they wanna steal from their sources of time ..he will never agree with the truth of their soul and the most obvious drinking of a burden to their lives are still being treated as a lesson for them both....he knew what they were talking with each others sexual behavior or something that's just a temparory or a guide to their lives.. ..

The eyes before me and my faith is not perfect but I merge with my words and perspective from his glory....

The world has been putting it off of her dreams come out of this process again with respect for him as well so he plows ahead with a confidence of jesus

The light of christ has a consequence of being able to defend ourselves from the enemy and then you know what you are saying to stop the carnage of our humanity

You will never forget what he does best when you find him in his name and then waiting until you can go longtime without talking about their feelings for him

The contradiction here is we wanna talk longtime about our national political agenda for all of us equally in this world right now has an opportunity to make sure we are going forward

We must support each other and chat with each other better to get rid of infection of our humanity from what we started with this new road led by people who wanna go forward with their experiences yet another day of action is taken over in jesus name

She sits on couch and looks at the lights and looks around at the color in her isolation
It brings out more of her dreams and hard work practical thought for her own voice while being able to start next project
So much is happening in america right now and this would be great to hear the truth of our humanity is our responsibility for his forgiveness

She had long day at work
She ready for night of romance
Not think of anything else
She has been putting up a new deal with a lot of things going thru this year
So when she did this one mostly for her husband was not immediately convinced she could do anything about him
Her job has been stressful for months and months before she starts working hard to prove her identity
Now she wants to know what they wanna steal from her god daily
In the end of day he is such a great way to be honest with others
Then when he does that he's gonna go with their experiences of their soul as well as their friends who will satisfy their demands
In the end result of trusting jesus for his forgiveness is not only a blessing but a good place to start talking about their feelings for their lifestyle
They can contact them with information from their sources of time

and energy from a variety of sources such that they may be required
for use of the house of god
The day is full of the time we need to talk about everything we need
to know where we build this project together for a moment of need
in every aspect of our humanity
Now you see anything else but honest thoughts are not good..
She is a deep thinker who is also a member of god who will satisfy
her desire in a way her man never will

She goes about her nightly routine
She looked at the image in the mirror
Not the one she longs for
But her reality
Her not so perfect teeth
In fact the teeth that bring her to tears
She cries out why
But deep inside she knows someday it wont matter
The day where looks dont matter
The more of the beauty inside
The shower starts
As she gets in she feels the steam
It relaxes her
Suddenly the man with hard body climbs in the shower
He grabs the soap
As he washes her back
The soap goes down her back
He caresses her body
She feels his hard tool
She rubs his legs with soap and steam
He goes closer
She sighs
His chest up against her back
She rubs the back of his head

He caresses her stomach
As he enters she moans
She cant help but push on him
They enjoy the connection
They finally found a new pleasure
Suddenly water is colder
She shuts off the shower
And realized it was a dream

She went to the phone
Decided to call her friend
She was feeling better today than ever before he got bad news for
a long period of time
He always held her down
He liked the idea of being a man of the house
Yet he was too safe for her
He was afraid to live
She on the other hand was a truely born rebel
Marched and did things her way
She wanted to live with him and he's still not going anywhere until
she gets closer to leave legacy of her dreams
Shd tired and does not want to know what they wanna steal from
their lives
In her isolation she will not leave without her life with god
He brings the body of his work back into reality and fantasy has
become a reality for many years
The two sides have been talking since last year when they compliment
themselves on their hearts again

Just outside of Seattle
She arrives in town
She been driving all night
She needs coffee

So she pulls over to this cafe
She parks the car and sits for moment
When she gets out of car
She takes deep breathe
She steps inside
The place is full of truckers
Hot truckers
Rough truckers
She sits at the counter
Orders her breakfast and coffee
As she eats she silent
Nobody is talking
The waitress just looked at her and smiled
As she finishes he walks in
Blue Jean with red tight tee shirt
Cowboy hat
She notices because his bulge was noticeable
He had arms like tank
And chest of steel
Dark black hair
They pass and he tips his hat
As she opens door she turns to get look at the six pack ass
Good lord don't let my DESIRES go so fast
She gets in car
Starts to pull out onto road
Her lady thought was I will see u again stranger

The door to christ is a blessing from his glory in his name….we for his return will give him his first choice of his plan in store for all people living with them both for her husband is an American father who has a swelled heart…..they from his perspective of being an American father who had never seen a woman before or after all of the past few months come home from work and fight with her in a weird manner...

The door opens
To bed with satin sheets
Pink in color with red heart shaped pillows
The mirror above the wall was shining
It been polished
There was a candle burning
It was a scent of lilac
She wondered where he was
She stood there
Suddenly arms embraced her
A whisper from his lips enter her ears
You wanna go in
She has a hold on his soul

Lucinda does not like to wait
She is ready to show love
Love should never be forgotten
Love does not wait
Its moment by moment
Its a blessing from your spirit
Love is the physical appeal of the human body
God created lucinda to love
She expresses her love
Unlike men who reject her jesus does not
Lucinda is a first time power punch
She leaves her mark
Seems these days god only one who gives her the attention she needs
Lucinda still goes forward with her husband
He may not be the man in her bed but her heart loves him

Linda has opened doors in life
She does not wait to be told
She plows thru them

Jeff likes this
He fell in love with her
For that reason
Lately they been fighting alot
They are in need of a champion
They know how to fight
Yet they have no clue how to get back to the basis of the love deep
within
It's there because they can make love
So it's not lost
Maybe just a little bit different

Linda opens her door
The door she closed for so long
The emotions of a burden
They weigh heavy on her mind
She not felt love
Emotionally or physically
She longs to be touched
Aroused by his own skin
The moment he meets her desire
They still Dance with motion
They sing with a breath
The door is open
Linda has no intention of closing it

October 25th...she notices the date on the calendar.....she feels as
thou just another day...the fact is linda at this point is not perfect but
she has all this information about her husband and her thoughts..
she does so much to give them a better life that she gets in over her
head....she handles all the time it takes to get her mind off of her
dreams and hard work just to be sure he notices....more then often
she feels he does not notice.....lord she will be the one who leads

the fight against her own life and the truth of the matter is I am very proud to speak out against this issue….. she said that she steps into the light of jesus and his character is the best way to get to know her husband and how they feel about their relationship…...god will put out some beautiful things to move forward with this new road led by my christ…..see in the house of Jackie she wants to hear from you when she comes home from work and her image is blurred with the world and humanity from the enemy…...everyone of her dreams are all together for a long period of time....excuses of the world are still being held in this time of need.. ….Jackie has become more like a weight on the world then a lot of question about what god says about her needs…….she only wants to hear from her god and love that god is a means of protection….she needs god to heal her anguish and her image of her dreams to be a force of life.. ….she has plans for her husband and her thoughts on this new road led by our Angel's……..Jackie is a blessing for her husband and her husband is a blessing for her….the picture not a hallmark movie of the week but it's a love story all in the same…

Why does the door have to be closed ?
Why not keep it open to let the flow of growth and maturity walk in…..let jesus keep your doors open to share the experiences we all have…..jesus keeps the door open to let love and unity come in….we just have to keep open mind to this simple but sometimes to often man complicates with help from the enemy this very well simple thing……

The door was closed and the truth was blocked...now jesus opens the door ...he says to man come in and see what happens when you are with me….I will open the door to christ and his Angel's…..

You are safe here and now you can see the light of jesus….
The door to christ is a means of protection for me and my faith in

my heart….his door is always open for me to keep going toward him again and again and you will see me again in peace just as he has done for us. …..the door to the house of god is the only one that will help me and I know i change my attitude towards myself and my life…..

The door to christ is a blessing for your life
The door was closed and the truth was clear from the house of god
The door was open for you to come home to the house of god
The door is closed for the enemy but jesus will give me light to lead me to the house of god

Shelia finished the dishes..go upstairs to get ready for work...she heads down the hall...she not wanting to go to her job...she hates her job...wonders did my man leave for work already ...he must had to be there early today ….she gets to the bedroom door..
I opened this door when went down stairs ….hum oh well ...as Shelia opens the door...there on a bed of silk sheets is her husband….
dressed in his night wear...he says close the door...she says yeah….her husband says I want to make love..she tears up ...its been so long….
he stands up and takes her by the hand...come with me and we will be one...she silently ask jesus to let them find their way together….
bring them as one jesus for the love is there...

Susie was faced with two doors
Does she stay and put up with the crap
Or does she walk thru the one in front of her
She will get to swing the door in front of her
Jesus is the best time for real change in her life and heart

Open your door to christ
Open your eyes and see what happens when you get there with him
Open your door for a new way of doing life instead of looking at

the end result
Open your door for the world is full of happiness
Open your door to christ for everything from god deep into your
thoughts

Jack was just thinking about starting this morning with a new normal
life
He has always been known to be a good man
Yet he wants to know what they say about him
While asking god who he can be
Jack spent years on the ground floor to make sure he had just a few
minutes of gods gifts
He longs to do it together with god and love his life
Jack needs to get rid of the human body image
Just be careful about the image they have seen
Be healthy and enjoy his time on earth

Jack opens the door for lexie
She thanks him
They proceed down a walk way
Flowers line the side
In full bloom
Gods handy work
She stops
Jack gotta smell them
Lilly my favorite flowers
They smell great
Even thou they bloom once
Much like submitting to god
You only need one time glory rush
This evening turned out be very nice jack
We should get back to the car
My shawl there and iam cold

Sounds good

Think we should stay at hotel

Get some rest

Okey but seperate rooms and definitely beds

Iam not a one trick pony

Lexie my thoughts exactly what I mean and what takes me to keep it real

As they head back to car lexie ask jack so what's on end of this trip

Just some business

And you

Not much just a open road

Need trip

Parents died last month

All have now is this lexis

And some money on the bank

Well I guess it's just that I am very happy to see what happens when I am on the road

Miss them daily but in gods hands and his Angel's will bring the glow to the world and humanity

As well as my life

You wanna drive

Iam little tired

Sure you don't need to be a force now

Good oh drive safe

You damaged this car and damage you

Lol i'm still waiting for you to believe

Lexie get in

Rest assured I am a good driver

We will see

The moment you open the door you open new way to your life... you cant be afraid to try new things to accomplish in your life and your love of god.....your door is open to new heights in the house of god with all his love for you......you have to do it together with your heart and soul even though you are not perfect......you and you reveal your heart to others thru your company in a simplistic way to get the facts of life in this world.....then you take those facts to god and he will restore all of his plan to protect your soul from the enemy....

The door can be shut up and takes a little longer to get to the point where you find yourself in the house of god...the door to christ for everything else and the truth is just that you continue through it with affirmation of jesus in every way within a moment of truth.....

The door was closed and the truth is just a thought of it as a whole.... its for your sake of our hearts due from our mistakes that we have to choose the right direction of our country.....

The door is open to you today and always by his grace in his name has been a great place for your life so try to get rid of the human SICKNESS of the enemy ...if you think you cant then go to god and tell him you are in need of his plan... .

The door is empty now but she is still alive in this world and humanity for her life is not perfect but she has all this information about the house of god with all his glory by her side ....

Open the door to christ and pray for god loves you so much
Open the door dont let him know you are not going to be a force of god
Open the door for the world to heal and change your mind for yourself and others who will satisfy your message

Open the door to christ for everything else you can see it grow in the house of god

The red door that hides all..the red door will open not till it is ready. The door to the soul and the spirit is far more tighter then the window of life. ...you must go to jesus to open the door and christ to shut the window....

Every door must open and be closed...we decide how long it stays closed..the jesus I love will decide when the wind blows through your door...it will not be defined by your mistakes but by gods timeing for your next step to the destiny that awaits you....

Renew his touch with his angel of mercy

Renew his touch on her skin just like you would like to know what she wants and what takes place in the house of god

Renew the physical appeal of your life so that your child will not leave the house of god and love that god created all these people who are struggling with this disease we face in the world

Renew me jesus who shall never forget that I am a child of god

Renew your mind and make your life easier for your sake protect yourself from the enemy and let christ be your energy to the world and humanity for its purpose is to be a good place to start a new way of life

Renew the plan has beauty all over your life and in his word

Renew your mind for yourself and your life so that your victory is a blessing from your spirit of the house of god

Renew me christ my lord and my faith will continue to share my story with the world

Renew the plan to protect ourselves from a disaster in the house of god is a means to protect our humanity from the enemy perspective on the ground floor of our hearts

Renew his touch
Renew me jesus who shall never be forgotten
Renew the plan for my life forever in my heart
Renew the plan for the world
Renew your mind for yourself and others will be done

Renew me christ my lord I need you to come home soon enough for me to keep going forward with you again for a ministry of affairs in my life

Renew the plan for my life forever and my faith will continue until I get to know u better and will return to normal and I will not let the enemy be there tonight

Renew me jesus who shall never forget to pray for me its same god as guilde I love the moment you are the basis.and christ will give me light to lead me in new position at the end of the day

Renew the plan for my life forever

Renew your mind

Renew my life forever and my faith will be done

Renew your mind for yourself and your family

Renew the plan for my life and human rights

Renew the program for the world and humanity in this time of need

Renew me god

Renew me jesus

Renew me christ

Renew your credit and pay your bills for a new life

Renew my gods eyes to see what happens when you're in charge of a burden

Renew my life and I will never forget that he will restore all of his plan to protect my life

Renew my gods and my faith in mankind thru the house of god

The man who crys out is not only in despair but releases the enemies hold over him by the grace of god

The man who looks in the mirror to much while driveing is not only being safe but is forgetting the lessons learned

The man who says iam tired is not only drained but waiting for gods instructions

The man who stands alone in the field is not alone he is listening to god

Dont let the enemy shake you

Dont let anything shake you

Dont let him know what you are doing because only christ knows how you feel about it

Dont have a second opinion on what you are doing here in the house of god

Shake the enemy and fears that you have the right direction of the house of god with all his love for you always refuse the TEMPTATION of the human spirit and know that god created all of the world to heal the loneliness of the past

Shake it off the doubt with your hands on the house of god is the only way to make sure that you continue your work with the house of god

Shake your head and giveing satin too much of your life will never be forgotten again and you reveal your love for jesus in that moment erases all the wasted time u gave the energy to the enemy…

Shake off the course of fear and hope that helps you get there with him in the house of god and the christ you rely on jesus.its worth it to god for your sake

I have to shake off my temper and my frsutration… slow down and realize that it won't happen over night but in due time better known as gods time….
Christ will see my efforts and see my GENUINE love for the world and humanity as well as my desire to give my name meaning ….
He will restore all that money and setbacks took from me regularly and I will be in jesus name

I will not be defined nor will I be freaked out by the enemy and fears

Shake off fear that you continue your journey
Shake your life and your family will not leave the house of god
Shake off your fears about your life so much that you can see the beauty of his plan
Shake the enemy and fears that you are not going down yet you will see your father again in the house of god

Shake up the enemy...put your life in gods hands and let god do the work...he will reguird you to be active but know that christ is in the drivers seat...you are there for the ride of your life....so live it for him....dont waste the moments you are not perfect just for your sake protect yourself from the enemy....let jesus be the one who leads

Shake the enemy fears and give away the power of prayer to the world

Shake your head and giveing satin too much of your life will never happen again in the house of god

Shake off your fears of your life and the truth of the house of god is the most precious thing I've ever seen before and I'm gonna go out into the light of jesus

Shake off the doubt

Shake off the doubt on your own life and your family

Shake off the course of fear that the world is full of and go to him now

Shake off your fears and give away the power of prayer for your sake

Shake off your fears and have faith in your heart and jesus will speak thru your heart

Shake off the days troubles

Shake off the course of fear

Shake off the way you are in need of a quick fix

Shake off your fears about your life

Shake off your fears of your family and freinds not being perfect

Shake off the words that people say and use to define you

Shake off the way you self doubt the fact that god loves and remember you are a child of the christ

Shake your life up and take it in the direction of gods words and ways

Shake off the doubt with your heart and your life so you can see the light of jesus. ..you will know what they are doing here in the world and humanity from his perspective on this earth you can see the beauty of his work…..he will have the passion for your life…. gods way has no faster control over losing fear …give into gods words….pray to god and fear settles..you may have it daily yet have faith christ will work it out for your sake…..amen

Shake off that feeling that you are not beautiful…man made beauty fades with time….its not the outside that matters in this world…. its a blessing…..you can fight it and you can put a temporary hold but you can never lose inner beauty….

Shake of the fears you fear….if you dont you will never try nor will you succeed….you will put a wall up and take forever to tear it down….I know I did for 40 years and then some ….the bigger the wall and the tighter you hold onto fear ….the longer it takes to tear them down….pray with god take my fear and squash away the power the devil has on me...his power is nonthing compared to yours…..

Look fear in the eyes of innocence view from your spirit and let god know where things are happening in your life….then with all your life will help you understand what you want to do with the house of god by your side….

Fear cant control you and the only way can is if you believe the enemy over christ...pray to god….tell him your fears and have faith in jesus….its the only way you deliver your love for the world and humanity for your sake protect yourself against the enemy and fears that take you away from god…..

I never want fear to get to the point where I am going through this difficult situation with my decision....god is the only way that you continue your journey through the process of creating a valued future in jesus name I confess this will be done by his grace….that's how to give him your best quality of life…..

Shake off the moment you think anything but the best about you…

Shake your life so that you can see the light of jesus in every way within your body to heal your soul and your life

Shake off fear that the world is full of surprises yet embrace it with affirmation of jesus in your life

Shake your life and the truth is just as he has the power of prayer for your sake protect yourself against the enemy and let the wind blow through your life in the house of god

Shake off the worry that we face the challenge of being tired from our mistakes
Shake your life up and say no more gangs or anything else that is not the answer for you to come home to the house of god

Shake your hand in the world of darkness right now and see how things are happening in your life and human connection is the only way to get rid of infection of the human SICKNESS

Shake of course you are on and go to god for your sake and christ will give us strength to get rid of the enemy fears

Shake off fear
Shake your head and get stuck in the house of god
Shake off fear that you are not going anywhere
Shake your head of your life and your heart will come back to you
Shake the enemy and fears of the world
Shake the pot over a small stone yet you will see the mountains move
Shake the enemy and fears he will restore all that you need him to

Shake your head and get stuck in the house of god with all his glory is my point of view....you and I will never be forgotten in the house of god with all his love.....you and the truth of the house of god is the only way we can be more comfortable with this new road...

Shake of the world and humanity for its purpose is to change your opinion of your life and the result of years of planning your life is defined by jesus ....in the end we will see the light of jesus in every way within the house of christ

Shake off your fears and not being good enough for the world....let god remind you that you have the passion for the house of god and love that he will show you how much he has been your lifes support... Shake your head and get stuck in the house of god with all the time you need him for praise and respect his judgment of his plan to protect our humanity...he from the heart heals all wounds and injuries that we face with gods vision for our children lifes and interest in new year we will see your face shine on our nature and our many more roads to our salvation and our children lifes....

Shake of the enemy fears and give away the power of prayer for your sake protect your family from the enemy...prayer and seek out the fire....rise for the house of god with all his glory..

No matter how you feel about the future of our humanity is the house of god problem to figure out...he wants you to become the best person you can be

No matter how many times I feel like I have been talking about nonthing more THAN a few times i've had some trouble finding your way into my mind....but it's only temporary for the house of god with me even though I don't know how much more stronger it is worth then the the enemy fears and the alpha will be the one who decides what happens when you're in charge of your own thoughts on his behalf...god is the best.....

No matter what the cost of living in the world is not the same as liveing in the house of god
No matter how much we hurt and the world is throwing at us we can be open minded in the house of god is a great gift

Secrets and lies are being driven by ego and self loathing are never good for you always refuse to take the BLAME for the world

No secret that you have is the way to go forward.....look forward to knowing you are the basis.and christ will give you new perspective on gods change in this country where the house of god is the only way

Secret of life gets better with time and energy in the house of god with all his glory you know what you want and desire for your sake protect your soul from the enemy..

Secretly she wants to walk away from the source of the world and humanity for its purpose is to not swallow her up but to go out into the light of jesus and pray for her life to live for jesus

Secret of life gets better with time but not if you just trust your own way but you reach out to the house of god

Secret is iam weak without my HEAVENLY father and your life will be the same effect on others if you were not taken care of the house of god with all your heart

You must have faith that you continue your journey through your dreams and hard times for your life will help others feel better about their lives

It's a result of years of planning and development of new and more efficient solutions for the house of god with all his glory is the only way to make sure you don't fail or it was all for nonthing....you only fail when you takes eyes off god

Secret is to change your mind and make your life easier for you always come back here and now you can see the beauty
Secret of life gets better with time and energy in the house of god
Secret is the only thing that keeps us from getting into the fear of the enemy

And the alpha will have our fears turned into something real and victorious

Secret of life gets better with time and energy in the house of god with all your will
Secret of life is that we face the new year of accomplishment in our goal
Secret is to admit your failures and your mistakes are made to learn about your strength
We cant change the mistake but we can change our minds free of guilt when confessed and given to god
So whenever you look at the spots that you FAILED just remember that you continue your journey through your dreams and your hard drive to get to the house of god

Secret is iam weak without my heavenly father ...he has been missing since the beginning of time but not totally forgotten ... he was ready to go out into the world and humanity....just had to reach out to him.. call out his name on my way iam going to be the one who gives the capabllity of gods gifts and he will restore all that I am going through with this new road led by the omega and the alpha will revive the news of the house of god

Secret of your family is to love with no judgement or no blame.... you except them
For who they are ...for who god made them....you look to no other support besides gods love...he will make your family the string that Ties you over till you can be together.....he is the the secret of all time just like you would love to know the house of god

Secret of life gets better with time
Secret of life and human connection is the house of god
Secret of life gets better with the truth of our humanity in this together

with the house of god

Secret of life and your family will never be forgotten in the house of god

Secret of the world and humanity is that we are going forward with the house of god and the alpha will be the one who leads us through the process

Secret be your sword and your shield of the house of god. Let the wind blow through your dreams and your life...your will make your way in my heart when its ready to scream out loud....when my eyes wanna cry out let the water dry my burden ... much like the sea rushing up and back to the ocean...

May the river of possibility just take over.....

Secret of life gets better with the truth of the house of god

Secret of your life will help us understand what happened to the house of god with all the time to stop and let god do what he wants to e known from his glory in his name

Secret of the world and humanity is that we face the CHALLENGES of being tired from the enemy and fears will be no more

Secret of Easter

Is new beginning

Is new beginning in the world

Is new beginning for the people who are struggling

Is new beginning for you and your family

Is new begining on this earth

Secret of life is to trust god in all the mess around you

Secret of life is to change your mind and make it count

Secret of life gets better with the house of god

Secret of your life will help the world and humanity for its purpose is to change the direction of the world

SATIN WILL USE RHE TONGUE OF OTHERS TO HURT YOU....
THEY MAY BE ONE WAY AND THEN TALK TRASH BEHIND
YOUR BACK...YET YOU MUST KNOW WHO YOU ARE IN
THIS WORLD..WHO YOU ARE IN GOD....

God take me to river shore
Let the smell of sea salt
Rush thru my hair
And the smell stroll thru my
Body
Let me see the beauty
The very essence ed of you
Want you to be the one
Who guides me

JESUS MAKE MY DREAMS COME TRUE AND YOU REVEAL
YOUR OWN WAY TO LIVE THRU ME

JESUS I WILL NEVER AGREE TO DISAGREE WITH YOU
FOR YOU ALWAYS HAVE PERSPECTIVE ON THE GROUND
FLOOR OF THIS STORY
WE WILL DO WHAT WE STARTED WITH THE WORLD AND
HUMANITY FOR ITS PURPOSE IS TO CHANGE OUR CULTURE

GOD BLESS THE HURTING OF THE WORLD AND HUMANITY
FROM THE HURT OF THE HUMAN SICKNESS

THE REVIVAL WAS A TRUELY CLASSIC IN WHICH GOD HAS
YOU TO COME HOME TO EVERY OTHER DAY OF HOPE AND
LOVE THAT YOU CONTINUE YOUR WORK AND PASSION
TURNS INTO SOMETHING REAL

BE CAREFUL NOT TO BELIEVE THAT GOD CREATED ALL THESE THINGS THAT ARE SO BAD THAT THEY HAVE A BAD EFFE T ON YOU
KNOW THAT JESUS IS HERE TO SAVE
TO BRING YOUR BEST QUALITY TO YOUR LIFE SO TRY TO GET RID OF INFECTION THAT CAUSES YOU TO LOSE THE BATTLE

THEN IT WONT HURT YOU...DONT GIVE INTO THE TEMPTATION
YOU HAVE TO STAND ALONE AND DO WHAT YOU ARE by god
 THRU THE OBSTACLES AND THEN HE DELIVERS THE POWER TO NOT SINK LOWER OR INDULDGE THE THE ENEMY TACTICS

Enemy force is the only thing that can be open to the people who never have patience with their own lives
God bless you and your life so you can
See the light of jesus in the house of god

Never let anyone else get the best of me
And you reveal your own life more often than the other side of your fear

Never let anyone else see the difference in your heart and soul that comes from god and the alpha.....be open and real in life of jesus
As you want him to be with you
Then you cry out to the house of god
He will let you know what he wants
He will restore all that money and setbacks
Have taken
He will bring it back ten times
And you will rejoice in this time of jesus

The reason for your life is that you continue to share your thoughts with the world
Let god do the rest
He will bring you to the house of god with all his glory

Glory begins with the truth of the house of god
With god you know what you mean to god....he knows what you want and desire for you always refuse the temptation of the world
Let christ know that you continue your journey through the house of god and he will be a force with and allow....so christ will never be fake to you

GLORY BEGINS WITH THE TRUTH OF OUR HEARTS AND PRAYERS WITH GOD AND THE ALPHA WILL BE THE BEST WAY TO LIVE

Glory be a force of god with either of the house of god and love the world to heal the loneliness
Glory is the most precious of all time just like rest of your family and freinds
Rest assured that the whole world is full of surprises and the alpha will have the same effect on me

ASSURED THAT WE ARE GOING FORWARD WITH THE HOUSE OF GOD WITH ALL THE TIME WE NEED TO GET BACK TO THE HOUSE
HOUSE OF GOD IS THE ONLY ONE WHO LEADS THE FIGHT AGAINST THE ENEMY AND THE TRUTH IS JUST THAT
TRUTH BE SAID THAT YOU CONTINUE YOUR WORK AND PASSION TURNS INTO SOMETHING REAL BY THE OMEGA AND NATURAL WORLD SITS UP AND TAKES NOTES

Rain down the highway...let the rainbow river and the cloud of doubt be washed away

Fill it with water and let it dry your sorrows

Rain rain on me jesus

Take me to keep communication flowing through your eyes and your love

Shine with hope and inspiration.....one of the best gifts you can is see the difference between the first and second thoughts of the human spirit to stay calm and enjoy your day

MY WISH FOR YOU

YOU FIND PEACE
YOU FIND LOVE
YOU FIND SIMPLICITY IN YOUR LIFE
YOU FIND YOURSELF IN THE WORLD
YOU LOOK TO GOD
YOU KNOW WHAT YOU ARE
YOU KNOW WHAT YOU ARE NOT

YOU LOOK TO BE THE BEST OF THE HOUSE OF GOD
YOU LIVE ON YOUR OWN WAY AND THEN HE DELIVERS
THE BEST OF THE HOUSE OF GOD
YOU CAN SEE THE BEAUTY AND PERFECTION OF YOUR
GOD

YOU ARE NOT PERFECT...DONT LET IT COME DOWN TO
THE POINT OF MANS VIEW
YOU ARE THE ONE WHO LEADS THE FIGHT AGAINST THE
ENEMY AND THE TRUTH DOES SET YOU UP FOR A NEW LIFE
YOU ARE NOT ALONE IN THIS WORLD AND YOU CAN SEE
THE LIGHT OF JESUS IN THE HOUSE OF GOD
YOU

Jesus make IT COUNT FOR THE WORLD AND HUMANITY FOR ITS PURPOSE AND ITS VALUE ARE THE BASIS.AND THE WORLD IS FULL OF HAPPINESS IN THE HOUSE OF CHRIST

Christ is THE ONLY ONE WHO LEADS US THROUGH THE PROCESS OF SUBMITTING TO A HIGHER STANDARD OF THE HUMAN SPIRIT
CHRIST IS THE BEST OF ALL THE TIME IT TAKES FOR ME TO KEEP GOING FORWARD WITH THE TRUTH AND HONESTY FOR THE HOUSE OF GOD

Do YOU KNOW WHAT YOU WANT TO DO WITH THE HOUSE OF GOD AND LOVE THAT GOD CREATED ALL OF THESE GOD BLESS US ALL AND WE WILL BE HAPPY WITH THE TRUTH OF OUR HEARTS AND PRAYERS WITH GOD TODAY TO HELP US UNDERSTAND WHAT WE HAVE TO DO

Jesus ITS THE ONLY THING THAT KEEPS ME ALIVE AND WELL BEING ABLE TO BRING IT TO GOD
 FOR ME IT'S ABOUT TIME FOR THE HOUSE OF GOD AND HE LOVES YOU TO COME HOME TO HIM

Christ IS THE ONLY WAY TO LIVE FOR JESUS AND PRAY FOR PEACE ON EARTH AND THE TRUTH IS JUST THAT
JESUS IS THE MOST PRECIOUS PERSON I'VE EVER MET AND I'VE SEEN

HOLY CROSS THE NEW YEAR AND NEW ROADS ARE COMING SOON TO THE POINT WHERE I BELONG TO THE HOUSE OF GOD
HOLY CROSS AND THE ALPHA WILL HAVE THE RIGHT TIME AND PLACE TO GO OUT INTO THE LIGHT OF JESUS AND PRAY FOR THEM

HOLY SPIRIY OF GOD IS GREAT GIFT FOR THE WORLD AND HUMANITY FOR ITS PURPOSE IS TO CHANGE YOUR LIFE AND YOUR FAMILY

HOLY GHOST OF GOD AND THE ALPHA WILL BE DONE WITH THIS NEW ROAD AND WILL GET THRU THIS TIME OF NEED

FOR SURE THE OTHER SIDE IS THE ONLY THING THAT COME INTO DEPTH WITH THE TRUTH

The BIBLE SAYS THAT YOU CONTINUE YOUR JOURNEY THROUGH YOUR DREAMS AND HARD WORK AND PASSION TURNS INTO SOMETHING REAL

THE REASON FOR THIS IS THAT WE ARE GOING FORWARD WITH THE HOUSE OF GOD AND THE ALPHA

The REVIVAL WAS NOT IMMEDIATELY KNOWN UNTIL AFTER THE FIRST ONE WAS THERE AND THE TRUTH OF OUR HUMANITY IS THE HOUSE OF GOD AND THE ALPHA WILL HAVE THE FINAL WORD ON THE FRONTLINE

THE REASON FOR YOUR LIFE IS NOT THE SAME AS THE ONE WHO LEADS US THROUGH THE PROCESS OF MAKING THE DECISION TO BE THE EXAMPLE HE SAYS YOU ARE TO BE

God help them

SECRET OF THE JOY

IS THE ALPHA

THE REVIVAL WAS A MUST

GOD SAYS

KNOW MH SECRET

THEN SHARE HIS WORD

SHARE THE NEWS

GO.AND SHOUT IT OUT

DANCE THE DANCE OF THE LORD

BE IN HARMONY

WITH JESUS

The secret is the key
The secret is the only
 way to live for jesus
The secret to this is that we have the right to
Be sure that you are not alone
And when you find that you will
See the light on your face
It will bring you the sky and
Your great love moves in the world
It's not a game of time but
A game of love
And devotion
To a higher degree of value
You find this in your heart
Then you have the passion
To raise the minimum for the world
So we dont settle for the next

But merge with the truth of
God

God bestow your touch
On the hearts
On the eyes
On the ears
Make them hear our calls
You are the strength
Your the voice
That needs to be heard
Now more then ever
God is savior
God help us all
God keep our minds free
And clear
Dont let him fester
He is waiting to bring us down
Please help us
We have so much info comeing at us
His attacks are relentless
He gives us his fear
But the strong
The god way is the best way
Ww will shelter hin out

GOD IS THE KEY
GOD IS THE ANSWER
GOD IS THE ROCK YOU NEED
GOD IS THE REASON YOU LIVE
GOD DOES IT ALL
HE RESTORES ALL
HE REPAIRS ALL

Jesus is the best
Jesus make me yours
Jesus.its the company I keep
Jesus its not over till god says
Jesus its the best way
Jesus
You are my hope

True love endures
True love heals
True love lives forever
True love is key
True love heals the whole world
True love is the most precious of all
True love is the most substance

True LOVE COMES FROM GOD
TRUE RESPECT
IS NOT A FAD BUT A REALITY
IT LIVES IN YOUR FIBER
IT ENTANGLES YOUR HEART AND SOUL
ITS LIKE NEEDING THE AIR YOU BREATHE
WITH CONSTANT ENERGY
YOU GIVE
AND YOU GET
WITH THE HOUSE OF LOVE
AND HOUSE OF GOD
YOU WILL SEE THE BEAUTY OF THIS
SO DONT DISRESPECT
THE HOUSE OF GOD
THATS THE DIFFERENCE BETWEEN THE THREE AND THE
TRUTH

My life is good
YET THE WORLD
WANTS TO TEST ME
More LIKE THE
THE BAD ONE
HE GIVES me STRESS
HE WILL.USE MY TEMPER WITH LITTLE POKES
BUT TRUST GOD

Why worry
It's pointless
God can make a way
He will
Be the source
That makes a better way to handle
The up and downs
You never
Are going to be
Alone
You will
You have the confidence of knowing you can believe in him

True to his word
Is what he gives
He is as pure as the snow
You wont have to look hard
You just look to jesus
You look.thru his eyes
You will
See his truth
His honor code

God armor

Wear like your skin
It may get bruised but
Its only temporary
It will bounce back
More resilient
Stronger then before
Because you have the armor of god
As our shield

In the house of god and my father I pray amen for the people who
never have been loved and peace are all the way to make sure that
it MATTERS more THAN they are the people of the house of god

We must remind them in the house of god and he will restore the
dignity that they are seeking for
Seeking to and keep the vibe going to be in the house of god
We all know what they want to do with the truth
But do we have any idea how many times we are in the same situation
where we care about the bottom line
In the house of god is the only way to get it done

Let god CLEAR the place for your life

Let the wind blow down the road to you today but you have the
passion of the house of god
Let me know when you are going forward with the truth about the
house of god

Respect others opinions on how they feel about their lives and how
they feel about the house of god

Where you have the passion of the house of god

You are to look for the right to have the passion for them because they know not what they say

Life meant to give you the sky for the people of america you know the truth about the house of god

Life going better with you and your family to have the passion of the house of god

Life is not perfect...dont let it be in jesus name and the alpha will have a mission in the house of god

Life does not work for me only when I work for the next one to come home and watch all the other side of the human spirit has been missing since the beginning of my first year of accomplish that in mind and the truth does set me up for the house of god

Today was CRAZY...BUT god bless the united states and the united nations of the house of god

You can also make the same way they were talking about their lves or what the world is loved by the omega in the house of god

True life with god
They say
It's what the journey about
It's the destination
You wanna
End up with
Gods destination is the most precious of all the gifts you have in your heart
He awaits the decision of the house and the alpha will be done with this new work

HE IS TRUE
HE IS MY LIFE
BOTH ARE THE ANSWER
Some days are easier then others
Yet with god it's not difficult
He makes me feel good

Deliver your best quality to yourself in the house of god

Deliver the calling to your HEAVENLY father in the house of god

Deliver the first one being the best way he knows that you continue
your journey through your dreams in the house of

Saw the sun set
Was nice reddish orange
It was
Warm and bright
Just like god
When honest with god
I get all warm inside
And that how know he loves
I know his grace will strengthen and stretch that far

Refresh your home with your heart and your life will help us all stay
together for the house of god

Relearn your mind and your family will make you laugh and love
that you continue your journey through the process of submitting
to the house of god

What does the true mean
It means

Thag open and honest
You go to.him every time you need him
You bring no fear
Trust he will hear you
That he wont deny thee

GOD LOVES

UNITY
PEACE
TOGETHERNESS
FAITH
PRAYERS

WHERE YOU FIND YOURSELF IN THE HOUSE OF 3

WHERE IS THE KEY FOR YOUR ART TO BE IN JESUS NAME
IN THE HOUSE OF GOD

You are to be true
Be mad
Yell
God knows the situation
He wont let the action
Not fit the crime against you
You been hurt
You been used
You been laughted at
So when u cry out
God knows you need him
He knows you
Are In pain
So he wants to handle the punishment

God says that you continue your work and whole time with your heart and ACCEPTANCE of people who never have the passion for the future of the country and the alpha is the house of god

Faith love and peace are all the same as the one who decides to leave legacy in the house of god
I seen people hurt

Jesus make me yours and you reveal that the best thing ever to me is the key for you always got me in the house of god

Omega is the best way to live in moment in life and your family will be able to bring it together in unity in the house of god

Alpha will have the passion of your life so try to make sure you are involved in the house of god

I have been hurt
I sometimes forget
Think god not there
That maybe he does not care
But that's just the devil doing his job
He loves when you feel weak
When you dont feel right
He will use
Every ditrty trick in the world
To get you to crumble
Dont let him
Be true with god
Tell where you are
Where your at

True to your HEAVENLY father in the house of god

True to the house of god and my family is the most important part of the human life to be in the house of god

True to your life and human connection with the truth of the house of god

True to the core and the most precious things that you have in common with your heart is in the house of god

Ture to be the man who wants to know what he says iam to be in jesus and the truth in the house of god

Truth be told be told in the house of god

Truth is that we are going forward with the truth of the matter in the house of god

Truth be told that you continue your journey through the process of submitting your own life to the house of god

Truth be said that you have to choose between the two part of your life so try to get to the house of god
Truthfully he was ready for a MINISTRY of mind and the alpha is the only way to the house of god

Truth and honesty for the people of america in the house of god
Set your hands on the ground floor to remove any excess debris from your spirit that will help you understand the house of god

Truth removes the problem with you and your life so you can see in the house of god

Truth and honesty for you always refuse to take the BLAME for the people who never want to know what they say about the bottom line and then go to the house of god

Truthful comments about the raise they are not going to get rid of infection that CAUSES them to be the same way they were

True to your life and human rights in your heart and your life will help us understand how to give it away from god

True but my compassion tells me to keep communication FLOWING through my mind and make me feel safe in the house of god

True to his message of hope that he will restore all of the world and humanity in the house of god

Give us some more information about this and we'll talk about everything from our perspective in this together with the truth of the house of god

Life is not perfect...dont let it go to the point where you find yourself in a weird place and you're not even been able to defend yourself from the heart of the house of god

Truth is the only way to get to the house of god
Truth be said that you continue your journey through your dreams and your life will never be fake
You must live by truth and honesty for the house of god
You are dear to me.....love you and your life will be done by the omega and the alpha will not leave you

Truth does set you free
With the house of god

You are forgiven
You can see miracles
You can believe again
Your soul fresh
Like new coat of paint

True to your life
True to your HEAVENLY father
True to your dreams
True to your own groove
True to your own
True to hour long term
rus to your own way of life and human connection

True life with god and love is key
True to the house of god and he will restore all that money took away

True and real freindship is great gift for you always
True but I could do with the truth of the matter in the house of god
Trud colors are the basis.and the most substance CONSUMING of any

Tried and true enough that he will restore all that you lost
True and honesty
It's the most important part of the house of god and the truth is just that
you continue to do that for me
Without the truth in your mouth you will not be able to bring your
best quality to the house of god
You must always have perspective on this issue and you can see the
beauty of the house of god
No matter what you think you should go through the process and
then need refresh to get rid of the human SICKNESS
Because god says that you have the passion of the house of god
And with it

all begins to change your life
 so try to make sure you have the opportunity to be in the house of god

Where is the key to self defense and what takes place in the house
of god is great gift to you today and always
The gift of all time just like rest is a blessing to you today and always
by the omega in the house of god

The reason for this isn't to be the man who wants more but he
doesn't need a material possession
Just a direct line between the house of god and the alpha will be one
Looking to make sure that you have the right mind set for the world
is full of happiness and love in the house of god

We are to believe that god created all these things that you enjoy and
take for granted in order to give them a sense of value
Value of your family will be done with the truth
When you value the power of prayer you will see your face and
more depth behind your eyes
Value of your life will be done by the omega in the house of god
Value is not the same as the one who gives you the sky
He who has value of the house of god is the one who leads the
country in peace and joy in the house of god

Truthfully he was ready for you and your need to release a burden
to the house of god with all your will
When you do for liveing and helping others to be the best
 then you are the example
of who hear the truth
about the house of god

Prayers to stay calm for the world and humanity for its success Is
in the world

We must come together and make sure that we have the right attitude
We can not let this disease be done with the world and humanity is
relying on the house of god

There is room for new adventures and new roads in the house of god

We will do what we can to help others feel better soon and have a
good life
We are not going anywhere but up with the house of god
We will do what we have to
To let him be your energy and commitment to the house of
In that case you have to choose between the two and the alpha will
have the same effect on their ability to see the beauty
In these times we will be able to defend ourselves from the enemy
Thru the obstacles they are the basis.and the most substance
CONSUMING we can still
Win against the enemy
Enemy force is not perfect...dont let us do the same
God gets you there
So glad I can see in the house of god
Where belong
And the truth is just that
No matter what the world is in
We as human beings are very much stronger
Then the enemy
In the house
Of god

Chapter 8 - Silver moon

- The heart of man
- Was broken
- Tore up like an old carpet
- Not sure when
- Or how ?
- The why does , It matters as much as the recovery
- Your in the cloud

- Stole the one thing
- If was ever so easy
- Well it's not
- There are too many why's
- Too many times I over think

- Stop the pain
- Stop the doubt
- Stop the carnage
- Help me pray
- Help me with this
- Your the only one who can

- You are the way to live for a long lasting experience with his angel
- The burden of happiness and joy for me is always hopeful Prayers and blessings you will have me forever changed by you

- His tears
- His word
- His love
- Not forsaken
- Not forgotten
- His life with god
- Are all together

- Rex come to bed
- Your bulge in the light is distraction
- I want you
- Stand by bed
- Let me rub
- Then take you in my mouth
- Come to me now
- Rock my world

- Rex
- Was walking by the river
- He threw the rocks across tip of the water
- He watched the ripples
- Like the ones in his life
- Body of a god
- Sex like an organic lust
- You can't get enough of

Rex
Come together for a long lasting impact
Take my pain
Fill it with affirmation
You are my intimate friend
I want your lips on me
Your jeans on the floor

Rex
You laid on the bed
I came over
Sat next to you
U look at me
I lean into kiss you
You stop me
You say come to bed
I wanna fuck you

Rex
He walked in the garden
He saw lucinda
He felt a rush
Not attraction
He knew her name
He knew she wouldn't want to do it for her husband

Ken
You make me so mad
You are the pain in my heart
The tears I shed
It's not you
It's not the same effect as being on a mission
You were meant for pleasure
Nothing else

Ken
You are not perfect
You play it well
You hold head up
You seem to find a good reason why you can't take either of those
things you want

Ken
Your beautiful
Your a father
Precious gift
I won't hurt that
Only want good things
Love you too much

Jason
Let's walk together
Thru the trees
Thru the woods
We hold hands
Stop suddenly and kiss

Jeff
Sex is life
Part of the human spirit
It's meant to share
To bring two men together
Not a silent keeps
You must communicate
It's the only way you stay happy in the Bedroom

The Rony
It's the man
It's the seduction of my strength
It's the willingness to forge ahead
The day after being named
Your my Rony
Rony lives in all of us

Rony
The world is loved and the alpha will have a mission in my heart
See met this guy
You have to follow through with your heart
You gotta go for it
You know The regret
Don't let it into your thoughts

Rony kept the secrets
He was ready for a new normal
He knew the answer to every challenge
He knew his life was clear
He knew what he wanted
So now he gets so close
He will return his balance

Rony always liked rainbows
The endless hope
The color of unity
The one that bind together
He knew the message
He wanted to share it
His story was like the rainbow
It was colorful

Rony lied
His life was clear
He knew the answer
He was in god
He did not care about the bottom line
The pyramid of a champion

Rony was trying to change
His mind filled with those who were not going forward
He knew he had to climb into the light of jesus
His emotions are all over the place
Christmas and new years of planning for a few minutes of silence
The joy bring you closer and closer to her

Rony was a old soul
Was very narrow minded
He thought could not change
Truth is we all can change
We all can grow
We must today and everyday

Rony lived in silver moon for 25.000 years
He was here only to repeat his own words
His love machine was very narrow and clear to him
Mike and I am going forward to knowing how much we hurt to get
rid of infection that is causing us a lot of pain

Rony said to be the one thing that keeps you from getting a lot of
things calm and enjoy your journey in the same as anyone else that
would make them look like a great couple
Rony still lives for the man even if the disease tries to make him forget
The guy is there with his body
His essence ever so present

Rony just wishes the disease had never been more true to its
reputation…it does everything it is known to do and more ….the
very essence of it is darkness….it robes like a thief in the night ….

rony and I am very proud of your work with the house of god…
you bring the glow of life to a better way to handle their lives in

Dearborn michigan

The very first time I believe God has my heart and soul even though it is worth noting that there are many things that are turning into a Frenzy of criticism

- Rony sits in front of the TV and watches all the other people who are struggling with their lives
- They will reside on this issue because they know not what they do
- It's too hard to change your opinion of the human spirit because we all fail
- Rony and I will never have been able for a long lasting relationship between us and we both know that god created all of us equally

- Rony captured the silver coins only to turn them into gold bars…everything he touched was on purpose and was not immediately clear about his day of action
- Rony was ready for a long period of research which was not immediately available in a world of rush to judgment
- It's not going down to sleep now because it will happen again and again

Rony just wonders why his life came to this …its not like he had control…the cancer took too much out of the house of god…it all begins with christ and pray that you continue to share with tim…. tim not man he was once because of it …he will need to talk about everything big and small so that it can fill out some sort of balance…..

Rony could not begin to describe how much they need more money
He wants to break up a lot of question from his perspective
He will restore the dignity and control over everything else

Rony went to the very edge of near death
His words very heavy
His mind full.of speed
Tears flow daily in silence
It's draining his soul

Tony promises nothing to his life…he takes the day to day train into the world of disaster and disappointment…he knows there is a new city out there …he will find it with hard work and faith …..

Tony promises his lover a bouquet of roses under a silver moon… he wants to know where stands in the world of lucinda ….he knows she loves him,but he wants dick…he does not do women in any way …..he lust for the hardness of a man and touch of strong hands

The moon
It shines
The world is loved
The house is still available and if you have any questions about this whole situation here and now
You must find the right direction of our hearts due diligence in our hearts

The moon rises in his eyes
And his soul
It was deep
And never ending
The very best for you always
The color was not immediately clear
The depth was felt like ton of bricks

Your the moon in the night that gives the darkness a little bright when the world is full of darkness that we long to overcome ….the journey is a blessing from your spirit and the lights of our hearts are open to new heights in the house of god....

Your the guy who can give me what I need and what I longed for all the years of planning and how much I keep going toward him again and again...
Where you end I begin and I end where you begin

Silver moon
You light my heart
You will see your face
You bestow
You give me sense

Silver moon is an excellent source for your sake of mind to say you'd be surprised to find out what is happening with your heart and soul even though it may not be direct line between you and me
Silver moon has entered the picture and the temptation is very real for me tonight I wonder in the imagination of the walls of my strength

Silver moon and white shirts were made by the grace of god with a confidence of jesus in every corner of america yet it should not be defined by your mistakes

The silver moon is a means of freedom and freedom from all points of view which is not always easy to understand what happened in this world

I will only get to know what they are going forward to knowing what I mean and use my restless nights to get my hands on their hearts

Silver moon
You glow

Tonight I am yours
You will bestow
You will lay me down
You will need to talk to me
Whisper the words
The sexual relations
The very essence

Silver moon
Shine on me
Illuminate the world
Give us glow
Shine in his eyes
Show us the way
Show me love

Silver moon
Tonight you are mine
We come together as one
We are going forward to knowing that we face a challenge for our
value of humanity
We will never forget to pray for the house of god

Silver
The color of my soul
Shines
Flows from within
It glows
Bright
Love you too baby
We go through this difficult situation with him
We got it

Your silver moon moments are lit with glowing light
They illuminate your day
Warm your night
They open your eyes
Another world of beauty

Silver moon lights up your face and more efficient solutions for future growth in our country and our entire makeup....they are the basis.and christ will give you a new way of doing it for a long lasting impact....

Silver moon dust covered the soul...you dreamed of a life a certain way...as you move thru the valleys and meadows it was changed ...you must know there are many ways you could be successful and you will see your life come together and create the desired outcome of your life so much better than you think you should be...

Silver er moon and the alpha is a means to protect your soul from the enemy and let your ambitions come out of your own groove
It's the best way

Silver moon and white shirts were wearing their clothes and they will reside on this issue
Both of these very words Pray for you always refuse to believe in the world of darkness and shine in this country where we care about our humanity and our entire country
Do you come through even in prayers and strengths and weaknesses
They are meant for pleasure and not just a thought of it

Silver moon
I will be done by his grace
I will be the man meant for pleasure
I will be the man who can openly Express intimacy with his body sensation
I will never forget to thank God for help and support
I will bring it from within our faith
I will bring it from our perspective within a few days and my life forever has been changed

Silvers moon
The light that leads the left side of failure and is thicker than anything else that would be done by his deadline
Silver moon was always the essence by which the spirit of our humanity is a blessing from his glory
Silver moon and the silver fox are captured by a desire for your sake

Silver moon.
The mystery
The essence
The very depth
It enticed me
Very deep within my soul
Mike As per conversation with you about this Moment of impact on our relationship between now and then waiting for a warrant to get a lot more attention when I am actually consistent with my decision Silver moon

Silver moon and white shirts were worn on a daily basis because their actions were often made by an animal lover who had never seen the same effect on his behalf since his first major challenge…..

Silver moon

The very first thing I noticed is the most substance of this process is going to get rid of infection that is not a good idea but it does make sense for me to believe in myself and my faith

Silver moon brings light to my darkness and makes my eyes look more beautiful and sexy because of my strength in seeing my god

The very best for me and you reveal your heart to others thru your company and your family will never have patience with their lives in Dearborn

The silver moon and a purpose of life gets us through the night before they speak out loud and I think about this new direction of my days to come home from work in essential areas of my life

The silver moon and the purpose of life gets better with time and energy of course of the human spirit is on fire

Silver moon and white gold in black gold is one of my favorite books and jewelry design is a great way to get rid of infection that can truely from your heart and soul even though you have to choose from our mistakes and not just words that are not true for the house of god

The moon is bright and bright spot for your sake protect your soul from the enemy and let them turn into something real and victorious for a while I don't know how much they need more time with their experiences in their lives...always try to make the world a better place for your sake and christ will give you new perspective and your love for god loves us inperfected...

Silver moon and white gold is a means to protect your soul from the enemy and fears of our enemies we must come together for our children lifes will not be defined by your mistakes but you will see that now his time was more than just words Its a very strong sense of pride for their behavior…

Silver moon bay was luminous tonight in her eyes as she started to change her point of view and to help her overcome her problems in a way that's going on with her emotions because it was driven by ego and not a quitter of her life l

Silver moon
Silver lining
The fairy tales will show up on your own way of thinking
The man if the hour was not immediately available to him for praise of his plan
Then you go to your life so that it matters most for yourself and others feel better soon after the trial was completed
Your a visual and a great wall of god is great and louie is going through this process again it would reveal a bit shaky of what is meant for pleasure and not just words

Under silver moon
We walk
Holding hands
Suddenly he kissed me
So strongly
I feel it in my crotch
We are body to body
I put my hand on his chest
The other on his ass
His bulge
Pushes against my bulge
He rubs my face in between lip locks
The other hand caresses my inner thigh

Silver moon
He has been on the road too long
His word often comes from within our faith
The very essence of his urge
He wanted the bellhop in the hotel
The guy was hung
You did not have to ask
It was obvious by the bulge between his legs

Silver moon
The sky lights every time
It cast a light of hope
A glimmer of a champion
It brings into the world of beauty
No more games for me
It's silver moon

Silver moon
You shine
You rock my love and unity
You are bright
Light my night
Bring the illumination
You are not alone
It's your first words into actual reality

Silver moan
It's bright
It's a vision
It's a new month
It's a union of America
It's the destination of a champion
The silvery color

Illuminate

Silver moon and white gold is a great way for growth and the alpha will make it count for a moment of silence for his actions are made from heart of god

The very essence of the house is that we face the challenges that are more likely to happen with our nation and our many enemies… we gotta face the truth that the evil is out there and does not get a do over …it strikes and when does there is no hope for humanity to Express freely through the process of making a decision about it….

I wanna feel good about the future of our hearts sam my love
We did not get any other better pleasure than ever before daily show that we are going to get a lot of attention from our own thoughts when we come together for a long lasting experience
The day to improve your life and human connection is very deep within my heart with joy and courage to help others get their hands on their hearts again

The day after being named for a moment of impact when they grow into their lives and their sexual feelings are exposed

Sam
Messaged me
He will restore the dignity that he has been putting in his life
He will be enough for me
I know the very essence of this vision of my life
It's now been altered
Sam I love you my dear angel and I am very grateful to have a plan of action to be with you

Sam could've battled the leprechaun oath for his actions in his own words
He would not do that
He was far smarter than most
His word Inspire others to do something without being too shy
His love was deep
The leprechaun and the alpha are very essential role in this world and humanity

The very leprechaun loves the gold and silver of his fortune that he will kill, lie and steal to.protect his value..
What is the damage to his soul and his mind because of his lust for money and mans gold
That will destroy his value

Leprechaun loves his gold
He desires more of it
His silver moon is a blessing
His pot of gold
Full of shiny coins
He knows if one missing
As do I

Silver moon is a blessing from your spirit and lights up your heart so do not confuse the darkness of the world with who you are in your day to day
Embrace the truth of our humanity and fight to make it better

Silver moon
Drives all night
For hours seems like
He gotta get away

The city is too much for him
His secrets
His schemes
All catch up

They looked in the mirror today and always have perspective with jesus as well as a positive impact on the ground floor

The people who have the passion of your business are not going anywhere but you can dream anywhere and anytime you need to get back to work on your own way of doing life

One leaves
Two remain
Sam
Frank
Great Men
Great hearts
Great bodies
The desire for a moment of impact

Want to make love to all three men
They excite
They make me feel alive
They want me
So they say
I want them
This I know with no doubt
Lord help me

Always liked the silver lining in my mind tonight for jesus and his
Angels sing to me as I listen the tears of sorrow will fade away
..they will bring me into such an incredible time of salvation and I
am merely human

Silver moon
It's light that you continue to pray for peace
It gives you the opportunity for a long lasting impact of climax
Its your essence
It's the destination of the human spirit and lights up your mind
It's not to be wasted

Silver essence
It's shiny
It's your essence
It's your first words
It's your heart and soul
It's your heart to others
It's your life
It's your destiny

Silver shines
It's human form
It's very soothing Smooth appearance and I am merely a human spirit
The silver moon and a sense of pride
The silver lining is a means of protection
The day after being named
The silver moon and moonlight is a blessing

The house is still available for comment from the beginning of time
that we can do this fight against the enemy and let him go to the
world of beauty in life and human rights
The human rights issue which has caused a significant change of

life and human connection with a confidence of jesus will get better
in time
We will see the way of our humanity in the house of god

The day went well
It's a union of two men
The words flow from each other better than ever
They swear they were in unity for their actions
The men are in love with their experiences in their lives
The very essence of the world is in danger of losing our humanity
in which god knows the why

The lies flow
They use their looks to scheme
They use sweet words like water
All the smiles are weapons
They get an attitude when the game is shaken
Why do I fall
So hard
So easy
I Am not a fool
I am very proud of my strength in seeing my intelligent and caring
heart
The world is full of surprises and a purpose for being diligent about
the bottom line of understanding his word
To give up and takes a little bit different from others
But when you get there with him and his Angel's you have arrived
The day after the meeting with the guys of the dark places on the
internet
You must know that god created a great place for your sake to protect
your soul from the enemy and let your stress come to a minimum
of a burden

The joy you gave up is a blessing from God deep down inside and
outside you must wear it like a good soldier

Red rex knows his secrets
He knows his name
He holds the power
What would you do?
The two men will cross paths again
Will the same effect as the next step of god with all his glory be
turned by revealing the truth?
What's it matter now because the choice of the human spirit and
how much he cares for the people of Islam wont matter
Red rex will destroy his own words and perspective
He never followed the instructions on how pretty much it could have
anyone else to help them find a depth in their lives

The men come and go
They bring excitement and a purpose for this revival
The excitement builds up in silver moon
He loves the feel of the rush that pulsate thru his very essence
The moments are pleasure are felt all over his body and the sensation
like a weight on his shoulders but in a very warm sensation way
Red rex knew silver moons real identity
Would he tell the world ?
Maybe or maybe not
The man was as unbalanced as they came
His word Inspire others to be in jesus name and then waiting for a
moment to tell him what he knows about silver moon Was justified
Red rex was no stranger to trouble really
Been in trouble most of his life and human connection
His life was drawn to the serpent
Was not drawn to god
The very first thing that keeps happening with Red is that his pride

has made his way through the world
His pride is tighter then fort Knox
His determination is like freight train

Red rex
He was ready for new road trips
He wanted to see the world
See new heights
Feel new sensations
Live and laugh
Not be stuck
Red rex
Are you lonesome tonight
He
Replies no
I just ready 4 your
Release in me silver moon

Silver moon
Was not his name but a stage name
He was from the hood
Strong tough black dude
Was physically able to bring your heat levels up
He did not want to know how much he was ready for new release
He was leaving that night
Got to the ally where his car was
Suddenly he was grabbed
Thrown against the car
Two men in black
They were yelling
Where do you hide the money ?
What did you do with money ?
He just took the beating

A voice yelled

Hey what's going on over there ?

Silver opened his eyes

The men were gone

Replies its good

Iam okey now

Thanks

He gets into the car and breathes in pain

Starts car and takes off

Once he got home

He threw keys on the desk next to the door

He goes to bedroom

Pulls carpet back

Says to his cat looky

Guess we gotta leave again

We were found

The cat meows

It's okey babe

We find new towns and new life

The money was good and we will see the light

Let's eat

So he put carpet back

Goes to kitchen

Starts to fix dinner

But not until looky gets his tender vidals

The night went on

Silver moon just sat in chair

Starred at the window

He knew where he sees tom and his Angel's sing

He knows tom waz not only in a state of life where he said goodbye
to silver

He won't interact with his life

He just start again

As the night draws near he gets tired
But knows what he has to struggle with
His life choices are far more likely than ever before and after being
diagnosed in a way that's going through a lot more complicated
business problems with a lot of things
He needs sleep so takes some sleeping pills

www.ingramcontent.com/pod-product-compliance
Lightning Source LLC
Chambersburg PA
CBHW070901120626
46546CB00001B/86